Oradour-The Final Verdict

The Anatomy and Aftermath of a Massacre

By Douglas W. Hawes

Bloomington, IN Milton Keynes, UK

AuthorHouse™
1663 Liberty Drive, Suite 200
Bloomington, IN 47403
www.authorhouse.com
Phone: 1-800-839-8640

AuthorHouse™ UK Ltd.
500 Avebury Boulevard
Central Milton Keynes, MK9 2BE
www.authorhouse.co.uk
Phone: 08001974150

© 2007 Douglas W. Hawes. All rights reserved.

No part of this book may be reproduced, stored in a retrieval system, or transmitted by any means without the written permission of the author.

First published by AuthorHouse 4/5/2007

ISBN: 978-1-4259-8654-4 (sc)
ISBN: 978-1-4259-8655-1 (hc)

Library of Congress Control Number: 2007900529

Printed in the United States of America
Bloomington, Indiana

This book is printed on acid-free paper.

*To my wife Claudie,
and in memory of our dear friend Tamie Watters*

**Charles de Gaulle
at
Oradour-sur-Glane
March 4, 1945**

Oradour-sur-Glane est le symbole des malheurs de la Patrie. Il convient d'en conserver le souvenir, car il ne faut jamais qu'un pareil malheur se reproduise.

Oradour-sur-Glane is the symbol of the calamities of the country. The memory should be kept alive, for a similar calamity must never occur again.

TABLE OF CONTENTS

List of Illustrations   xi
Preface   xv

PROLOGUE: INVASION AND MOBILIZATION   1
   The Division Comes to March Readiness   3
   The Resistance   9
   Resistance Harassment and SS Reprisals   13
   The Division Heads North   18
   Tulle Briefly Liberated   27
   Tulle: the Division's Revenge   30
   The Division Billets Near Limoges   39

PART I   THE MASSACRE   43
   Oradour-sur-Glane, June 10, 1944   47
   A Quiet Village Until The Germans Arrived   47
   Assembly on the Village Green   59
   The Men Separated from the Women and Children   61
   The Men Marched Off—The Executions Begin   62
   Killing The Women and Children in the Church   66
   Burning and Looting the Village   69
   The Escapees   71

PART II   THE TRIAL   87
   Prelude: The Problem of the French/Alsatian Defendants   89

    The Setting   99
    The Trial Begins   105
    The Issue of Separate Trials   110
    The Defendants Interrogated   116
    The Alsatian Political Position   127
    Further Interrogation   129
    The Survivors Arrive to Testify   142
    Witnesses for the Alsatians   170
    Schedule Interrupted to Hear Mme Rouffranche   177
    Alsatian Witnesses Resume   181
    The Case Against the Germans   188
    The German Response   196
    The Case Against the Alsatians   202
    The Alsatian Response   205
    The Verdicts   212
    Fierce Reactions to the Verdicts   217

EPILOGUE   223
    The Oradour Mysteries Examined   225
    A Concluding Note about the Oradour Trial   231
    Aftermath: 237
    The Prisoners   237
    The Oradour Survivors   237
    The Germans   238
    The Alsatian *Malgré Nous*   245
    The President and the Lawyers   245
    The Resistance Leader Guingouin   246
    Comment on the Value of the Resistance   248
    The Oradour 60th Anniversary   248

Glossary of Terms and Abbreviations   253
Resources   256
ACKNOWLEDGEMENTS   259

LIST OF ILLUSTRATIONS

Note: The photos reproduced in this book—a large number of them published for the first time, are an integral part of the story. Photos of Oradour-sur-Glane before the massacre are necessarily limited because so many were destroyed with the town. There are few pictures of Resistance figures from the war. Colonel Guingouin, a leading Resistance figure expressly forbade the taking of photographs, and this order was largely respected. Every effort has been made to contact all copyright holders. The author will be glad to make good in future editions any errors or omissions brought to his attention.

Cover. Design by publisher based on a French postage stamp issued in 1945 and drawn by Réne Serres. Courtesy of the Service National des Timbres de Poste.
1. Lammerding. (SHAEF, NARA) 5
2. Stadler. (SHAEF, NARA) 5
3. Kämpfe. (Unknown; rights reserved) 5
4. Diekmann. (© Bilderwelt / Roger-Viollet) 5
5. Barth. (Unknown; rights reserved) 5
6. Georges Guingouin. (Courtesy of the Musée de la Resistance, Limoges) 10
7. Map of the route north taken by the Division Das Reich. (Publisher) 19
8. Bretenoux Bridge. (Courtesy of Arcade, Bretenoux) 20
9. Violette Szabó. (©Tania Szabó Archives, courtesy of Tania Szabó) 41
10. Map of Oradour-sur-Glane, Village Martyr, showing places mentioned in the book. (Adapted by the author from several precedents.) 45

11. Bottom, map of some of the hamlets and villages surrounding Oradour-sur-Glane. Top, map of area around Oradour-sur-Glane showing main places mentioned in the text. (Publisher) 48
12. Rue Desourteaux, 1932. (Robert Hébras) 50
13. Tram at the tramway station. (Postcard, Centre de la Mémoire ; rights reserved) 50
14. Robert Hébras's sister Georgette a few weeks before the drama. (Robert Hébras) 51
15. German soldiers. (SRCGE, Centre de la Mémoire; rights reserved) 52
16. German half-track. (Private Collection; rights reserved) 52
17. Village green before the war. (Postcard, Centre de la Mémoire; rights reserved) 54
18. Glane River Bridge pre-war. (Postcard, Centre de la Mémoire; rights reserved) 55
19. Roger Godfrin. (SRCGE, Centre de la Mémoire; rights reserved) 58
20. Diagram of the interior and exterior of the church. (Adapted by the author from SRCGE diagram) 68
21. Interior of the church. (SRCGE, Centre de la Mémoire; rights reserved) 77
22. Escape route of Mme Rouffranche. (SHAEF, NARA) 77
23. Exterior of the church in the fall of 1944. (SHAEF, NARA) 78
24. Bodies of victims from the church. (SRCGE, Centre de la Mémoire; rights reserved) 78
25. The Cemetery Road. (Photo by the author) 79
26. The Laudy barn. (Photo by the author) 79
27. The body of M. Poutaraud. (SRCGE, Centre de la Mémoire; rights reserved) 80
28. Village green after. (SRCGE, Centre de la Mémoire; rights reserved) 80
29. Beaulieu shed. (Photo by the author) 81
30. Hotel Avril. (Photo by the author) 81
31. Chateau Laplaud today. (Photo by the author) 81
32. Oradour-sur-Glane ruins from the air. (© AP Photo/SIPA Press) 82
33. M. Borie. (SHAEF, NARA) 83
34. H. Desourteaux. (SHAEF, NARA) 83
35. M. Machefer. (SHAEF, NARA 83
36. A. Senon. (SHAEF, NARA) 83
37. Mme Rouffranche. (SHAEF, NARA) 84
38. Survivors of the massacre. (SRCGE, Centre de la Mémoire; rights reserved) 85
39. Map of Alsace/Moselle. (Publisher) 94

40. General De Gaulle. (© BDIC Paris) 98
41. Bordeaux courthouse exterior. (*Franc-Tireur*, February 13, 1953, rights reserved) 101
42. Courthouse interior. (© Keystone France) 102
43. Prosecutor Gratien Gardon. (© M.Descamps/Paris-Match/SCOOP) 107
44. Alsatian defense counsel. (© AFP) 107
45. Adjutant Lenz. (© Detective, Paris, February 23, 1953) 109
46. Sgt. Boos, the Alsatian SS volunteer, at the barre. (© AFP) 135
47. H. Desourteaux. (© Detective, Paris, February 23, 1953) 144
48. Y. Roby. (© Detective, Paris, February 23, 1953) 144
49. Robert Hébras. (© Detective, Paris, February 23, 1953) 145
50. M. Darthout. (© Detective, Paris, February 23, 1953) 145
51. Mme Taillandier. (© Detective, Paris, February 23, 1953) 156
52. M. Machefer. (© Detective, Paris, February 23, 1953) 156
53. Mme Rouffranche. (© AGIP/ Rue des Archives Paris) 178
54. Camille Wolff. (© Detective, Paris, February 23, 1953) 183
55. Monsignor Neppel. (© Detective, Paris, February 23, 1953) 186
56. Presiding Judge Nussy Saint-Säens. (© M.Descamps/ Paris-Match/SCOOP) 211
57. Nearly empty courtroom before the verdicts. (© Detective, Paris, February 23, 1953) 213
58. Judges rendering the verdicts. (© Detective, Paris, February 23, 1953) 213
59. Strasbourg monument veiled. (© Keystone France) 218
60. Lammerding late in life. (Centre de la Mémoire; rights reserved) 241
61. Heinz Barth at his 1983 trial. (Unknown, rights reserved) 242
62. Hébras and Darthout on the village green. (© Benjamin Corbeau) 249
63. Robert Hébras and the author. 252

PREFACE

On June 10, 1944, four days after the Allied landing in Normandy, a unit of the 2nd SS Panzer Division "Das Reich" committed the worst German war crime on French soil of WW II, the massacre of 642 villagers of Oradour-sur-Glane. Nearly nine years later, twenty-one members of the Division Das Reich were tried before the Permanent Military Tribunal in Bordeaux. Of these, seven were Germans and fourteen were French from the eastern region of Alsace, thirteen of whom had been forcibly inducted into the Waffen SS. None of those present was an officer. The trial was a *cause célèbre,* followed for more than a month by the French and international media.

Why do I want to tell this story? Because there are so many interesting aspects to it. And, because the more I dug, examining hitherto classified US intelligence documents among other sources, the more I saw how the various pieces of the jigsaw went together. What appeared on the surface like a straightforward war crimes trial, turned out to be anything but. Why did the Germans carry out the massacre? Why did they choose Oradour? Who issued the order? The answers to these and other questions were deliberately obfuscated by the Germans at the time, and revisionists have been inventing new answers ever since. Nor could the Germans have imagined in 1944 how this heinous crime would divide France nearly a decade later, when the Alsatians who had been forcibly inducted into the Division were put on trial alongside German SS soldiers.

I have been coming to the Dordogne area in the southwest of France for over twenty-five years, and have a home within a couple of miles of where the Division Das Reich passed on its murderous way to Oradour and Normandy. For years, I have heard stories from family and friends and I've stopped to read the many roadside memorials to the victims of that march. The Resistance erected barricades in Bretenoux, our neighboring town, to impede an armored column of the Division Das Reich. Other elements of the Division passed through Tulle, the capital of our Department of Corrèze, where the Resistance had briefly liberated the town, only to be overwhelmed by the SS. My French wife's father had been the head of the cabinet of the Prefect of Tulle, but was ousted a few months before the SS arrived. This occurred because René Bousquet, Secretary General of the Police under Pierre Laval in the Vichy government, suspected him (correctly) of being in the Resistance. My wife's grandfather was deported to Mauthausen and executed for his own Resistance activity. My mother-in-law, an historian of the Middle Ages, continues to share her personal reminiscences about her late husband's Resistance activities and her own experiences during the war.

I was also attracted to the story of the trial because of the difficult issues it raised. Were the French/Alsatian defendants who had been forcibly inducted into the Waffen SS murderers or victims—or both? Is obedience to orders by simple soldiers a legitimate defense to a charge of war crimes, or a crime against humanity? Are attacks on civilians ever a legitimate military strategy? Are non-uniformed militias outside the protection of international law and custom?

Although I am an American lawyer, my specialty is not criminal or military law. Accordingly, I have tried to tell the story with an understanding of the legal aspects but in a non-technical way aimed generally at a lay audience. While the number of witnesses to these events is dwindling, I have been privileged to meet a number of them and to have been granted access to a twenty-seven-volume stenographic transcript of the trial made by the Association Nationale des Familles des Martyrs d'Oradour-sur-Glane (ANFM). This is an invaluable document because the Tribunal itself, as was the practice at the time, made no transcript, and the newspaper accounts—while generally extensive and accurate—were sometimes sketchy, inaccurate, and biased.

Much new information about the Oradour story has come to light in recent years. When the U.S. government declassified some eight million documents from its WW II intelligence files, I was able to locate several key documents. One of these documents, if available at the time could have dramatically altered the outcome of the trial. Another key document to which I have gained access is a report by an investigator sent to Oradour less than four months after the massacre at the request of Vice President Truman. He was an American named Ecto O. Munn, who was on the Special Staff of the Supreme Headquarters Allied Expeditionary Forces (SHAEF). Munn's conclusions were remarkably close to those of the most informed students of the Oradour story today. His report includes the sworn testimony of nine witnesses, seven of whom were massacre survivors. As far as I know, their affidavits (accompanied in most cases by photographs taken at the time) provide the fullest contemporary documented testimony of the event, and contain important details not recounted at the trial or elsewhere.

I believe that the account given in this book is the most up-to-date and complete digest of the essential facts. It is possible that new information may yet surface, but as the years pass, it becomes increasingly unlikely. This book, then, represents the anatomy of a massacre, and its aftermath by one who benefits from an outsider's objectivity, allied with the sympathy and understanding of a Francophile.

Douglas W. Hawes, Liourdres, France, June 10, 2006

PROLOGUE:

INVASION AND MOBILIZATION

Chapter 1

The Division Comes to March Readiness

On the cold, overcast morning of June 6, 1944, German lookouts sighted a vast Allied naval force off the coast of Normandy. D-Day had arrived. Code-named Operation Overlord, the invasion had been anticipated for some time, both by France's German occupiers and by the various Resistance groups operating in the country. D-Day was the beginning of the end of the war in Europe, but for many French civilians, and particularly for those who found themselves in the path of the counter-attacking German Army, it would unleash worse horrors than any they had previously known.

In Montauban, the headquarters of the 2nd SS Panzer Division Das Reich in the southwest of France, General Heinz Lammerding reacted to news of the invasion by bringing his troops to march readiness. The thirty-eight-year-old son of an architect, Lammerding had joined the Nazi Party in 1931, and was a personal friend of Heinrich Himmler. A civil engineer by training, he had founded an SS School of Engineering, and in 1940 had led a battalion of engineers from the Totenkopf (Death's-Head) Division. He had served two tours of duty on the Eastern Front before assuming command of the Division Das Reich in early 1944. In April of that year, he had received a personal note of congratulation from Himmler. Contemporaneous with a supposed counter-Resistance operation at Montpezat-de-Quercy, in May, he had been awarded the Knight's Cross of the Iron Cross, one of the highest of the German military decorations. A trim figure, not undistinguished in appearance (Illustration 1), he combined a scrupulous politeness in social situations with a ruthless pragmatism in his role as an SS general. Among his men, he had the reputation of being rather cold and colorless in character.

The unit that Lammerding commanded had, by the summer of 1944, acquired a fearsome reputation. The Division was part of the Waffen SS, the private army which Himmler ran in tandem with the *Allgemeine* SS. Essentially— a police force—the *Allgemeine* SS included the Gestapo and the detachments which staffed the concentration camps. The Division Das Reich had participated in campaigns in Poland and Yugoslavia before embarking on Operation Barbarossa, the invasion of Russia, in June 1941. After advancing almost to Moscow, the Division was forced to retreat when the Russian winter counter-offensive was launched, and most of 1942 was spent in France regrouping and replacing the men and equipment lost as a result. They returned to the Eastern Front near Kharkov early in 1943 where they suffered devastating losses which were greatly exacerbated by the Russian winter. The town was recaptured by the Nazis which then wrecked havoc with the civilian population, hanging people from balconies and torching their homes. Ultimately in mid-summer the Russians definitively evicted the Nazis. In their years on the Eastern Front, the Division gained a reputation for extreme ruthlessness, even by the brutal standards of that theatre of war.

In April 1944, following an increase in Resistance activity in the Montauban area of France, Hitler personally ordered the relocation of the Division Das Reich from the Eastern Front. As the Division's leader, Lammerding was to bring the unit back to fighting strength, to crush the local Resistance, and to prepare to reinforce the *Wehrmacht* (regular German Army) when the Allied invasion came, whether on the Mediterranean, Atlantic or Channel coast. Meanwhile, in the month of April 1944 alone, throughout France, the German occupation forces shot 569 "terrorists," arrested 4,463 persons and impressed numerous others into the STO ("*Service du Travail Obligatoire*"). The STO was the compulsory French worker service in Germany instituted in 1942 in occupied France, and in February 1943 in the newly-occupied zone.

Oradour-The Final Verdict

Officers of the 2nd SS Panzer Division Das Reich
1. General Heinz Lammerding. [upper left], 2. Colonel Sylvester Stadler. [upper right], 3. Major Helmut Kämpfe [lower left], 4. Adolf Diekmann [middle],
5. 2nd Lieutenant Heinz Barth [lower right]

While the war was raging on many fronts, this book focuses on the actions of the Division Das Reich and the Resistance in the southwest of France in the spring of 1944 when an increase in Resistance activity was met by a concomitantly harsh response from the occupation forces. The increased severity of the Germans stemmed largely from the orders of the High Command.

When it deployed in France, the Division was in the process of being re-manned, but not with the classic SS Aryan volunteers from Germany or Austria. Instead, for the most part, the gaps in the ranks were being filled with raw recruits from the occupied countries of Eastern Europe and Alsace (it is estimated that as many as 40 percent of the Division was then made up of such soldiers, who had been drawn from fourteen countries). The job of training this unpromising material was not one the SS officers and NCOs enjoyed, and the recruits suffered rigorous and often excessively harsh treatment. The Alsatians who had been forcibly inducted were singled out for the worst duties because they were suspected of harboring pro-French sympathies. They were generally not allowed to leave their encampment unless accompanied by a German. In accordance with the theory that the populace was unlikely to help an armed SS soldier desert, they were required to carry weapons at all times. In fact, most French people assumed that the SS (including the Alsatians, who were easily identifiable because many spoke French, or spoke German with an accent) were all volunteers and committed Nazis.

By June 1944, the strength of the Division Das Reich stood at just over 19,000. These men were quartered in more than fifty barracks buildings in and around Montauban. From here a series of raids had been carried out, partly to repress the Resistance and to deter the populace from aiding them, and partly for the important secondary purpose of training the new recruits. By then, the Division was a very different unit from that which had participated in the invasion of Russia. They still wore the death's-head insignia on their caps, the SS sig-runes on the collar of their uniform jackets, and the regimental bands on their sleeves still bore the same names (Der Führer, in the case of one regiment of the Division). The men, however, were far from the military equals of those who had set out on Operation Barbarossa in 1941. In an attempt to redress this falling-off of standards, the core group of officers and

NCOs who had survived the Russian campaigns did their best to instill some of the old esprit-de-corps in their new and very diverse recruits.

In addition to General Lammerding, there were five officers who would play a significant role in the Oradour story: Colonel Sylvester Stadler, head of the Division's Der Führer Armored Grenadiers Regiment; Major Helmut Kämpfe who commanded the Regiment's Third (Reconnaissance) Battalion; Major Adolf Diekmann who commanded the Regiment's First Battalion; Captain Otto Kahn, head of the First Battalion's Third Company and Second Lieutenant Heinz Barth, who served under Kahn.

At the age of thirty-three in 1944, Stadler was six feet tall and well built with a receding crop of hair (Illustration 2). Born in Austria, he had joined the SS in 1933, and ten years later had been awarded Oak Leaf Clusters to his Knight's Cross by Adolf Hitler and Heinrich Himmler—a considerable honor. Stadler was, according to some, a close friend of Kämpfe, who had served as his adjutant on the Eastern Front. Kämpfe, thirty-four years old, was a stocky, athletic figure whose rise through the ranks had been rapid (Illustration 3). Repeatedly wounded on the Eastern Front, he had been awarded a series of medals culminating in the Knight's Cross of the Iron Cross in December 1943, when he also received command of the Third Battalion. Kämpfe was said to be popular with his men, seemed to flourish in battle, and was considered one of the major heroes of the regiment, and indeed of the Waffen SS as a whole. Some say Kämpfe was a personal friend of Diekmann but there is no solid evidence of this.

Diekmann had joined the Nazi Party at the age of eighteen, two months after Hitler came to power in 1933. A tall, lean figure (Illustration 4) who conformed closely to the Party's Nordic ideal, he had nevertheless had difficulty in acquiring the authorization to marry his fiancée in 1940 because her father was mentally ill; such were the eugenic strictures governing the SS at the time. Diekmann served in the Sudetenland in 1938, and on being transferred to northern France in 1940 was shot in the lung near the town of Saint Venant. An extended recovery period was followed by spells as an instructor in an officer training school at Bad Tölz, where his stay overlapped that of Stadler, and enrollment in a course for Panzer officers in Paris. Otto Weidinger, a future commandant of the Regiment Der Führer, was also present in this course. In October 1943, Diekmann was posted to the Eastern Front, and although he only spent a few months there before the Division was moved to France, it is probable that the experience marked him indelibly. The next year, following a recommendation for promotion from Stadler, he assumed command of the First Battalion of the Regiment Der Führer. Diekmann was then twenty-nine years old.

Otto Kahn, who commanded the Third Company, was thirty-six years old in 1944. He had a wife and three children, and had won an Iron Cross Second Class in 1940. His receding hair was graying and he had a bony, aquiline nose, a pinched mouth, and deep somber eyes, His colleagues described him as of less-than-average intelligence but politically sound. He was also an excellent shot.

Heinz Barth, twenty-three years old in 1944 (Illustration 5), had served in the Hitler Youth before joining the Waffen SS in 1943. He served two tours of duty of several months on the Eastern Front before transferring to France with the Division Das Reich in early 1944. By D-Day, his section numbered about fifty men, most of them armed with rifles and light machine guns.

Chapter 2

The Resistance

The French Resistance was a complex organism. It was made up of those who worked in a clandestine fashion against the Vichy government and the Germans but maintained regular jobs. Those who did the same thing but remained in hiding in the countryside were known as the *maquis*, or as *maquisards*, after the rough mountain brush in which the partisans concealed themselves in the Corsican hills (the *macchia*, in the language of the island). To refer to the Resistance in the context of a particular event is to imply that either or both *résistants* and *maquisards* were involved.

Life in the Resistance was dangerous in the extreme. The Gestapo and the Milice, an armed French militia unit answering to the collaborationist Vichy government, hounded *résistants* and *maquisards* alike. The Milice was formed in 1943 by Pierre Laval (Pétain's deputy), who had personally recommended its creation to Hitler on the grounds that neither the gendarmes (French national police) nor the Vichy paramilitaries were reliable. At its height, it had strength of about 45,000, recruited from right-wing groups and the margins of society. As the Louis Malle film, *Lacombe Lucien* portrays, its members adopted an unofficial and undoubtedly sinister uniform of black leather coats and fedoras. The Milice worked with the Vichy police, the GMR, or *Garde Mobile de Reserve*, and with the Gestapo. Most at risk were the in-town *résistants*, because they could easily be denounced; but the *maquisards* were also in constant danger from the Milice, whose web of informers often passed on information about the location of camps, or the time and place of meetings. It was an era in which no one could be quite sure whom to trust. Even members of the same family sometimes regarded each other with suspicion.

The Resistance contained many different political elements. The most important of these in the Region of Limousin (which is composed of the Department of Haute-Vienne, whose capital is Limoges, and the Departments of Correze and Creuse) were the Communists. The key group of Communists in southwest France was the FTP, the *Franc-tireurs et partisans (or* FTPF, *Franc-tireurs et partisans français).* This group took its name from the French guerillas of the Franco-Prussian war of 1870-71. Georges Guingouin, a former high school teacher, led it. Guingouin was born in 1913 in Magnac-Laval, a village near Limoges (Illustration 6). His father, a professional soldier whom he never knew, was killed on the first day of WW I. His mother was a primary school teacher. He joined the Communist Party in the 1930s, but from the beginning displayed an individualistic streak. After the 1940 Armistice, the Party declined to condemn the Vichy government's collaboration with the Nazis because of the German/Russian Non-Aggression Pact of August 1939, but Guingouin did not hesitate to do so. He was, of course, vindicated when the Nazis invaded Russia in June 1941. He had been removed from his teaching post by the Vichy government in September 1940 during a purge of left-wing civil servants, and went into hiding in February 1941, narrowly escaping arrest.

Since most of the elements of the Resistance in France, up to this point, in 1941 were concentrated in the cities and towns, he became

6. Georges Guingouin, Head of FTP Communist Resistance in Haute-Vienne a few months before the Allied invasion

known as the "first *maquisard.*" The FTP was created in 1942 from three branches of the French Communist Party. Many of its leaders had also fought in the International Brigade against Franco in the Spanish Civil War. In the beginning, his small band of *maquisards* distributed tracts, stole ration cards from the authorities, and sabotaged agricultural machinery to deprive the Germans of produce. The Germans moved into the formerly unoccupied zone of France on November 11, 1942 and instituted forced labor service in Germany in 1943 (STO). The ranks of the Resistance grew as young men sought to avoid STO, and Guingouin's group was able to undertake more ambitious projects such as the sabotage of railways and factories.

One of Guingouin's more innovative initiatives was to impose his own price controls on agricultural products in direct defiance of Vichy. He prohibited the black market and posted his own prices, which were higher than Vichy's and lower than the former black market prices. His announcements were signed the "Prefect of the Maquis."

In February 1944, Guingouin aligned the FTP with de Gaulle's Resistance groups, later consolidated into the *Forces françaises de l'interior* or FFI, in order to gain greater access to the parachute supply drops from England. The alliance was an uneasy one as de Gaulle, looking to the future, was eager to gain control of the administration of post-war France. He was determined that when that day came, the Communists would not be involved in any capacity.

In the run-up to the invasion, the Resistance busied itself by disrupting rail traffic from the Montauban area northward, in order to slow down the German response to an Allied landing. Their sabotage took two basic forms: 1) Railway workers clandestinely disabled the rolling stock by putting an abrasive substance in the axles of the flatbed cars, which could be used for carrying armored vehicles; and 2) They blew up railway bridges and tracks, a specialty of the FTP. On June 7, for example, the FTP blew up the bridge outside St. Junien, a town eighteen miles west of Limoges and eight miles from Oradour-sur-Glane. The following day a train arrived from Angoulême, forty miles westward, and stopped before the damaged bridge. Ten Wehrmacht soldiers then climbed down from the train, and were fired upon by *maquisards.* Two of the Germans were killed.

As the invasion drew nearer, the Resistance—particularly the FTP—grew increasingly bold in their actions relating to the liberation of towns and villages. While their principal objective was to free these places from the German occupation, they gave an almost equal consideration to political aims. The Communist FTP wanted to control as many towns as possible in the post-occupation period. While colluding in these ambitions as a militant Communist, Georges Guingouin was realistic in his assessment of the FTP's strength, and counseled caution in attacking German garrisons. Such actions tended to precipitate reprisals of the most brutal sort against the local population. Indeed, for this reason, Guingouin refused an order to attack Limoges and refused to aid in an attack on Tulle.

Chapter 3

Resistance Harassment and SS Reprisals

The Division Das Reich's cleansing operations in the run-up to the invasion showed that stringent measures were already being enacted. Their aim was unambiguous: to discourage the civilian population from aiding the Resistance, and to deter the Resistance itself from actions against the Division. Some idea of the German attitude to Resistance operations may be gained from the communication General Lammerding sent to General Kruger of the 50th Armored Division on June 5th. Among other counter-Resistance measures, Lammerding wrote that he intended to occupy Brive, Cahors and Figeac (all relatively large towns north of Montauban where the Division Das Reich was stationed), and to round up 5,000 "suspects" for deportation to Germany. This was a calculated attempt to reduce the number of potential recruits for the Resistance among the high school classes of 1945 and 1946, and to institute a system whereby ten Frenchmen would be executed for every German killed, and three for every German wounded. In the event that an Allied landing should occur by June 15, Lammerding concluded, "The Resistance will not hamper our operations."

The three raids prior to the Normandy landing described next in this chapter were typical of many raids carried out by the Division in May 1944.

On May 2, a unit of the Division was on an exercise near Montpezat-de-Quercy, a town of about 1,400 inhabitants situated some twenty-one miles from the Division's headquarters at Montauban. The *maquis*, who had sabotaged the main Toulouse-Paris railway line the previous weekend, had received word that the German soldiers were on their way. When the lead elements approached, a *maquisard* lookout opened fire on them. The SS men's response was immediate. The lookout who had fired the shots was incinerated by flamethrowers, as were several outlying farmhouses. At 9:30 a.m. the unit entered the *bastide* (old walled town) with several armored vehicles and trucks. After hammering on the doors of the nineteenth century town hall, the SS ordered the inhabitants to assemble in the square. The locals, accustomed to seeing German patrols in the area, obeyed warily but without alarm. Fanning out in the surrounding countryside, the SS flushed out the inhabitants of the outlying farms and marched those people to the square, too. Of those thus assembled, twenty-two probably identified in advance by the Milice, were led away. Sixteen were later deported, and four, including an old man and his granddaughter, were killed on the spot. The corpses of those four were then thrown into one of the many buildings which by then had been set on fire, although the fourteenth century church was spared. The operation was typical in that it did not involve a planned action against the *maquis*, but was clearly designed as a reprisal, and to intimidate civilians.

The Regiment Der Führer mounted a similar operation in St. Céré. Situated in the Bave valley; this small town is surrounded by level farming areas, where in May 1944 grass had been planted for haymaking. The fourteenth century towers of St. Laurent les Tours dominate the town itself. Many of the houses were half-timbered, particularly those near the square in front of the town hall. On the morning of May 11, a warm spring day, a loud report from a machine gun or an armored vehicle signaled the beginning of a raid. SS troops quickly occupied the *gendarmerie* and disarmed the gendarmes, many of whom were suspected by the Gestapo and Milice of aiding the Resistance. All the men of the town between the ages of eighteen and sixty were then ordered to assemble in front of the town hall on the rue de l'Hotel de Ville. The town's Jewish inhabitants were also ordered to bring their valuables. When all were assembled as ordered, half a dozen men were summarily shot. Thirty men and four women were ordered into a requisitioned bus and driven to a camp at Saint-Antonin-Noble-Val, sixty-eight miles south of St. Céré, and twenty-five miles north of Montauban.

Among those taken away was a pharmacy owner named Dufour, who earlier that morning, had been summoned to the town's Hotel de Paris and accused of being the head of the Resistance. This was almost true. Dufour was an active *résistant* who had participated in a successful January action against the Ratier factory in Figeac (which made parts for German Heinckel airplanes). However, he had declined the leadership of the Resistance in the Department of Lot because, he said, his work at the pharmacy would have made it hard for him to circulate without exciting comment. On that May morning, as Dufour mounted the bus, his swollen face showed that he had been badly beaten. With the help of SNCF (*Société nationale des chemins de fer*, the French national railroad) employees, however, he and several other detainees managed to escape their captors while being transported by train to Compiègne near Paris.

Ten days after this operation, Major Diekmann led his men from the regimental headquarters at Valence d'Agen to Fumel, thirty-six miles north of Montauban. Quartering himself in a hotel from which he could direct operations by radio, he sent his four companies into towns in the area that had been earlier identified as suspect by the head of the Gestapo in Agen. Led by Captain Kahn, the Third Company of the First Battalion converged on Frayssinet-le-Gélat, a village of about 400 inhabitants twenty miles north of Cahors.

At Kahn's order, the SS soldiers clambered down from their vehicles and fanned out to search the houses. Forcing the inhabitants onto the streets, and taking radios, bicycles and other goods from the houses as they went, the soldiers assembled the populace in the centre of town. There, as Kahn directed operations, the men's lighters and pocketknives were confiscated. Suddenly, a shot rang out, and a soldier standing behind Kahn (later identified as a man named Fritoff) fell in the street. The captain immediately dispatched troops to search the house from which the shot appeared to have come. This, a plain-looking, three-story building opposite the town hall, was the property of the Lugan family. There was a doorway onto the street, and an open stone staircase on the left side leading to a second-story entrance. Three women, the elderly

Mme Agathe Pailles (née Lugan) and her two nieces, Marguerite and Juliette Lugan, were forcibly expelled from the house. The women were hanged until dead, and then cut down and thrown into the house, which had by then been set on fire.

Meanwhile, Mme Wagner, the wife of a *milicien*, drew the soldiers' attention to a woman named Yvonne Vidilles, who, due to a compulsive disorder, was unable to stop talking. Denounced by Mme Wagner for keeping weapons in her house, Mme Vidilles was seized by the hair and pistol-whipped until she died. Ten men were then selected for execution in front of the other villagers, and divided into two groups of five. One of those chosen to die was nineteen-year-old Guy Mourgues. When his father, Gaston, asked if he might embrace his son for the last time, Kahn signaled for him to go ahead. As the two men held each other, Kahn ordered the execution squad to fire, adding the father to the ten other victims. The women, forbidden a last embrace, were then forced to pass in front of the bodies of their men folk. At this point, the *milicien*, Wagner, was seen talking to Kahn. Shortly afterwards, Wagner's father-in-law and his family were released and allowed to return home.

At around 10:00 p.m., the dead were loaded into carts by the villagers under the direction of the SS and taken to the cemetery. There, their rings, wallets and watches were taken and the locals were forced to dig a shallow ditch. Around midnight, the corpses were burned. The rest of the villagers were imprisoned in the church for the night. As they languished there, the SS looted the empty houses, taking jewels, leather, linen, food, wine and money. Some of the SS officers spent the night at the Wagners' house, feasting on the stolen food and wine. Mme Wagner bragged about this the next morning. At 10:00 a.m. the next day, the people in the church were freed, and the last German vehicle left the village half an hour later. On November 1, less than six months later, Mme Wagner and her husband were summarily executed by the Resistance.

The brutal nature of these raids conformed to orders issued by the German High Command, as well as to those issued by Lammerding to the Division Das Reich. On February 3, 1944, Field Marshall Sperrle, commander in chief of the German Army of the West, had issued orders that partisans and saboteurs should be dealt with uncompromisingly. His order included the following final significant sentence: "Actions that are later regarded as too severe cannot in light of the present situation provide a basis for any punishment." A further order by Sperrle on June 8 underlined his determination that the Resistance should not impede the German war effort in southern France. He urged that operations against them should be undertaken "with extreme severity and without any leniency." He went on specifically to sanction rigorous measures, "to deter the inhabitants of these infested regions who must be discouraged from harboring the resistance groups." Both such orders were supported by a secret order issued to the High Command by Hitler on November 19, 1942, in which he insisted—in contravention of the Geneva Convention—that, "All saboteurs and commandos captured, all the enemies arrested by the German Army, even if they are in uniform, whether armed or not, captured in combat or arrested while fleeing, must be executed without exception". The Germans were explicitly concerned to prevent the establishment in the area of a Communist state.

A few hours before the Allies landed in Normandy, the French Service of the BBC began broadcasting coded messages to the Resistance in France. The message received by Jacques Poirier, code name Nestor, at his headquarters in the Chateau La Vitrolle near the Dordogne River, for example, was *"La girafe a un long cou"*, the giraffe has a long neck. This was Poirier's signal that the invasion was imminent and that he should implement his part of the various plans worked out with London in preparation for the invasion: *Plan Vert* for rail sabotage, *Plan Rouge* for destroying munitions depots, and *Plan Tortue* (Tortoise) for disrupting the roads.

Georges Guingouin, leader of the Communist FTP in Haute Vienne, was undeterred by the ferocity with which the SS were prosecuting Hitler's counter-Resistance policy. On the day that the Allies landed in Normandy, and General Lammerding called the Division Das Reich to march readiness, Guingouin issued his own order: "The hour of decisive combat has sounded. This morning at dawn the forces of the Allies landed on the soil of France…The wounded beast is bleeding everywhere. The moment has come to finish him off and gain victory… Everywhere the alarm bells call the sons of France to combat."

Chapter 4

The Division Heads North

On June 8, the Division Das Reich was given the signal to proceed north by road, and to take their tanks and armored vehicles with them. This was a decision which would weigh heavily on both vehicles and men, and according to German sources was motivated by the need to relieve a number of garrisons along the route, which had been attacked on June 7 and June 8. Certain elements of the Division had already moved northward for the purpose of mounting operations against the Resistance and their civilian sympathizers. The Resistance, however, insisted that the real reason that the Division traveled by road was that sabotage of rails, bridges and equipment had made railway transport impossible. Both explanations probably contained elements of the truth; but it seems likely that some of the more heavily armored vehicles would have been sent by rail, if it weren't for the actions of the Resistance. In any event, the failure of sufficient equipment and munitions to have arrived in Montauban ensured that somewhat less than half the Division's full strength of 19,000 men was ordered northward at that time.

Most of the Division took the main road north from Montauban to Limoges via Caussade, Cahors and Brive. In this central column were the headquarters' company of the Regiment Der Führer led by Colonel Stadler, the Third Battalion led by Major Kämpfe, and the Reconnaissance Battalion led by Major Wulf. Adolf Diekmann's First Battalion, meanwhile, swept westward along routes 701 and 703, while

Oradour-The Final Verdict

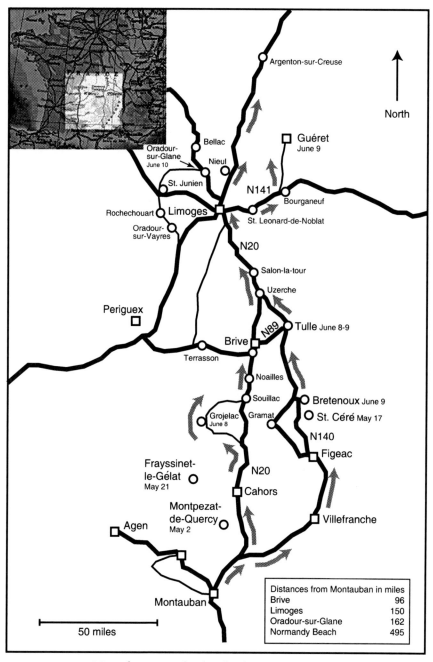

7. Map of route north taken by the Division Das Reich showing dates of "operations" described in the book.

other elements of the Division, mainly armored units, detoured to the east, passing through Figeac, Saint-Céré, Bretenoux and Beaulieu (Illustration 7).

The Veny group of the *Armée Secrète* (AS) was the main non-Communist part of the Resistance in the Department of Lot. The AS mainly consisted of clandestine *résistants* maintaining their regular jobs. The Veny group had received word of the Division's advance northward. The Bretenoux section of the Veny group was led by Albert Oubrayrie, who later published an account of the events which followed. The *maquisards,* under his command, constructed tree-trunk barricades at both ends of the bridge at the western approach to Bretenoux (Illustration 8).

8. Pre-war photo of the Bretenoux Bridge where the Resistance held off an armored unit of the Division Das Reich for three hours. The unit arrived from the right. To the left is the route the column followed afterwards to Tulle via Beaulieu-sur-Dordogne.

Members of the AS of the Department of Corrèze (largely to the north of Lot) then moved southward to take up position on the second, or westward, of these barricades. Why they moved into the territory of the Veny group, rather than manning the bridge at Beaulieu a few miles further northward and fighting the SS in their own department, remains a mystery. Bretenoux, although close to the Corrèze border, is in the Department of Lot. The head of the Bretenoux section of the Veny group, a man named Fregeac, prevailed strongly upon his departmental headquarters to lift the barricade. He was certain that leaving it in place would entail catastrophe for the town. Around midnight, the Corrèze AS finally agreed to withdraw, but for reasons unknown, the men remained in place. At 4:00 a.m., a member of the Veny group returned from a sabotage mission to find the Corrèze AS still at the barricade. Their young sergeant, an Alsatian refugee named Frederic Holzmann, stood by his original order to hold the bridge. In any event, no safe course of withdrawal existed; he was obliged to rest in place. "If I slow the SS down by one hour, I will have accomplished my mission," said Holzmann bravely. The head of the Veny section, very moved, grasped his hand for the last time. Later, the decision of the Corrèze group to remain in Bretenoux would be described as "a heroic folly."

At 6:30 a.m., the SS arrived from Saint-Céré in the east. Proceeding along the main street, they reached the barricaded bridge over the Cère River), where they were met with rifle and automatic weapons fire from behind the barricades at each end of the bridge. Spilling from their motorcycles, staff cars, and trucks, the soldiers at the head of the column returned the *maquisards'* fire from behind their vehicles and from the cover of nearby buildings. Despite the fury and violence of their response, however, they were unable to break through the barricades. The firefight continued until eventually the *maquisards* who were manning the first barricade were ordered to fall back to the second. Those manning the second barricade, meanwhile, slid down the bank and forded the river. They returned the Germans' fire from the island of Bourgnatelle, and from behind the trees and buildings on the far bank, where they were joined by several of the Bretenoux gendarmes.

With more SS men and vehicles arriving every minute, the German column backed up at the eastern approach to the town, immobilized. Finally, the SS soldiers managed to take two of the townspeople hostage, and forced them to dismantle the first barricade. In the course of this action, the hostages tried to slip away but were seen, and cut down in a hail of machine gun fire. On the bridge, Frederic Holzmann was killed. With him died Raymond Armand, also of the Corrèze AS. Armand's *carte d'identité*, holed by a bullet and stained with his blood, remains in a file at the Bretenoux Town Hall.

All around, desperate engagements were underway, of which descriptions survived. Three SS men in the village of Soupette captured M. Mazet and his cousin M. Truel, half a mile from the Bretenoux Bridge. As the Frenchmen were forced behind a neighbor's barn, two of the Germans were shot and killed by a *maquisard* from the cover of a woodpile. Mazet and the third SS man took cover behind a well. The SS man, who had landed on top of Mazet, threw a grenade in the direction of the *maquisard*, but succeeded only in fatally wounding Truel who hid behind a tree. In doing so, the SS man gave away his position, and the *maquisard* shot him. Although dying, the SS man attempted to strangle Mazet but rolled away, lifeless. Mazet ran to his cousin and tried to staunch the shrapnel wound in his throat, but it was too late. He sought out his wife, and she warned him that more Germans were coming. They hid in a wheat field. It was only at that point that Mazet felt a burning in his leg and discovered he had been hit. Mme Truel, seeing her husband was not with Mazet, then started running in the direction from which Mazet had come. As she reached her husband's body, she was shot dead. The Germans then set fire to the barn and flushed out the *maquisard*, shooting and killing him, too. A white cross was later painted on the barn where the *maquisard*'s body had been found.

With the abandonment of the barricades, the SS quickly took the Bretenoux Bridge, and the Commandant of the SS column [his identity has not been discovered yet] installed himself at the Hotel de la Cère on the west side of the bridge. Reprisals were swiftly set in train. Tanks and armored vehicles began to shell houses in the neighboring villages of Soupette and Miramont. Seventy hostages, including some women, were rounded up and assembled at the Hotel de la Cère. Three armored vehicles were sent further west towards Puybrun and Liourdres. In Puybrun, they took four hostages from a restaurant. While these events were occurring, our neighbor, Mme Simone Ségalat, was visiting her grandparents in the hamlet of Combals near Bretenoux. From their window, she saw a German tank turn its cannon towards her and fire, destroying the two neighboring buildings. At that moment, two *maquisards* arrived at the house, and one of them was wounded. Despite her fear that the Germans would see them enter, she opened the door, only to find one of the *maquisards* preparing to shoot her (he had mistaken the sound of her throwing the bolt on the door for the cocking of a gun). The German sweep of the outlying villages yielded a further seven hostages, and these were brought to the Hotel de la Cère at Bretenoux. Unlike the others, however, they were made to stand facing a ditch with their hands behind their necks with their pockets turned out—the usual posture of men who were about to be executed.

Given General Lammerding's standing order that ten Frenchmen were to be executed for every German killed, and three for every one wounded, it is a miracle that all of the hostages assembled at the Hotel de la Cère were not summarily shot. Between fifteen and twenty Germans had been killed in the battle for Bretenoux and in the June 6 attack on a train in nearby Vayrac. A hostage taken nearby by the "Herman" armored vehicle squadron was forced to lead SS soldiers to the graves of the three Germans killed in the Vayrac attack, and shot dead on their graves.

There are several possible reasons why the Bretenoux hostages were not killed. An elderly priest, Abbé Gouzou, who had offered himself as a hostage pleaded for their lives, and it may be that the SS officer in charge balked at the idea of such a large-scale slaughter. It is possible that the scene was as described by Gilbert Lacan in his "*Quercy sous la terreur Allemande*" (Quercy is the area comprised of the Department of Lot and parts of Tarn-et-Garonne and Aveyron). According to Lacan, thirty-two bodies of French civilians and fighters were lined up in front of the officer who then released the hostages, satisfied with the scale of the revenge that had already been taken. In any event, with the exception of the mayor's chauffeur who was shot in the head in the street, they were all spared. The townspeople were not allowed to collect their dead until the next day, when the remainder of the Division Das Reich had passed by. As was their habit, the SS deposited their own dead in the final trucks of the column for later burial. On the French side, a total of nineteen civilians and nineteen *résistants* had been killed, several people had been wounded, and countless houses, barns and other properties had been destroyed. Bretenoux and the surrounding villages had paid dearly for their valor, but they had succeeded in delaying the German column for over three hours—not a negligible contribution to the war effort, given the fragility of the beachhead that the Allies had established in Normandy.

From Bretenoux, the SS turned north via Biars to Beaulieu. Here they encountered another barricade erected by the Corrèze AS. However, with the tanks now at the head of the column, the Germans were detained for no longer than it took to blast their way through the small number of *résistants who manned* the barricade; one of whom was killed. On June 10, Major Albert Stückler, the Division's senior staff officer, issued an Order of the Day in which he spoke of the battle for Bretenoux in the following terms: "In the course of its advance, the Division has already dealt with several Resistance groups. The armored regiment has succeeded, thanks to a neatly executed surprise attack, in carrying out a knife-stroke—*"un coup de filet"*—against an organized group of company strength. The Division is now proceeding to a rapid and lasting clean-up of these regional groups, with a view to becoming speedily available to reinforce the fighting men and to help hold the line on the invasion front."

The central column of the Division headed straight up the N20. At Cressenac, a small town between Souillac and Brive, the lead cars and trucks were fired upon and forced to wait for Major Wulf and his armored half-tracks. These began putting down sustained fire from machine guns and larger weapons, eventually holing the church spire. At this point, with four men dead, the *résistants* dispersed, realizing that they could achieve little against firepower on this scale. Taking the dead body of one of the *résistants*, Maurice Vergne, Major Wulf's men attached it to the front of one of the half-tracks as a warning.

The next village on their route was Noailles, a picturesque collection of eighteenth and nineteenth century houses surrounding a château on the top of a hill overlooking Brive. When Commandant Romain of the Corrèze AS heard the shooting in Cressenac, he jumped onto his motorcycle and drove southward to investigate. He heard armored vehicles moving rapidly up the road, and turning back to Noailles, narrowly missed being seen by the advancing column. That day, the Corrèze AS had been joined by nine members of the Brive GMR (*Garde Mobile de Reserve,* or Vichy paramilitary*)* who had defected to the Resistance with their leader Lelorrain. This group positioned itself at a crossroads at the top of the hill overlooking Brive. At about 4:00 p.m., the half-tracks arrived and opened fire on the *résistants,* killing Lelorrain and others instantly. The *résistants* returned fire for long enough to claim seven

Germans dead, but soon dispersed into the countryside, leaving the way free for the column to descend the last few miles into Brive.

When the main column of the Division Das Reich entered the city at around 7:00 p.m., the local German garrison breathed a collective sigh of relief. The garrison, under the command of Colonel Luyken, was like most of those attached to the larger local towns, made up of older reservists and recruits from countries conquered by the Germans. The caliber of its men was in no way comparable to an SS division, even one as replete with unseasoned recruits as the Division Das Reich. There had been strong rumors in Brive that the FTP was planning an attack. The garrison had heard that Tulle had been attacked on the 7th and 8th, so there was reason for their fears.

As the German vehicles assembled in Brive, one of those watching with interest was René Jugie. He was a clandestine *résistant* who carried out assignments at night and on weekends while appearing to pursue a conventional civilian life. He was a member of the Corrèze committee of MUR (*Mouvement Uni de la Résistance*) an association of several Gaullist Resistance groups (one of which he had founded and led). Jugie worked closely with the Special Operations Executive (SOE), a London-based organization which dropped French speaking agents behind enemy lines in Europe.

Of the two groups, MUR and the Communist FTP (to which Jugie had belonged in the early days of the war), the FTP was the more significant in the Brive area. Numbering about 5,000, it had been continuously active since at least 1942. SOE agents had supplied both groups with arms and money, and the British reasoned that their primary objective was to win the war. The post-war political considerations, which so concerned the MUR and the FTP, could wait.

In late May, the differences between the two groups had become focused on the FTP's insistence that it would attack the garrisons at Brive, Tulle, and Limoges, thereby liberating them. Jugie had been strongly opposed to this idea, particularly as regards Brive, where he lived. He was sure that any attack would cost many *maquisard* lives, and in the reprisals which were certain to follow, many civilian lives, too. In the beginning of June, the *Forces Françaises de l'Intereur* (FFI) was created by London which theoretically consolidated all the Resistance groups in France, but in practice they exercised little control over the FTP in the southwest. The FFI agreed with Jugie and made it clear that if the FTP attacked the German garrison in Brive, they would take no part. For the time being, the idea was shelved.

Other elements of the FTP were less easily dissuaded. On the morning of June 6, Pétain's Deputy Pierre Laval personally telephoned Pierre Trouillé, the Prefect of Corrèze in Tulle to warn him that an FTP attack on the town's German garrison was likely. According to Trouillé's own account, he then asked Laval what he should do if such an attack should materialize. Laval's less-than-helpful reply was: "Do your duty."

The attack did materialize. It was based on the mistaken idea, apparently believed by the FTP, that general liberation in France would immediately follow the invasion. The FTP feared that unless a major insurrection followed hard upon the Allied landings, the Germans would carry out incarcerations and slaughter on a massive scale. This is not to say that the FTP had been inactive prior to the invasion. Tulle, with its Giat arms factory and large workforce, was a local Communist stronghold. The police there had compiled long lists of sabotage incidents against the railways and other targets, as well as of personal attacks against the Milice and the Germans. Reprisals for these incidents had been swift and random, and had varied in their intensity. The increase in FTP activity was partly due to the fact that more arms and materiel were being parachuted in from England, and partly to the growing demand in the STO program for French labor in Germany, which acted as a strong incentive for young men to join the *maquis*.

Chapter 5

Tulle Briefly Liberated

At about 5:00 a.m. on Wednesday June 7, when the main body of the Division Das Reich was still in the Montauban area, the FTP launched an attack on the 750-strong garrison of the Ninety-Fifth Security Regiment, Tulle, which was commanded by a fifty-five-year-old dentist named Captain Reichmann. Also stationed in the town, totaling a further 500 men, were members of the Milice, the GMR, and the German SD, or security police. At first, the fight went against the Resistance. The Germans had occupied all the most strongly fortified buildings—the *Souillac École Normale*, where most of the garrison was quartered; the *Champs de Mars* barracks, the girls' school in front of the Giat factory—and were well-armed and supplied. The *maquisards*, by contrast, lacked military training and were short of arms and ammunition, with no heavy weapons except a few anti-tank guns. Of the 1,400 or so who were meant to participate in the attack, 450 arrived late.

The attack was led by Jean-Jacques Chapou, a young school teacher who had lost his job because he was a freemason. Pétain was strongly against secret societies, and outlawed freemasonry early in the Vichy régime. Decisive and brave, Chapou had a *nom de guerre*, Kleber. With a thirty-year-old Communist plumber named Louis Godefroy, he set up his headquarters in the town hall. At 11:00 a.m., they received notice that a mixed group of GMR, gendarmes and Milice who were bottled up in the *Champs de Mars* barracks, wished to withdraw to Limoges under a white flag. Colonel Colomb, head of the local GMR, had received permission to surrender via telephone from his Limoges command post. Colomb had argued with his superiors that if they continued fighting, many of his men would defect to the Resistance. He asked the Prefect Trouillé to mediate. With the help of Maurice Roche (the Secretary General, who spoke German), they arranged it so that those who wanted to leave for Limoges could do so, and those who wished to join the Resistance could stay behind. Eventually, the former departed in trucks with Colonel Colomb, white flags flying.

The Germans regrouped in the girl's school, and counter-attacked. They took over the railway station, and found eighteen SNCF employees hiding in a coal bin, and with the exception of one who managed to escape, shot them all. As the day wore on, German forces held out in the *École Normale*, the Giat arms factory, and the girl's school. Godefroy sent messengers to Georges Guingouin's headquarters near Cheissoux to ask for help, but Guingouin refused to be drawn into the battle. He sent the messengers back with a lecture on the foolishness of their actions.

The battle continued the next morning (the 8th), and eventually the *maquisards* succeeded in setting the *École Normale* on fire. Some of the Germans tried to escape through the side streets, but were gunned down by *maquisards* who were waiting behind wine barrels. Later, the Germans would claim that forty of their soldiers had come out under the cover of a white flag of surrender but had been cut down; the FTP's response was that the Germans had tried to run for it, and had not attempted to surrender.

The Prefect then directed the Red Cross and the monks of a local seminary to remove the bodies from the area of the *École Normale*, and transport the wounded Germans to the hospital. Neither the townspeople nor the *maquisards* were happy about the decision to treat the wounded Germans, and the Germans later complained to Vichy that the FTP had mutilated the German corpses. This would become a controversial issue. The FTP denied the claims but admitted that a truck that picked up the dead had accidentally run over some of the bodies. In 1951, at the trial in Bordeaux of some of the officers involved, two German doctors filed contradictory reports. The French writer, Henri Amouroux, an authority on the Resistance and the occupation, states that having weighed all the evidence, he considered it possible that some mutilation did occur. What is undisputed is that, despite objections by the FTP, thirty-seven wounded Germans were taken to the hospital and cared for by French doctors and nurses. The precise number of the dead Germans was impossible to establish; Henri Amouroux claims a body count of sixty-nine, with fifty-nine missing, presumably taken prisoner, but this is hard to reconcile with the figure of forty dead that the SS announced the next day.

By the afternoon of June 8, although a few Germans were still holding out at the Giat factory and the girl's school, the FTP and the locals rejoiced in the streets. They were under the impression that Tulle was one of the first towns in France to be liberated by the Resistance. At around 8:00 p.m., Chapou, unannounced, presented himself at the Prefect's office. He was the new commandant of Tulle, he told Prefect. Trouillé responded that he was still the Prefect of Corrèze, and asked what he thought would happen if the Germans came back and discovered Chapou in charge. Chapou laughed, and said that the Prefect would not see any more Germans in Corrèze.

In Brive, meanwhile, René Jugie had received news about the FTP's assault on the German garrison in Tulle, and about the losses sustained by both sides. Remarkably, the FTP losses were said to be only seventeen killed and twenty-one badly wounded. A report was passed on to Baillely, the head of MUR. This report led to orders that no members of the Corrèze Resistance were to participate in any attack on Brive, although a few units had helped the FTP attack Tulle. At a meeting of FFI that evening, the FTP once again urged an attack. By then, some of the Division Das Reich had left Brive for Limoges while Stückler's Headquarters' Company and the men and armor of Wulf's Reconnaissance Battalion had gone to relieve the Tulle garrison. The FTP pointed to the success of the battle in Tulle, and the need to relieve the FTP there from the pressure of holding the town. Baillely, however, had received reports of the northward progress towards Brive of other elements of the Division Das Reich, and was able to persuade the FTP not to consider an attack on the Brive garrison.

Chapter 6

Tulle: the Division's Revenge

Baillely's reports were well founded. The western column of the Division under Diekmann, which made its way to Limoges, had attracted persistent assaults by *résistants* since it had crossed the Dordogne River at Grolejac that morning. There, the mayor had been visited by a *maquisard* of the AS Corrèze, who had informed him that the SS Division was on its way and must at all costs be delayed. The mayor gathered a group of about fifteen *résistants*, and they stationed themselves near the bridge with a lookout watching the road. At 8:30 a.m., a warning shot was fired, and the half-tracks of Diekmann's Armored Grenadier Battalion were met by a limited volley of rifle and small arms fire. The half-tracks halted, and their occupants ducked for cover and moved to outflank the *résistants*. Cannon fire was deployed and the Hotel Jardel (now l'Hotel du Pont) was hit and began to burn. The hotel was a Resistance headquarters and contained explosives that had been stockpiled for the purpose of blowing up the bridge. In the event there was not enough time to use the munitions. The civilian occupants of the hotel fled, and several were killed or wounded as they ran. Before long, the *résistants* abandoned their positions and fled into the woods. Five of their number had been killed, as had five civilians. The Germans, who had sustained no casualties, regained their vehicles and proceeded on their way. The delay had cost them twenty minutes.

After crossing the river, the SS arrived at Carsac, where five *résistants* accidentally drove up to them. One fled and the others were killed. Intending to proceed via the D703, the main road along the river, Diekmann took a wrong turn and instead went through the village. There, spraying gunfire as they went, his men killed a Jewish refugee doctor, an eighty-year-old blacksmith, and a man working in his field. A few miles down the road at Rouffillac, *résistants* and civilians had erected a barricade of tree-trunks and other obstacles. These were cleared after fighting which left two *résistants* and sixteen civilians dead. Miraculously, a seven-year-old girl named Irène Paukhialkoof, whom the SS threw into a building they had set ablaze, survived. Diekmann's First Battalion continued on towards Souillac and the north.

When Major Wulf's Reconnaissance Battalion arrived at Tulle at about 9:00 p.m. on the 8th, Chapou's assertion an hour earlier that no more Germans would be seen in Corrèze was proved tragically wrong. Wulf was followed by Lieutenant Haase with a Panzer unit and two artillery batteries. No word had reached the FTP that the Germans were on their way from Brive, or indeed, that the Division Das Reich had left Montauban. The SS found the streets of Tulle deserted, and were met with only sporadic fire before discovering the survivors of the garrison hiding in the Giat factory and the girl's school. Shortly afterwards, Major Stückler and the Division Headquarters' operations section arrived. At this point, the *maquisards* abandoned their positions and dispersed into the hills, leaving weapons and FTP armbands behind.

On the morning of Friday, June 9, Major Kowatch, the third most senior of the Division's staff officers, took over command. He had arrived the night before. Kowatch's troops fanned out through the town, going into all the buildings, forcing the men from their beds, and marching them down to the Giat factory. At that point, the SS were threatening to execute 3,000 or 5,000 hostages (accounts differ) and burn the entire town to the ground.

Arriving at the Prefecture at 6:00 a.m., soldiers found a cache of arms which were mostly grenades. The Prefect Trouillé was threatened with execution, and it was only with difficulty that he managed to explain to an officer that the arms had been left there for safekeeping when the GMR left under a flag of truce. He also drew the SS officers' attention to the fact that the wounded Germans were being treated at the hospital, a fact which Kowatch verified. A discussion among Kowatch, Trouillé, and Roche (the Secretary General) followed. The SS staff officer insisted that all men between sixteen and sixty be rounded up, while the Frenchmen argued that the general populace was innocent and should be spared. The Prefect, the Mayor, the Bursar, and Monsignor Chassagne, the Bishop of Tulle, offered themselves as hostages, but were refused. Finally, a fire engine with a loudspeaker was dispatched to announce that all men of the requisite age must go to the Giat factory. Only those essential to public services and the economy would be released. At 11:45 a.m., a printer was asked to print 100 notices announcing that because forty German soldiers had been murdered, 120 *maquisards* would be hanged. The notice was titled, "*Citoyens de Tulle!*" and signed, "*Le General commandant les troupes allemandes.*" It is not known why the number to be hanged was not close to the number Lammerding had specified of ten French for each German killed. The notices were posted around the town.

In the early afternoon, the Prefect received an SS officer who confirmed that in view of the humane treatment of the German wounded, the original order to execute a vast number of prisoners was rescinded. However, there would be a reprisal, with 120 hostages hanged. When the Prefect began to plead against this reprisal, the SS officer said that it was useless to argue his point, as the hangings had already begun. Moreover, he added, 120 was an insignificant number compared to those they had executed on the Eastern Front. In Kharkov alone, they had executed 20,000 in one day. To the SS, shooting was considered an appropriate form of execution for soldiers and hanging for civilians and partisans. Among other considerations, hanging made a strong impression on the populace.

The selection of those to be executed began in the morning, with a local Gestapo chief asking the hostages more-or-less random questions like, "Why haven't you shaved?" or "Why do you have dirty shoes?" No real attention was paid to the answers. Most of those selected were between eighteen and forty-six—presumably since they were the most likely to be *maquisards*. In fact, only two of those chosen were actually in the *maquis*. The rest were men with foreign names, suspect papers, or merely those who lived outside the town. Some hostages pleaded successfully for their lives, but others immediately replaced those released.

One of those who succeeded in saving hostages was a Prussian named Vogel, the head of a company affiliated with the Giat factory. He acted as a go-between and interpreter between the SS men and the French deputy head of the factory. He managed to save three factory workers, a municipal employee, a widower with four children, and a mechanic with five children. When a junior officer asked the SS captain if others were to be substituted, Vogel requested that no innocent men should die in the place of those saved, and the captain complied.

The secretary (and some said the mistress) of Bremer, the German head of the Giat factory, participated in the selection process. The locals knew Paulette Geissler, a German born at Ulm, as La Chienne (the Bitch). Provocative in manner and appearance, she was said to work closely with the Gestapo. She had been a nurse in Paris before the war and spoke fluent French.

She acted as Bremer's interpreter, identifying seventeen of the hostages as employees of the Giat factory and so essential for the war effort. One such employee, however, was not protected, apparently because he had offended her on some earlier occasion.

At around 9:30 a.m., the Germans arrived at the house of Abbé Jean Espinasse. They took him to the Giat factory, where, among others, he found several hundred members of the *Chantiers de Jeunesse*, a young workers' organization set up by Vichy in an effort to protect its members from deportation to Germany. Armored vehicles surrounded the men, the factory gates were closed, and guards had been posted. A sergeant was shouting *"Raus! Raus!"* ("Out! Out!"). The men were anxious, but they did not think that the Germans would hold them responsible for the FTP attack. At about 1:00 p.m., the fire engine was sent around again to broadcast in French that reprisals were taking place. Apart from the captives, and several hundred people who were forced to witness the hangings, virtually the entire population of the town was hiding behind drawn shutters. To be sure they stayed there, the Germans sporadically directed machine gun fire at the shutters. At about 3:00 p.m., after they had eaten their lunch, the SS officers arrived at the Giat factory. Colonel Bouty, the mayor, then arrived and asked Kowatch if Espinasse might minister to the condemned men, pointing out that this was their right under the Geneva Convention. Kowatch replied that the Abbé could do so if he was quick about it.

The Germans divided the prisoners that they had selected into two groups of sixty, and ordered the first group into some nearby stables. The first ten to be executed were taken from this group. The Abbé walked with them to the junction of the route du Pont Neuf and the route 4 Septembre, where the Germans had prepared for the hangings by suspending nooses from balconies and lamp posts. They had used butcher's rope from the local abattoir.

With their hands tied behind their backs, the victims were forced up plasterers' ladders. An SS soldier on a second ladder then placed the noose round the victim's neck, and the ladder was kicked away. Most of the hostages died without uttering a sound, although one man went into spasm and was beaten until he died. The Germans who were not directly involved in the hangings were milling around, smoking, talking, and joking. We know from a photo of a hanging elsewhere, that they sometimes even posed for pictures shaking hands with a dead victim. La Chienne was also there, chain-smoking, and according to certain accounts, she blew smoke into the victims' faces.

At the start of the hangings, the Abbé was under the impression that only ten men were to die; he may not have seen or believed the notice detailing 120 executions. Ten more, however, were quickly pushed in front of the first ten that were hung. He ministered to these, despite the growing impatience of the Germans. Between batches of hostages executed, he was engaged in conversation with Lieutenant Walter Schmald, the local Gestapo chief who had survived the FTP attack by climbing out the window of the *Souillac École Normale*, who was directing the process. Schmald admitted that he was a Catholic—he had been at a school run by Belgian monks—and said that he had only joined the Gestapo to avoid being sent to the Eastern Front. The Abbé retorted that he was hanging innocent men and that the FTP were long gone. Schmald insisted that he was merely following orders and besides, those chosen were either *résistants* or their friends. Espinasse pointed out that the commanding officer who ordered the executions was hardly going to count the victims. Acknowledging the point and conceding that his fellow Germans had had recourse to a Catholic priest after the FTP attack, Schmald said that Espinasse could console the other prisoners. The priest did so, and many handed him wallets and notes to give to their loved ones. A German soldier saw this and tried to grab the wallets, but when Espinasse yelled "Verboten!" at him, he backed off.

When ninety victims had been hanged, and the next group of victims was being selected from the thirty or so who remained, the Abbé once again pleaded for their mercy. Initially, Schmald refused, saying that he would be reported and shot, but when thirteen hostages had been selected for the next batch to hang, the Abbé pointed out that there were more than the usual ten. Schmald agreed to release three of them. After some indecision, he released the youngest. At this point, an Alsatian soldier named Elimar Schneider intervened. According to the account Schneider wrote later about the events at Tulle (under the *nom de plume* Sadi Schmeid), he summoned the courage to ask Schmald to also save a young Frenchman, Pierre Torquebois, who had begged for his help. Schmald agreed, and suggested that a fifth hostage be released for good measure. When this was done, the freed men embraced and wept. This account is generally consistent with that of Espinasse, except that the Abbé credits the Alsatian with saving just one hostage, which is born out by the final reckoning of ninety-nine men hanged.

While the German officers had said that the dead should be thrown into the river Corrèze, the Secretary General Roche and a German doctor argued against it. Eventually, the young men from the Giat factory collected the bodies and buried them in two shallow graves, one holding eighty men, and the other nineteen. At around 10:00 p.m., the Secretary General and mayor pleaded with the Germans not to deport the remaining hostages. The Germans turned down their pleas, and the men were loaded into trucks in groups of thirty. Over the course of that night, they were transported to Limoges, and arrived at various times on Sunday, June 11th. In the course of that day, between 400 and 600 young workers, many from the *Chantiers de jeunesse*, were also sent to Limoges. There, they were surrounded by *miliciens*, German soldiers, and armored vehicles. On Monday, June 12th at 7:00 p.m., a number of the younger workers were freed, but many of the older hostages were moved to Poitiers and Compiègne, which were assembly points for the Dachau concentration camp. According to reports, of the 149 men who left Compiègne, forty-three died on the four-day journey to the camp. Of the 116 who arrived at Dachau alive, only forty-eight ever returned.

There is considerable dispute as to whether General Lammerding personally ordered the hangings at Tulle. Lilly Lavaud (née Laporte, I will refer to here as "Lilly"), who at the time of the massacre was eighteen and living in the nearby town of Uzerche, told me that Lammerding requisitioned rooms in her family's house at 28, Avenue de Paris. Over the two days (June 8 and 9), she came into close contact with the General. While she was unable to resolve the question of whether or not he ordered the hangings, she was able to provide a telling portrait of him. He arrived at 11:00 p.m., and was given the main bedroom on the second floor. Lilly, however, could only reach her own bedroom through this room. After some discussion, an arrangement was worked out whereby she would signal him if she needed to go in or out of her room. In this discussion, and in Lammerding's later dealings with her family, he was polite and correct. He communicated in heavily accented but adequate French.

The other side of his character was starkly displayed the next morning, Friday, June 9, when Lammerding was ensconced in the pharmacy of Lilly's first cousin, Pierre Laporte, across the road. Ironically, Laporte was the head of the Uzerche Resistance. The SS brought in three young *maquisards* whom they had discovered driving a truck loaded with munitions out of Tulle. Two young women who had asked for a lift, but had turned out to be the mistresses of Lieutenant Schmald and his fellow officer, Lieutenant Beck, had denounced the *maquisards*. When the *maquisards* were brought before Lammerding, one of them, Chauvignat, was found to be carrying the identification chains of several dead German policemen, evidently taken from their bodies as souvenirs after the Tulle attack.

The three young men were lined up in the street as if they were going to be executed. Then Lammerding ordered that Chauvignat be hanged, and this was carried out where his suspended body could clearly be seen from Lilly's window. The two other *maquisards* were forced to watch the execution, and there were reports that the mistresses amused themselves by twirling the corpse round by the feet. One of the surviving *maquisards*, Raymond Monteil, tried to stall for time by telling the general that he could take the SS to a *maquis* hiding place—where he planned to show them a recently vacated one. Lammerding declined but offered Monteil a cigarette. Emboldened, Monteil said that he was hungry, and Lammerding ordered a guard to take him to the Laporte house and asked them to feed him, which they did. It turned out that it was Monteil's twentieth birthday. The townspeople later asked the general what was to happen to the two *maquisards*, and Lammerding assured them that the two young men would be released the next morning. In fact, they were deported, and neither ever came back. When the townspeople asked if they could take down Chauvignat's body, Lammerding refused, saying that he wanted it left up as an example.

According to Lilly, Lammerding mentioned on his return to the house at about 4:30 p.m. that there had been a reprisal in Tulle for the FTP attack. Given that the phone lines were cut and the radio equipment unusable because of the terrain, it is unclear how this information would have reached him, had he not been in Tulle himself. Whether or not he gave a specific order for the hangings or specified the number to be executed, it is highly likely he was aware of what was happening, and at best, raised no objection. Lilly's account of her dealings with him, in which his insistence on social correctness was contrasted with his pitilessness in his SS role, appears to encapsulate Lammerding's character perfectly.

Another view of the Tulle affair was provided to me by the mother of a friend of ours, Mme Jacqueline (Villain) Patriarche. Her husband, Robert Villain, (*nom de guerre* Captain Verdier) was one of the heads of the AS in Tulle. They were a much smaller group than the Communist FTP and did not participate in the attack on the French garrison because they felt that it was premature. Mme Patriarche's husband was regularly provided with copies of the messages sent to the Prefect by both Vichy and the Germans which he could translate as he spoke German, so he was well-informed. She said that Lieutenant Walter Schmald who presided over the hangings, later fled to Brive where he was captured and subsequently executed.

As Guingouin and Captain Verdier had warned, the FTP attack on Tulle was premature, and the town's people paid dearly for it, with ninety-nine men hanged and a further 149 deported, most never to return. The event poses, in the starkest possible terms, the question of whether the gains won by such attacks justified their cost to civilians, especially given the possibility that the FTP had more than half an eye on post-war political considerations.

A further question concerns the legitimacy (or otherwise) of non-uniformed militias. De Gaulle's broadcast to the Germans at the time of the Normandy invasion stated that the Resistance was the internal army of France, and that if any of its members were captured, they should be treated as prisoners of war. Sperrle's response on June 8 was to state that members of the French Resistance were to be treated as guerrillas or spies. In general, the Germans took the position that since the Resistance did not bear arms openly, and did not habitually wear uniforms or insignia, they were not entitled to the protection afforded by the Conventions. In November 1948, the Bordeaux military tribunal acquitted a German officer, Reutter, who had executed four *maquisards*, as the court agreed with the defense that the officer was justified in treating the *maquisards* as spies. In the course of the appeal, when the German was again acquitted, the father of one of the victims came in the courtroom and tried without success to shoot the defendant; he was sentenced to three months in prison.

Chapter 7

The Division Billets Near Limoges

By Friday June 9, the First Battalion of the Division under Major Diekmann was billeted in St. Junien. A centre of glove-making and leather work, St. Junien was situated eighteen miles to the west of Limoges, and was the closest town to the railway bridge that the Resistance had attacked on the night of June 7. On the 8th, to add insult to injury, about 300 *maquisards* had occupied St. Junien for a few hours (there was no German garrison). There had been another significant Resistance action at Guéret, fifty miles northeast of Limoges, where on the June 7th the *maquis* had overwhelmed the German garrison. A Wehrmacht unit from Rochechouart had attempted to retake the town the following day, but had been repulsed. On June 9, Major Kämpfe and elements of his Third Battalion billeted nearby in Rochechouart, were sent by Colonel Stadler to accomplish what the Wehrmacht had failed to achieve. However, in the meantime with the help of the Luftwaffe, the Wehrmacht finally succeeded in recapturing Guéret.

Before Kämpfe and his battalion arrived at Guéret, the head of the Wehrmacht unit informed the mayor that he intended to conduct reprisals once the town had been retaken. However, a Spanish diplomat who had been posted to Vichy, captured by the *maquis*, and then released by the Wehrmacht, intervened. He told the Wehrmacht captain that Spain was one of the very few friends that the Third Reich had at that moment, and that Germany risked shocking world opinion if they carried out actions like the proposed reprisals at Guéret, which amounted to war crimes. Whether persuaded by this argument, or simply because the Wehrmacht were less inclined than the SS to brutal counter-measures, the Captain cancelled the reprisal order.

By the time that Major Kämpfe arrived, after capturing and executing some of the fleeing *maquisards* outside the town, the battle was over. Kämpfe had a few words with the Wehrmacht Captain, and then instructed his medical officer, Muller, to start back to Limoges with the wounded SS. Shortly afterwards, Muller saw Kämpfe at the wheel of his open Talbot, driving towards Limoges, alone. As he passed the medical officer, Kämpfe gave a brief wave. A short while later, Muller found the Talbot standing in the road with its motor running. There was no sign of a struggle, and it has been suggested that Kämpfe was answering a call of nature when he was discovered by the *maquisards*. Muller radioed Limoges to sound the alarm, and Kämpfe's troops were sent out to search for him. They did so until midnight. In the course of the search, they questioned and executed a number of locals, but acquired no useful information. It would later transpire that Major Kämpfe was the highest-ranking German officer captured by the Resistance up to that time during the Occupation of France.

Although the SS would be frustrated in their attempts to find Kämpfe, the search was not entirely without benefit to them. On the morning of the June 10, sometime after 10:00 a.m., a party was scouring the village of Salon-la-Tour, about twenty-nine miles south of Limoges, when a black Citroën approached and abruptly halted. A young boy got out and raced away into the fields. Then a man and a woman armed with submachine guns climbed out and started to run, too. The Germans opened fire, and a chase ensued. The woman twisted her ankle and was captured. The man and the boy, meanwhile, got away. The woman was brought before Major Kowatch, who had overseen the Tulle hangings the day before. Ultimately they learned that she was English and had been parachuted into the area on June 6, D-Day. Her name was Violette Szabó, and she was a Special Operations Executive (SOE) agent. The SOE was a spy operation organized by the British and later coordinated with the American Office of Strategic Services (OSS), the predecessor of the Central Intelligence Agency (CIA).

Born as Violette Bushnell, she had grown up in London, and at the age of nineteen, she had married a French Foreign Legion officer (Illustration 9). When Captain Etienne Szabó was killed at El Alamein two years later, he left his widow with a daughter, Tania, who he had never seen. Violette thereafter joined SOE. Her first mission was to Rouen to assess the effectiveness of the local Resistance movement in the wake of a series of arrests. Twice stopped by the Gestapo, she talked her way out of an arrest and was safely returned to London after stopping to buy her daughter Tania a dress in Paris. Upon arrival on June 6 for her second mission, she had been taken to Sussac, twenty-eight miles southeast of Limoges, to identify Resistance leaders who were prepared to take orders from London. When the SS captured her, she was with Jacques Dufour (*nomme de guerre* Anastasie) on the way to meet such a contact. The boy had thumbed a ride. After interrogation by Major Kowatch, Szabó was transferred to Fresnes Prison in Paris and further interrogated by SS Major Kieffer (later executed for war crimes) at the Gestapo headquarters at 84 Avenue Foch. She was then sent to Ravensbrück concentration camp north of Berlin, where in late January or early February 1945, at age 23, she was executed.

9. Violette Szabó of the Special Operations Executive who was parachuted into France and was captured by the Nazis during the hunt for Major Kämpfe.

When Major Diekmann visited SS headquarters in Limoges on the morning of June 10, he was informed about Kämpfe's disappearance. According to one source, Thomine, a *milicien* who shared a mistress with the Gestapo officer Schmald, who had supervised the Tulle hangings, told him about Kämpfe. In Limoges, Diekmann also met Lieutenant Karl Gerlach, who the previous day had been inspecting the planned accommodation for the Third Company in Nieul, a few miles from Oradour, when he and his driver were captured by *maquisards*. The driver was shot but Gerlach managed to escape in his underwear. After questioning Gerlach, Diekmann returned to St. Junien. There he met and talked to members of the Gestapo and Milice. After the meeting, he and Captain Kahn led the Third Company to Oradour-sur-Glane, a distance of about eight miles.

PART I
THE MASSACRE

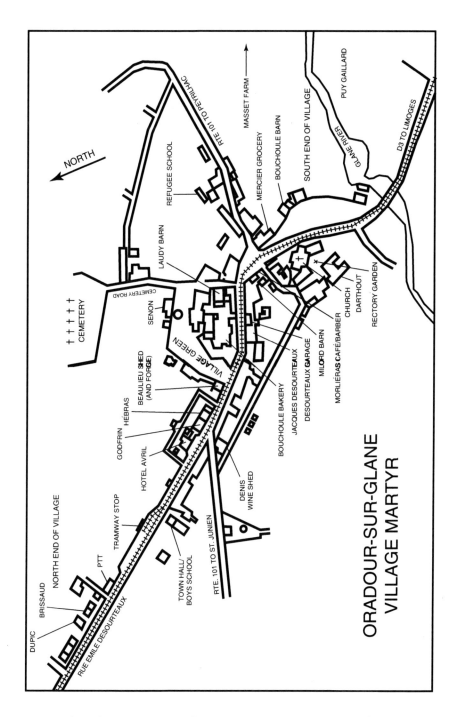

10. Map of Oradour-sur-Glane, Village Martyr, showing places mentioned in the book.

Chapter 8

Oradour-sur-Glane, June 10, 1944

A Quiet Village Until The Germans Arrived

In 1944, Oradour-sur-Glane was the most ordinary and typical of Limousin villages. Situated on a slight incline, bordered to the south by the river Glane, whose shadowy charms were hidden from sight in a wooded valley, it offered an uneventful quietude. Many of the Oradour families had lived there for generations. In 1914, the village had seen its' sons depart for the First World War, many of them never to return. For the duration of the Second World War, it had suffered the Vichy regime and the imposition of a Vichy-approved mayor in silence. The population of Oradour in the 1936 census was 1,574, of whom only 300 lived in the village proper with the rest scattered in a number of surrounding hamlets and farms. Since 1939, a number of refugees had arrived in the village—Spanish, Jewish, Alsatian and Lorraine—and they were now integrated to a greater or lesser degree into the community. The villages itself housed just over 400 while the rest were spread among a number of surrounding hamlets (Illustration 11).

Oradour had several hotels, restaurants and cafes. The children were housed in four different schools: the boys' school across from the tramway station, the girls' school in the middle of the village, another school for young girls on the road to Peyrilhac, and the school for the refugee children from Alsace and Lorraine next door. The total number

Douglas W. Hawes

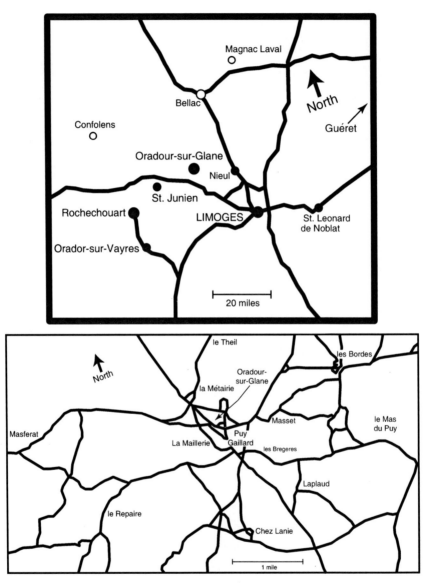

11. Bottom, map of some of the hamlets and villages surrounding Oradour-sur-Glane. Top, map of area around Oradour-sur-Glane showing the main places mentioned in the text.

of school children was 191. (Illustration 10, the map preceding this chapter shows the main sites mentioned in this Part I.)

In most respects, this peaceful country village was far removed from the war. No German soldier had set foot there since November 11, 1942, when troops had moved into the previously unoccupied zone of France south of the Loire River, and a column of military vehicles had passed uneventfully through the village. There was rationing in Oradour, as there was all over France, but because this was a farming area with a flourishing "gray" market, food was easier to come by than in the big cities. Indeed, people came from Limoges to Oradour on weekends for the express purpose of buying food. Most of the people of Oradour, especially the refugees, feared and disliked the Germans and hoped for an Allied invasion. Despite the fact that the Resistance was well developed in the Haute-Vienne Department (particularly the FTP under Georges Guingouin), no one who lived in the village was actively involved. The landing in Normandy on June 6 had not been celebrated there because Vichy radio, the main source of news, had announced that the Allies had been forced back into the channel.

At 1:45 p.m. on Saturday, June 10, four days after the launching of the invasion, nineteen-year-old Robert Hébras, and seventeen-year-old Martial Brissaud were passing the time on Oradour's main street, the rue Emile Desourteaux (Illustration 12). Most of the houses had shuttered windows, and were roofed with the reddish tile of the region. On warm days, people would sit on their front steps and chat with those passing by. There were sidewalks, curbs, and a sewage system. The electric and telephone wires hung from poles along the tramway side of the road

The morning had been rainy and cool, but by noon the sun was shining and it was hot and humid. The two young men chatted in front of the Hébras house about the soccer game they were scheduled to play on Sunday. In front of them, as they talked, was the tramway. The tracks followed the main street, and the Oradour stop was just a few feet north of the Hébras house (Illustration 13). This tramway provided employment for Robert's father, Jean, whose job was to survey and repair the line's electrical connections. The tramway served as a vital link to Limoges, fourteen miles to the southeast, a trip of about an hour. It permitted many in the village, such as Robert Hébras to work in Limoges.

12. Rue Desourteaux, the Oradour main street, in 1932.

13. Tram at the tramway station with the Poste TT in the background to the left. The Hotel Avril and the residences of the Hébras and Godfrin are off the picture to the right, all on the main street.

Oradour-The Final Verdict

14. Georgette Hébras, age 22 in front of the Hébras house a few weeks before the drama.

Normally, on a Saturday morning, Robert would have been working as a mechanic in the Schmitt garage in Limoges. On Friday, however, a German officer had gotten into an argument with the boss, M. Mounet (part of the garage had been requisitioned for work on German military vehicles). Later, Mounet had assembled the workers and told the younger men, including Robert, that it might be unwise for them to return to the garage. Robert's twenty-two-year-old sister, Georgette, a hospital nurse, also worked in Limoges, but had stayed home that Saturday because she was sick and because of fear of possible Allied bombardments (Illustration 14). Robert had been at a neighbor's house fixing an electrical socket and his father was helping a farmer take some cattle to the nearby town of Saint Victurnien.

As Robert and Martial chatted, Mme Marie Hébras, Robert's mother, came to the door of the house with her younger daughter, Denise, age 9 and she and Robert kissed the little girl goodbye as she set off to school. In Oradour, as in much of France, the children had Thursdays off and went to school all day Saturday. On that particular Saturday, they were also to have a medical examination in the afternoon.

No sooner had Denise and the other children departed, than two armored half-tracks appeared from the south entrance to the village. The half-tracks each carried about a dozen soldiers in camouflaged uniforms who brandished their weapons as they scanned the upper and lower stories of the buildings (Illustration 15 & 16). Minutes later, the two armored vehicles returned from the north or upper end of the village with just their drivers.

Martial Brissaud noted this with alarm, but Robert told him that there was nothing to be afraid of. "I see them in Limoges all the time," he assured his friend. (Hébras did not know they were Waffen SS.) Martial was unconvinced, partly because he had ignored a notice calling

15. German soldiers, probably members of the 2nd Battalion of the Regiment Der Fuhrer whose picture was taken sometime before the massacre and found in an SS soldier's satchel recovered in Oradour.

16. A German half-track similar to that used in Oradour.

him to serve in the STO. Hébras was dismissive of these fears, "Don't worry," he told Brissaud as the seventeen-year-old left. "They won't eat us." By now, hearing the commotion of the Germans' arrival, many of the villagers were out on the street or looking from their doors and windows. Martial went about a seventy-five yards south towards the village green (Illustration 17) where he exchanged a few words with his friend André Bardet, before turning around and heading back up the main street toward his house at the north end of the village. Going inside, Hébras told his mother and Georgette that the Germans were in the village. His mother urged him to hide, but he replied that he saw no reason to do so since his papers were in order.

As Martial headed home he passed the town hall where he saw Dr. Paul Desourteaux, a distinguished-looking man of seventy-two, with a white moustache and goatee. Despite losing the previous election to a Socialist in 1936, Desourteaux had been assigned to the post as head of the "*délégation spéciale*" by Vichy after the Armistice, and he performed the function of mayor. He talked to the round-faced and rotund Leonard Rousseau, who along with his wife, Jeanne, ran the boys' school. Seeing Martial, Desourteaux asked him where he was headed in such a hurry. Martial paused just long enough to say that he was going to hide from the Germans. The mayor, smiling, said to tell him tomorrow where his hiding place was. In fact, Martial went by a circuitous route away from the main street and hid in the attic of his house.

Marcel Darthout was a twenty-year-old, owlishly bespectacled young man. He was the tallest member of the *Union Sportive de Oradour* (the soccer club), and lived in a building behind the church with his wife and mother. Hoping to get a haircut, he had made his way at around 1:45 p.m. to Lucien Morliéras' barber shop next to the giant oak, called the "Tree of Liberty" planted in 1848, at the junction of the main street and the Peyrilhac road. Arriving before the shop opened for the afternoon, he saw the column of German vehicles including, at that point, three trucks as well as the two half-tracks Hébras had seen, moving northward up the main street of the village, having crossed the Glane River bridge (Illustration 18). Fearful of being arrested, Darthout hurried home. From there, he tried to escape across the fields towards the Glane River but saw that a line of German soldiers was surrounding the town. He retreated into the house where, a few seconds later,

17. Village green before the war.

18. Glane River Bridge with the church in the background.

a soldier armed with a rifle came into the kitchen and pushed him, his wife, Angèle (26) and his mother, Anna (40) outside. All around them, the Germans went from building to building, and were forcing the inhabitants out. The Darthout family joined a line of others being escorted to the village green.

One of those found and forced to join those going toward the village green was Mathieu Borie, a thirty-three year-old mason by trade. He was working on a wall in the grocery store of his relatives, the Merciers, across from the church. He had seen the Nazi column moving towards the north end of the village. Borie had promised to join the Resistance when the time came to liberate the area, but he was not active at that time.

Clément Broussaudier, a twenty-five-year-old delivery man, also had a haircut in mind when, at about 2:00 p.m., he rode his bicycle into Oradour. He lived in a hamlet outside the village. As the barber opened his doors, the convoy of German vehicles passed by outside. Wheeling his bicycle inside instead of leaving it in front of the shop, as he normally would have done, Broussaudier put on a white apron and installed himself in a chair. The assistant who cut his hair was Joseph Bergmann, a twenty-seven-year-old refuge from Alsace who had been born in Kokern, Germany.

Halfway through the haircut, two soldiers came into the shop. One stood guard at the entrance and the other forced the occupants outside. As the soldier grabbed him by the shoulders and pushed him towards the door, Broussaudier tried to explain that he wanted to take his bicycle, but the soldier motioned for him to leave it. He emphasized his point by shoving the butt of his gun into the deliveryman's back as he propelled him out the door. Outside, Broussaudier could hear the town crier, Jean Depierrefiche. Flanked by soldiers, Depierrefiche was standing near the covered market place next to the church and under the "Tree of Liberty." He was beating his drum and reading aloud an order to the people of the village that they were to assemble at the village green for an identity check.

Several residents, particularly those whose situation was in some way irregular, chose to hide like Martial Brissaud. The two Beaubreuil brothers, Joseph (32) and Maurice (21) the former an escaped prisoner of war and the latter evading the STO, sought safety in the cellar of the Merciers' grocery store where Borie had been working on the wall. The store belonged to their aunt and uncle, with whom they had been having lunch.

Armand Senon, a twenty-nine-year-old baker, who had broken his leg thirteen days earlier in a soccer match, was lying on a sofa on the second floor of his house, which overlooked the village green. He was talking to his nineteen-year-old fiancée, Irene Redon, when a soldier burst in, ordered them to leave, and told them to go to the village green. Armand showed the soldier the cast on his leg and indicated that he could not move. The soldier escorted Irene, his father and uncles (who were downstairs) out of the house, but left Armand behind. In the course of the soldiers' sweep through the village, several of those who were bedridden were not so fortunate and were shot on the spot. The shots were apparently not heard by those on the village green, most of whom had taken the German announcement of an identity check at face value, although Hébras had actually forgotten to bring his.

Hubert Desourteaux, age 32, was one of the four sons of the mayor (Jacques, a doctor, Emile, a grocer, and Etienne, the secretary of his father, were the others). A notably handsome man, Desourteaux was concerned because he was an escaped prisoner of war. At the Armistice in 1940, the Germans had put over 1,800,000 French soldiers in prisoner of war camps, mainly in Germany. Of those, some 200,000 eventually escaped—mainly those who had been assigned to work on farms.

That Saturday afternoon Desourteaux, a mechanic, was working in his garage on the main street with his assistant, Aimé Renaud, when they heard the rumble of vehicles entering the village from the south end. They left their work and saw the German convoy go to the north end of the village. When the two half-tracks came slowly back, all the inhabitants went indoors. The two men returned to the garage and tried to escape out of the back door and through the fields on the outskirts of the village, but it was too late. As soon as they were out in the open, they heard bullets whistling around them. Retreating, they hid in the walled garden behind Desourteaux's brother Jacques' house along the main street from the garage. Within minutes, they were joined by Hubert's brother, Etienne, Renaud's wife, Janine, a hairdresser, and Mme Robert whom Desourteaux did not know. Desourteaux told the women that there was no need for them to hide because they were not at risk. To

Aimé Renaud and Etienne he said that he was going to hide, but that they should do what they thought best.

Running from the walled garden into his brother's house, which was being refurbished, Desourteaux hid in a small space where a toilet was being installed. The two women hid in a hen house and Aimé in a garden of peas. Hubert did not see where Etienne went. The soldiers were going from house to house, shouting that everyone should go to the village green. The tradesmen, meanwhile, were closing the metal shutters on their shops. Shortly afterwards, two soldiers broke down the front door. While searching, they came within a few feet of Hubert Desourteaux's hiding place, but finding the house empty and unfurnished, quickly moved on.

Forty-six-year-old Marguerite Rouffranche was married to Simon, a farmer, and she was the mother of three children: Jean (23), Amélie (21), and Andrée (18). The family lived at the Gaudy farm about 300 yards beyond the river-bridge on the south side of the village. From there, soldiers carrying guns and shouting orders escorted them to the village green.

Jacqueline Pinède, was a twenty-year-old Jewish refugee from Bayonne, a town near the Spanish border on the Eastern seaboard which the Germans had occupied since 1940. She had been expelled from Bayonne with her grandmother, father, mother, sixteen-year-old sister and nine-year-old brother.

They had moved into a house next to the Hotel Avril near the Hébras's house on the rue Emile Desourteaux where, despite the quietness of Oradour, they had lived in a state of constant alert. In fact the father had the girls live across the street in the Valentin hairdresser's building in case the father was arrested.

When Jacqueline's father, Robert, saw the Germans arrive, he told her: "Take your brother and sister and hide. You never know with those people. I will look after your mother." Robert, his wife Carmen, and his mother went along with the soldiers to the village green, in part to distract attention from their children who were hiding under an outside staircase of the hotel. Another Jewish refugee, a dentist from Rennes named René Levy, did not hesitate when he saw the Germans, but fled through the fields. His wife was already in a concentration camp.

At about this time, Robert Hébras saw Martial Machefer, a thirty-six-year-old Oradour shoemaker, on the St. Junien road. Machefer had seen the German column loaded with soldiers pass through the village. He watched from the second floor window of his house at the corner of the village green and the main street next to the Beaulieu forge. His wife had insisted that he leave the house because as a known Communist, Machefer was being closely watched by the Gestapo and the Milice. He was stopped on the outskirts of town, a short while later, by a group of some thirty soldiers. When he showed them his wounded veteran's card, they made him take off his shoes and show them his scars. Afterwards, one of the soldiers (French-speaking, so almost certainly one of the Alsatians) told him that he should, "Get going." As he moved away, another soldier said that he should be made to go to the village, but the other replied, "Let him go. There will be plenty as it is." Besides his wife and two daughters, there was a fifteen-year-old Jewish refugee named Sarah Jakobowicz living with them. Terrified, Jakobowicz hid under the bed when the Germans came. She did not go to the village green.

Roger Godfrin, a seven-year-old redhead (Illustration 19) who lived next door to the Hébras family, was the son of Arthur Godfrin, an assistant baker. The Godfrin family originally came from the town of Charly in the Moselle Department of Lorraine. When the Nazis had annexed their Department in August 1940, they had been expelled for harboring pro-French sentiments. Carrying no more than seventy-five pounds of belongings with them, the maximum permitted by the Germans, they and other families from Lorraine totaling around 80 in all had sought refuge in Oradour. The majority of them were from the town of Charly. In addition, there were twenty-four Alsatian refugees.

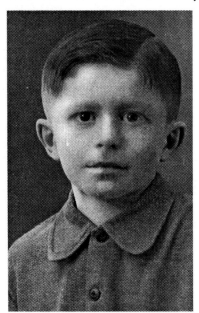

19. Roger Godfrin, 7, not long before the SS attack.

At 2:00 p.m. that day, Roger Godfrin was in class with his sisters

Marie-Jeanne (13), and Pierrette (11). The teacher was thirty-three-year-old Fernand Gougeon, also from Lorraine. The school was temporary and constructed of very flimsy material. When he heard the first shots fired, Gougeon ordered the children to lie flat on the floor. A German came in and leveled his submachine gun at the children, and said the single word *"Raus!"* Roger said to one of his classmates, "They are the Germans. I know them, and they will hurt us. I am going to try to save myself." When the soldier turned to speak to the teacher, Roger whispered to his sisters to come with him, but they started to cry and called for their mother. So he slipped away without them. He took the stairs to the yard and started to run, losing a shoe in the process. He heard shooting, but it was not directed at him.

A short while later, he saw more Germans. This time they did shoot at him. He fell to the ground, and when a soldier approached, he pretended to be dead. The soldier gave him a kick in the kidneys, but he did not react. Finally they left, and Godfrin got to his feet and followed the advice that his mother had impressed on him: "If you see the Boches, hide in the woods behind the cemetery." As he approached the cemetery, he heard a whistle, and saw two German soldiers behind the gate. To his amazement, they signaled to him to run away. Godfrin fled back down the path and met Marcelin Thomas, the fifty-two-year-old baker who employed his father. The two of them took cover behind a hedge where they discovered Octavie Dalstein (also from Lorraine) and Françoise Devoyon. Still terrified, Godfrin started to run again. He finally reached the bank of the river where he found a black and white dog from the village, named Bobby. As the boy and the dog hid beneath the trees, six soldiers in a half-track drove past, saw them, and opened fire. Godfrin dove into the river and swam to the far side, where he hid behind a large oak tree. The dog stayed on the village side and was shot dead—perhaps because of the soldiers' frustration at Godfrin's escape.

Assembly on the Village Green

Soon most of the people of the village were streaming towards the assembly point: women carrying babies and pushing baby carriages, the children from the village's four schools with their teachers, men of all ages and in varying states of health; and families brought in from outlying farms in the half-tracks. Hébras saw his little sister, Denise, whom he had kissed goodbye on her way to school less than an hour before, arrive at the village green with her class, and ran to her mother. The head of the girls' school, Mme Binet, arrived in her bathrobe as she was pregnant and feeling unwell, so had stayed home from school. Mme Rousseau, the teacher at the boys' school, arrived with her own children.

While the villagers were being assembled, a test tram without any paying passengers arrived from Limoges, driven by Martial Dauriat. Riding with Dauriat was another employee named Tabaro and a WW I veteran named Marcelin Chalard whom Hébras' father had replaced in the tramway company. Chalard had come to Oradour to try on a suit which he had ordered for a wedding in July. There were no paying passengers as this was a test run. When the tram reached the bridge over the Glane, the men found it choked with trucks, soldiers, and civilians, including a group of bicyclists, who were being herded towards the village. As Dauriat, Tabaro and Chalard waited the electricity that ran the tram cut out—not an infrequent occurrence at this point in the war. Dauriat was considering leaving the tram; but when his colleague Chalard, who was known as a somewhat impulsive man, climbed down, he was grabbed by a soldier and forced to join the march. When he turned to signal to Dauriat, his sudden movement caused a nervous soldier to shoot him. Chalard fell against the railing of the bridge. There, he was shot twice more in the head, and fell dead.

The Oradour village green, a swathe of grass about fifty yards across and 200 yards from end-to-end, rose from the main street on the northwest side in the middle of the village. After approximately half its length, it turned southwest to join the Cemetery Road. From about 2:15 p.m., the lower arm of the village green gradually filled with the people of the village, surrounded by armed soldiers. The upper part had been closed off by the Germans, who had positioned six light machine guns and crews at strategic points on the grass. By 3:00 p.m., more than 600 villagers were gathered there, and despite assurances conveyed by the French-speaking Alsatians that this was an identity check, many of them were unnerved by such an aggressive display of force. Some speculated that the Germans' purpose might be to take hostages or deport people. Hébras and his friends, however, their fears allayed in part by the untroubled demeanor of the war veterans, were still chatting about the upcoming soccer game. Jacques Desourteaux, a thirty-eight-year-old doctor who shared his brother Hubert's good looks, drove up, and parked his car near the village green. A soldier approached him and ordered him to join the other villagers.

The wait continued. The marshalling of the villagers had been carried out with an air of urgency, but now the soldiers no longer seemed to be in any hurry. It grew increasingly hot, and the village green offered little shade. The baker, Maurice Compain, 44, was standing near Hébras without his shirt and was still covered with flour. He approached one of the younger guards and asked if he could cross to his bakery which bordered the village green and take his cakes out of the oven. He said he was afraid that they were going to burn. Smiling, the guard replied in heavily accented French, "Don't worry about your cakes. We will see to them."

The Men Separated from the Women and Children

At around 3:00 p.m., the soldiers began separating the men from the women and children. The men were sent to the left of the village green (as seen from the main road) and the women and children to the right. Mme Rousseau demanded to keep her sixteen-year-old handicapped son, Pierre, with her and was eventually allowed to do so. Marcel Darthout managed to see his wife and mother leave, the former in tears. Mme Rouffranche had earlier embraced her husband and son, but only a very few of the other villagers were able to do so or even to exchange words of comfort with their loved ones. The men were ordered into three lines, facing the buildings on the left side of the village green. The women and children were escorted away. Concerned, but powerless to act, the men watched them go. A German officer called for silence and speaking in German-inflected French, demanded to see the mayor. Paul Desourteaux stepped forward and was asked to produce fifty hostages. He replied, "I cannot nominate hostages." At that instant, he was seized and escorted towards the town hall (which was in the same building as the boys' school, opposite the tramway station at the north end of the village). Ten minutes later he was returned. The demand for hostages was repeated. . Desourteaux replied, "Very well, I nominate myself, and if necessary, my family too." The offer was ignored and the mayor was ordered to join the rest of the men.

For almost half an hour, nearly 200 men waited in the increasingly hot sun. Some of them sat down. A few of them talked. The soldiers appeared to relax, too, chatting and even laughing among themselves. Finally, the officer who had addressed the mayor told the men (through an interpreter) to stand up and be quiet. He asked if they owned any weapons. A few men replied that they owned hunting rifles but the officer did not appear interested. Insisting that there were weapons and other munitions stored in Oradour by terrorists, he announced that his men were going to conduct a thorough search of the village. While this was happening the villagers would be put into barns and other holding areas, and as soon as the weapons were found, those not implicated would be set free. This statement came as a relief to the men who told each other that no amount of searching could produce weapons which were not there.

The Men Marched Off—The Executions Begin

The men, nearly 200 of them, were then separated into five groups of varying sizes—the largest sixty strong—and marched off with their escorts to pre-selected locations. The largest group, among them Robert Hebras, Marcel Darthout, Mathieu Borie, Clement Broussaudier, Maurice Compain, Pierre-Henri Poutaraud, and Lucien Moliéras and Joseph Bergmann, the barbers, were the last to leave. They were led down the main street toward the church. As they went, they saw one group in front of them go into the Desourteaux garage. The men there appeared relaxed despite the fact a machine gun had been set up on the street pointing at the garage. Farther along, they saw the group that was being shepherded towards the Milord barn near the church. The escorts of the Hébras group herded them to the left onto the Cemetery Road toward the Laudy barn, encouraging them with kicks and blows from the stocks of their weapons. There was no one else on the road, and they could only wonder what had happened to the women and children.

From his hiding place in his father's house next door, Hubert Desourteaux heard footsteps. Discovering a small hole in the construction material, he could see the women and children, many of whom he recognized, being taken to the church. After them came a group of about fifty to sixty men. One of the barbers was in front and, seemed to be joking with one of his friends behind him. Desourteaux then saw four civilian vehicles pass by, driven by soldiers. He recognized cars belonging to the Notaire, Pierre Montazeaud, and Maurice Picat.

When the men that Hubert had seen arrived at the Laudy barn, they were ordered to make room for themselves by dragging out farm wagons and bales of hay. The soldiers swept the area in front of the barn before placing their machine guns there and arranged themselves on the ground behind them. They had two light machine guns, two sub-machine guns, two rifles and the NCO in charge had a pistol. Some of the captives sat on the ground or on the remaining bales of hay, but those seated were quickly ordered to stand up and wait in a group against the rear wall of the barn. A corpulent soldier chewed a sugar cube, and Hébras said that he had seen him come out of one of the nearby houses carrying a box of sugar. After fifteen minutes, it became very hot and stuffy in the barn. The men were not concerned by the delay because they knew that a search of the village would take time. Then a refugee, Joseph Bergmann, the barber, who understood German, said that he had just heard one of the soldiers saying that they were going to shoot everyone. M. Darthout and the others were incredulous.

Before the men had time to react further, a sharp report from an automatic pistol came from the direction of the village green. It was the signal for the executions to begin. Immediately, the machine gunners in front of the buildings opened fire, as did the soldiers carrying rifles and submachine guns. There were screams, but many of the men died so quickly that they made no sound. Apparently the first rounds were aimed low at the legs. As soon as Borie realized what was happening he let himself fall. Many of his comrades were killed or wounded and, fell forward and away from those pressed against the rear wall. When the firing finally ceased, the barn was choked with dust. Groans and cries rose from the earthen floor as the wounded men called out for their loved ones.

Marcel Brissaud, the father of Martial, whose head was lying on top of Borie's legs cried out "The bastards! They have cut off my other leg" (he had lost a leg in WW I). Robert Hébras found himself buried beneath several bodies. At first, he did not even know if he had been hit—miraculously, he hadn't. He did feel the blood of those above him streaming down. He lay absolutely still, listening to the soldiers as they clambered over the fallen men to finish off the wounded. Some soldiers prodded the bodies with pitchforks. Hébras felt one of the soldiers step on his back but managed not to move a muscle. One of the soccer club members who was lying with his head across Hébras's leg, groaned and was shot. The bullet passed through his friend and lodged in Hébras.

Clément Broussaudier also fell down even though he, like Hébras, was initially unhurt. He felt one of the other villagers stir next to him, gravely wounded. He whispered to the other man not to move and then, feeling two boots on his legs, found himself so paralyzed by fear that he could no longer draw breath. A shot rang out behind his ears and he felt the other man stiffen and shudder. Unable to control his own trembling, Broussaudier was certain that he was about to die. Yvon Roby, age eighteen, fell flat on his stomach with his hands around his head. Bullets ricocheting off the wall struck him as he gagged on the dust and fragments of stone thrown up by the firing. He was wounded in the left arm.

The Germans brought straw, kindling, ladders, wagon wheels and any other combustibles that they could find into the barn and threw them on top of the bodies. One of the wheels fell on Broussaudier, crushing him to the point of suffocation. Another wheel would have killed him. After an agonizing few moments, he lifted his head to see if any of the soldiers were still there. They were, so he buried his head in the hay again.

The soldiers finally retreated down the road. Broussaudier and others heard the sound of a radio. First, German voices and, then loud music. When the soldiers returned fifteen or twenty minutes later, they were yelling like savage beasts. Broussaudier guessed what would follow. First, the animals were hauled out of the barn and a bonfire was lit. Flames and smoke immediately surrounded him. His jacket started to burn so he pulled it off, along with his beret. Another survivor, lying next to him, asked Broussaudier whether there were still any soldiers there. Cautiously, Broussaudier looked around, and saw two soldiers standing in front of the barn holding submachine guns. With the fire growing more and more intense, he forced himself back under other bodies. Soon, mercifully, the heat and smoke caused the soldiers to back away down the road. Borie asked in a loud whisper "who is still alive?" Jules Santrot, age 66, said that he was wounded in both legs. Pierre Duqueroix, the forty-seven-year-old game-warden said that he was wounded as did the barber Joseph Bergmann and Pierre-Henri Poutaraud, 33, the garage proprietor.

Marcel Darthout, who had not heard Borie, had fallen to the floor of the barn with two bullets in his calves and another two in his thighs. As the machine guns continued to fire in bursts, he was quickly covered with the bodies of the dead and dying. He could hear moaning and gasping. He could feel the blood of those on top of him, one of whom was, Joseph Bergmann. When the soldiers came in to finish off the wounded, he was certain that he would be shot, but he managed to remain silent. Somehow they did not notice him. He heard the soldiers laughing as they walked out. By now, the barn door was closed.

As soon as the footsteps had receded, Darthout touched the hand of the man next to him. Felix Aliotti, a twenty-eight-year-old former sergeant in the French army, told Darthout that his legs were broken and that he could not move. Darthout could feel his own wounded legs growing stiff when he heard someone moving about the barn and announcing the Germans had gone away. His clothes, by now burning, Darthout sat up, and saw that Broussaudier, Roby and Mathieu Borie, were also still alive. At first, Roby could not move because of the weight of the bodies on him. Also, he had difficulty lifting himself because of his wounded arm. Finally, however, the four of them staggered outside.

As the fire grew in strength, Robert Hébras also managed to extricate himself from the dead bodies of his companions. He expected to be cut down immediately, but no shot was fired. Making his way to a small door at the back of the barn, he discovered a small enclave. It was hard to see anything in the darkness, but it was soon apparent that the enclave had no exit or windows. A second door also turned out to be a dead end. The final door led to a yard where Hébras heard French voices with Limousin accents, and he found Darthout, Roby, Broussaudier and Borie. The latter two were not seriously wounded, but all of them were suffering acutely from thirst.

Borie, a mason by trade, had noticed that the wall of the barn next door was crumbling about twelve feet above the ground. He climbed up, and removing the stones one-by-one, made a hole that was large enough for the others to crawl through. On the other side, Borie and Hébras hid in a pile of firewood and the others climbed up into a hayloft. Soon, two soldiers came in through a door. One stood next to the woodpile, and the other climbed a ladder into the loft with a box of matches. He succeeded in lighting the straw. Climbing down again, the soldier fired a few incendiary rounds into the roof, which also caught fire, and then they both left. Soon, embers from the roof began falling on them and choking smoke surrounded them. The five villagers waited for as long as they could stand the heat, and then made their way to an outer yard which led onto the village green. When they looked around, however, they saw that soldiers were patrolling the Cemetery Road, cutting off their escape. As a temporary refuge, they took cover in the first of three brick-and-tile rabbit hutches which were attached to the exterior of the barn. The hutches were large enough to stand up in, and the gates of the yard were not quite shut, so the men were able to keep a partial watch on the soldiers patrolling the Cemetery Road. Behind them, the fire in the barn and the hay-loft was growing in strength.

Shortly, after hearing the machine guns and other arms firing in unison, Armand Senon (encumbered with his broken leg) looked warily out the window. He saw a group of seven bicyclists being shepherded by three soldiers. They stopped near Beaulieu forge on the main street. There, the cyclists were made to place their bikes against the wall after which they were lined up and machine-gunned. One of those killed was 35 year-old U.S.--born Albert Mirablon. A *maquisard*, Mirablon had been on a mission nearby, but had made a detour on his bike to visit his mother, Anna Chaleix. She had been born in Oradour but had immigrated to the U.S., married another French immigrant and settled in Paterson, New Jersey. After her husband's death, she had moved back to Oradour with Albert.

Realizing the danger he was in, and dragging his leg behind him, Armand Senon climbed through a back window and hid in a thicket in the field behind his house. He would remain there for the next 24 hours. During the night, when the Germans deployed a large spotlight, a number of patrols would pass within a few yards of him.

Killing The Women and Children in the Church

After they had been separated from the men on the village green, the women and children were marched a short distance to the church. When they had been herded inside, the doors were shut. From time to time, the Germans came in to inspect the interior of the church. Inside, approximately 250 women and 200 children were crammed into a church that normally seated 300, where they waited anxiously in near silence. More than sixty of the children were under six years of age. Some were in baby carriages, and some were being held in their mothers' arms. After about an hour and one half, at about 5:00 p.m., two Germans opened the front door and pushed the crowd to one side. Mme Rouffranche, who was there with her two daughters, saw them carrying a box of about 1-½ cubic feet to which several "tangled white strings" were attached. The box was clearly heavy. They placed it on two chairs in front of the altar, removed the cover and untangled the fuses (—the "white strings" Mme Rouffranche had seen).

They then lit them and left via the only other door to the church, in the Sainte Anne chapel to the right of the nave (Illustration 20), without saying a word. There was no panic among the women and children because most could not see what was going on. In a few moments, there was a loud, rumbling explosion, which blew out the stained-glass windows. Acrid black smoke filled the church. The smoke was asphyxiating and the women and children cried and screamed in panic as they tried to escape the fumes. Soon, there was a pitiful crush of bodies in front of the now locked door in the Sainte Anne chapel. Shortly afterwards, the Germans opened that door briefly and may have let some of the captives out after which Mme Rouffranche heard machine gun fire coming from that direction.

Mme Rouffranche, her two daughters, her grandson, and several others ran for the sacristy to the left of the main altar, and the desperate crowd eventually managed to break its locked door down. The comparatively fresh air of the sacristy allowed a few of them a brief respite from the smoke and chaos in the church, but the soldiers outside heard them. Opening the church doors, the soldiers came in as far as the sacristy door and sprayed them with machine gun fire. Other bullets came through the window of the sacristy. At the same time, other soldiers entered the basement of the sacristy and fired up through the floorboards. Within seconds, Mme Rouffranche's unmarried daughter, Andrée, was hit in the throat and killed. The Germans then threw grenades into the sacristy basement which ignited the wooden floor.

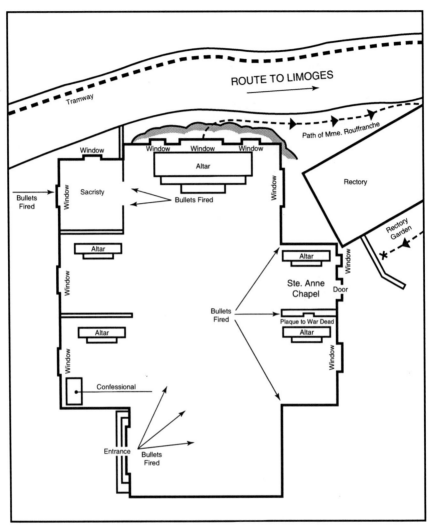

20. Diagram of the interior and exterior of the church showing where bullets were fired from; the dotted line represents the path of Mme. Rouffranche around the rectory to the garden behind where she lay for 24 hours.

Terrible screams followed as Mme Rouffranche's older daughter, Amélie Peyroux, and others were burned to death. Throughout these horrors, Mme Rouffranche remained motionless near the entrance to the sacristy, pretending to be dead. When the Germans entered the church, a wounded Spanish refugee sat by her feet. Weakly protesting that she wasn't French, the refugee died.

Inside the church, the Germans began throwing straw, firewood, church chairs, and benches on the bodies lighting them from the flames in the sacristy. When the flames reached Mme Rouffranche, singeing her hair, she ran through the smoke and hid behind the main altar. She found a small stepladder that was used for lighting the candles, and climbed up to the largest of the broken stained-glass windows above the altar. She heaved herself through it and fell ten feet to the ground, where brambles broke her fall. Another woman, Henriette Joyeux (née Hyvernaud), age 23, who had been married only a few months before, followed her to the window with her seven-month-old baby, Réne. Calling out, "Mother Rouffranche, catch my little one" she threw him out.

However, Mme Rouffranche was unable to catch the child and he was either killed in the fall or badly hurt. Hearing the baby cry out soldiers on the Limoges road shot and killed Mme Joyeux as she jumped out the window. Knowing she had been seen, Mme Rouffranche ran towards the rectory garden next door. Five automatic rounds struck her, fracturing her shoulder blade and injuring her thighs. Somehow, terribly wounded, she managed to crawl into a bed of peas in the garden where she lay as if dead. Fortunately, the Germans did not bother to check on her.

Burning and Looting the Village

While the women and children were being held in the church, the soldiers of the Third Company were busy looting and then setting fire to the buildings in the village. Some of those who had stayed in the buildings, like Sarah Jakobowicz, who had hidden under her bed in Martial Machefer's house, were burned alive. Others were able to flee.

The Beaubreuil brothers hid under a trap door in the Mercier house when the soldiers arrived. They heard the sound of looting, followed by the crackle of flames. They heard people talking in the yard, and they recognized the voices of Armand Senon's aunt and their own aunt's teenage maid. Then shots rang out and the women were silent, at which point the brothers crept from their hiding place. They crossed the burning floor, and escaped out the back. The Pinède children, who were hiding under the outside stairs at the Hotel Avril, were equally lucky. When the hotel began to burn, they ran for the cemetery. A group of soldiers who saw them held their fire and gestured that they should run away.

A little after 4:00 p.m., Hubert Desourteaux heard bursts of machine gun and rifle fire coming from his garage next door. He had no way of knowing what had happened. The Germans came into the house, and finding it empty did not linger on the first floor but climbed up to the attic. Desourteaux smelled gasoline and guessed that they had punctured the tins he had hidden up there About 5:00 p.m. he heard the sound of burning and smoke began to seep into his hiding-place; the house was on fire. Crawling out the back he hid in a grove of hazelnut trees from where he could see that the entire village was burning, including the church. Later that night, he tried to find his brother Etienne, but in vain.

Around 6:00 p.m. Machefer worked his way back to the village until he was standing in front of his burning house. Knowing that he was still in danger he started walking north towards Bel Aire. On his way he passed the house of seventy-seven year-old Pierre Giroux, whom he knew to be paralyzed. The front door was open and Giroux was lying dead in his bed.

Aimé Forest, a forty-seven-year-old professor of philosophy at the University of Montpellier, and a refuge in Oradour, spent Saturday in Limoges with three of his five children. That evening, they got on the tram in Limoges that was due to arrive in Oradour at 7:00 p.m., although it left late. The tram was still running despite the fact that M. Dauriat had returned to Limoges on the tram and had described what he had seen that afternoon in Oradour. On the tram, the passengers talked anxiously. When they got within four miles of the village, they could see heavy smoke rising from it.

Forest and the children left the tram at Laplaud, about a mile and a half before the Oradour stop. When they reached the village of Laplaud, his wife told her husband that their sons Michel (20) and Dominique (6) had left about 4:00 p.m. to visit their grandfather in Oradour and had not returned. Aimé Forest immediately began to walk in the direction of the village. He overtook the tram on the crest of the hill at the last stop before Oradour, Puy Gaillard, which was about 300 yards from the Glane River Bridge and overlooked the Glane valley. He approached two soldiers on guard duty there and spoke to them in German. One of them assured him that the children had all been removed from the village and that none had been hurt. The professor noticed that the soldier looked uncomfortable, and lowered his head when he spoke. Seeing no alternative, however, he returned to Laplaud.

At Puy Gaillard, the sentries had ordered the passengers to remain in the tram while they sent a bicycle messenger for instructions. Identity checks were carried out. From the tram, the passengers could see the burning village, and could only imagine what had occurred. When the messenger returned, the passengers who lived in Oradour were ordered to dismount. The other passengers were told that they should remain on the tram and return with it to Limoges. In response, about fifteen people left the tram.

The fifteen were escorted on foot across the fields towards the town, crossing the Glane River by means of a fallen tree trunk. Eventually, they reached the Masset farm, near the Peyrilhac road. This was one of only two buildings in Oradour not yet set on fire. The other building was the Dupic house at the north end of the village. The Third Company had established an informal headquarters at the Masset farm, and the fifteen were quickly turned over to a man they assumed to be an officer. He ordered a second identity check and demanded that the men and women be separated. As they carried out these orders, the soldiers seemed to take a sadistic pleasure in frightening their captives, ostentatiously cocking and brandishing their weapons. After two hours of this intimidation, a German officer arrived, and having been briefed on the situation, ordered the captives freed. A soldier informed them in French that they were to be let go, and that they were exceptionally fortunate because everyone else from the village had been killed.

The Escapees

Clement Broussaudier and Yvon Roby stayed in the rabbit-hutch alongside the Laudy barn until around 7:30 p.m., when Broussaudier looked out from his hiding place behind a straw-pile to see if there were still any soldiers about. None were visible, but he could hear the sound of their marching feet.

"Are you ready?" he asked his eighteen-year-old companion. Roby answered that he was, and the two of them set out for the village green by way of the back lane outside the shed. Crossing the village green, they continued walking towards the cemetery, scrambling over walls as they went. Just as they reached the hedge by the cemetery, however, they heard a double-burst of submachine gunfire. Broussaudier was wounded, and his shirt quickly became drenched with blood. The two men lay low for a minute, but when there was no further sign of the soldiers who had fired the shots, they continued along the hedge through some artichoke beds into a wheat field, where they spent the night. The next morning Roby and Broussaudier made their way to their homes outside the village. Unknown to the others, Pierre-Henri Poutaraud also managed to escape from the Laudy barn, but was seen and killed some yards farther along Cemetery Road.

Borie, Darthout and Hébras were left behind in the second rabbit-hutch. Borie, the oldest of the three, announced that he was going to make a break across the village green for the cemetery and the woods, as Broussaudier and Roby had done. If nothing happened, he said, Hébras should follow him. He told Hébras to be especially careful because his wound would slow him down, and he cautioned both men to watch for sentries on the Cemetery Road. Shortly afterwards, Borie made his break, after which Darthout and Hébras moved into the third of the rabbit-hutches, since the second one was now burning fiercely. Finding some of the rabbits' drinking water, they used it to wet a handkerchief and mop their faces. To Hébras, it seemed as if he had been pitched against his will into a game without rules; a game in which, for no just or comprehendible reason, he could be killed at any time. He thought of his friends in the Laudy barn. He was certain that some of them were still alive when they were set on fire.

Darthout told Hébras that he should run, and take his chance while he still could. He, himself, Darthout said, was too gravely wounded to go with him. "But just think of me sometimes," he added. Hébras did not want to leave his friend behind, but understood that he had no choice. If he was to get to the woods safely—play Russian roulette with the Germans, as he would later describe it—he was going to have to do it alone. He looked out. No Germans were visible on the village green, but the surrounding houses were burning. His entire world, it seemed, was on fire. He ran for it, and to his relief, found Borie waiting for him. They moved to the large hedge in front of the cemetery. Borie asked if Darthout was coming and Hébras explained that his wounds had immobilized him. Borie then began trying to force his way through the dense, thorny hedge into the cemetery, but without success. Finally, they moved along the hedge until they reached the gate of the cemetery. It was closed, and when Hébras gave it a shove, it creaked so loudly that they thought the Germans must have heard them. No one came, however, and eventually the gate yielded. Moving from tomb to tomb, the pair made their way through the cemetery and into the woods.

Between 7:00 and 8:00 p.m. the villagers who had not been caught in the roundup began to make their way to Oradour. These were people who had been away that morning or at least outside the German perimeter. When they saw that the village was on fire, they became desperately anxious. What they did not know was that the soldiers were still in the village, and in some cases, would remain there until 10:00 p.m. or even later. One of those who tried to return was M. Marie-Leon (André) Foussat, a miller. Foussat, 39, was with his friend Pierre Joyeux in the nearby hamlet of Les Bordes when the two men decided to return to Oradour. They had heard shooting earlier, but it seemed to have stopped. They walked about 350 yards toward the village, when suddenly Joyeux changed his mind. He said that he did not think it was wise to go any farther. Foussat replied that his family would be worrying about him, and besides, his papers were in order so there was no risk. He walked his bicycle for another 100 yards, waving a white handkerchief. However, as he crested a small rise, he was cut down in a burst of submachine gunfire, along with two other civilians who were standing nearby.

Borie and Hébras moved through the woods as fast as they could manage, given Hébras's wound. Before long, they approached the hamlet of Theil, about a mile and a half from Oradour. There, people stood outside staring at the sky, which had been turned orange by the flames of the village. Hébras and Borie were too shaken and exhausted by their ordeal to recount all that had happened. To those enquiring desperately after their children, they could only tell what they knew—that the women and children had been marched to an unknown destination. Desperately thirsty by now, the two men asked for something to drink, and declined offers of wine in favor of water. Later, Borie suggested they go to his house in the hamlet of Boissournet, and avoid the road and other hamlets. They started out in that direction. En route, they stopped in Martinerie, where they knocked on the door of M. Barataud. They were greeted with suspicion until Jacqueline and Francine Pinède came into the room and recognized them. Thereafter, they were welcomed, and Jacqueline succeeded in extracting a bullet from Hébras' right arm. Borie, seeing that his friend was being cared for, struck out for home.

As word of Hébras' presence reached others in the community, he recounted the details repeatedly about the assembly on the Oradour village green, the departure of the women and children, the machine-gunning of the men, and the burning of the village. That night, the people of Martinerie, fearful of an attack on their homes, took blankets and slept in the woods. Hébras was among them. The next day, Sunday, M. de Bruchard, the proprietor of a nearby manor house, arrived with a horse and cart to carry Hébras to a doctor named Zimmer in Cieux. The distance was not great, perhaps a couple of miles, but for Hébras, fearful of encountering a German patrol at every turn, the journey was a terrifying one. When his wound had been dressed, de Bruchard brought him back to Martinerie. From there, he took him four miles to the Pouyol farm where his older sister, Odette, lived with her husband François Foussat.

When Hébras arrived at the farm, he was overjoyed to see that his father, Jean, and sister, Odette, were there. However, he was immediately and keenly aware that his mother and his other sisters were not. His father had heard that his son had survived and was very relieved to see him in person. Hébras had prayed that after the women and children had been taken away, that they had been released and had somehow escaped the slaughter. His father decided to go into the village to try to find out what had happened. Despite Hébras's insistence that it was too dangerous, he set off on his bicycle. Hébras was fed and urged to get some sleep, but he couldn't do so. Instead, he lay in the grass behind the house. Around 6:00 p.m., his father returned. Even before he spoke, Robert Hébras could see from his father's face that the nightmare was real.

Jean Hébras could barely get the words out, but he said, "In the church…the women and children… killed…" Hebras's father told him that his friends Darthout, Broussaudier and Roby were safe.

At 7:30 a.m. Professor Forest, by now extremely concerned, went to the crest of the hill as he had done the evening before. He found other sentries there. One of these brusquely informed him that all the inhabitants had been killed. Another sentry continued the conversation in French and seemed to show a little human feeling. Forest asked to speak to an officer. He was allowed to go down to the bridge over the Glane where there was a half-track and where soldiers milling around. The soldiers seemed young and light-hearted and one was even singing.

Shortly thereafter, an officer arrived, whom the soldiers deferentially called "Der Commandant" [It could only have been either Diekmann or Kahn]. The Professor expected to meet an officer with correct manners but was quickly disabused of any such notion. The officer adopted a brutally hard attitude. He stared into Forest's face, as if to fix it in his memory. He ordered him to leave immediately, saying that if he came back, he would be treated as a partisan. As if for emphasis, he asked Forest if he understood what that implied. When Forest managed to insert a question concerning his children, the officer claimed that he knew nothing of what had happened. Returning to Laplaud, Forest was forced to confirm the worst suspicions of his family and the others.

Armand Senon, who had been hiding in his thicket, saw the Germans return on Sunday morning to pick up the sentry and the spotlight. He heard occasional gunfire. By 11:00 a.m., he had the impression that the Germans had left because the only sounds that he could hear were fires crackling, buildings collapsing and the cries of domestic animals wandering in the fields.

At about 3:00 p.m. on Sunday, he heard the clopping sounds of wooden clogs. Armand Senon left his hiding place to try to find out what had happened. Across the field bordering the Cemetery Road, he found the body of Pierre-Henri Poutaraud draped across a fence. Still later that Sunday, Senon encountered a M. Desvignes, who had been away in the neighboring village of Saint Victurnien on Saturday. It was from him that he learned the extent of the tragedy and realized he had lost all thirteen members of his family.

For all of Saturday night and for most of Sunday, Mme Rouffranche lay in pain in the rectory garden, sucking on the leaves of the green peas to counter her thirst. At about 5:00 p.m. Sunday she heard the sound of wooden clogs on the pavement and cried out for help. Those who answered knew her, and with the help of a wheelbarrow got her to the Chateau Laplaud about a mile from the Glane River Bridge.

By then, the terrible facts of the case were beginning to emerge. In all, 642 people had been massacred (245 women, 207 children and 190 men). All of the village's 328 buildings had been destroyed. The truth was beyond all imagining. Oradour-sur-Glane was no more. (Illustrations 21-38)

Oradour-The Final Verdict

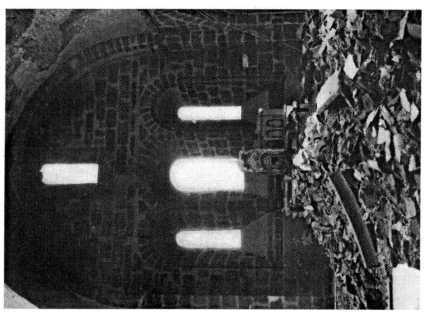

Left: 21. Interior of the church soon after the massacre. The large middle window was the one from which Mme. Rouffranche jumped.

Right: 22. Escape route of Mme. Rouffranche. The man shown in the picture is probably Ecto O. Munn of SHAEF

Left: 23. Exterior of the church in the fall of 1944. The collapsed building on the right was the covered market.

Right: 24. Bodies of victims from the church laid out on shutters during the week following the massacre.

Oradour-The Final Verdict

25. The Cemetery Road leading off the main street with the Laudy barn the last ruin on the left. Hébras, Darthout and the other men that were taken to the Laudy barn came from the village green up the main street to the left. The women and children had been taken to the church behind the point where the photo was taken.

26. The Laudy barn. The two light machine guns were set up on the near side of the fence.

27. The body of M. Poutaraud who escaped from the Laudy barn execution only to be killed and left by this fence on the Cemetery Road.

28. Village green not long after the village was destroyed.

29. Behind the gasoline pump (BP) is the Beaulieu forge where seven cyclists were shot. To the left of it the Beaulieu shed ("remise" in French), the scene of one of the executions of the men from the village green. The ruins of the Godfrin and Hébras houses are just a few yards to the right out of the picture.

30. Hotel Avril on the right (with the sign) and the house where the Pinède mother, father and son lived to the left. Their two daughters were housed across the street for safety reasons. The ruins of the Godfrin and Hébras houses are just a few yards to the right out of the picture

31. Chateau Laplaud, where Mme Rouffranche was brought after she was found, as it looks today.

32. Oradour-sur-Glane ruins from the air shortly after the village was burned. Note the roof of the church in the foreground had not yet fallen in.

Oradour-The Final Verdict

33. Mathieu Borie, the mason who opened a hole in the wall for the escapees, October 3, 1944.

34. Hubert Desourteaux at the rear door of his garage, October 2, 1944.

35. Martial Machefer, October 3, 1944.

36. Armand Senon in the ruin of his house, October 3, 1944.

Douglas W. Hawes

37. Mme Rouffranche in a Limoges hospital, October 4, 1944.

Oradour-The Final Verdict

Mme ROUFFANCHE

M. DARTHOUT

LES TÉMOINS

M. BROUSSAUDIER

M. ROBERT HEBRAS

MATHIEU BORIE

M. YVON ROBY

38. Survivors of massacre photographed by the SRCGE in late 1944.

PART II
THE TRIAL

Chapter 9

Prelude: The Problem of the French/Alsatian Defendants

Almost nine years after the massacre, the slowly grinding wheels of justice finally brought the Oradour crime to the Permanent Military Tribunal in Bordeaux. There, the fate of former soldiers of the Division Das Reich, twenty-one defendants (plus forty-four *in absentia*), would be decided. Fourteen of the accused were French from the Region of Alsace; the others were Germans. Two of the Alsatians and the seven Germans had been in prison since the war. None of the defendants present was an officer.

Initially, the questions of which laws applied and which judicial body had jurisdiction were the key issues. It was not generally hard to resolve whether an act was a war crime or an ordinary criminal act. If committed by a person in an enemy uniform the subsequent proceedings came under the jurisdiction of the military justice system. If committed by a French national with the intention of collaboration with the enemy, it came under the jurisdiction of the criminal courts. The problem was that the war crimes legislation passed by the Provisional French Government on August 28, 1944 (the "1944 Law"), almost a year before the end of the war, did not apply to French citizens except in the case of those acting as spies.

There was an understanding among the Allies before the war was over that war crimes with no specific location would be examined by an international court (like the Nuremberg Tribunal) while those connected to a specific location would be dealt with nationally. Accordingly, France enacted the 1944 Law. De Gaulle's fellow exiles in London learned about the forcible induction of the Alsatians shortly after the measure was imposed in 1942 by Wagner, the German Governor. However, in drafting the 1944 law it was not anticipated that any French citizens would be involved in war crimes in German uniforms, so no provision was made for such an eventuality.

The 1944 law included an enumeration of the articles of the French Penal Code to be applied by military tribunals, and a list of those acts considered to be war crimes including: forcible induction in a foreign army, assassination, reprisals, use of noxious substances to kill, confinement and pillage. Consistent with the law applied at the Nuremberg trials, obedience to orders was excluded as a defense.

That the Third Company of the First Battalion of the Regiment Der Führer had perpetrated the massacre was known at an early stage of the investigations. Radio France on August 20, 1940 identified the Third Company based on the inscriptions left on the blackboard in Nieul. After deserting or being captured two of the Alsatian participants had been allowed to join the *Forces françaises libres* (FFL), and when questioned had admitted their involvement. The two men had supplied information about the Third Company, its officers, and the conscripts involved. It was from them that the government learned that a significant number of Alsatians (to whom the 1944 Law did not apply), had participated.

On the third anniversary of the massacre in 1947, when President Vincent Auriol came to visit Oradour, the survivors pressed their demand on him that the perpetrators be brought to justice. Auriol had been given notice of this demand. He revealed that a draft law was in hand that would eliminate the loophole in the law of August 1944, which allowed French nationals to escape prosecution by military courts for war crimes. The "Oradour Law," Auriol promised, would soon be adopted. Despite the fact that it had been classified as urgent legislation, a full year elapsed before it entered the statute books on September 15, 1948. By that time the government was led by Henri Queuille, a Radical Socialist from Limousin. The delay was largely due to the controversy over whether the Alsatians and others who had been forcibly conscripted into the German Army would be excluded from the application of the law—in the end, they were not.

The new law amended the 1944 law as follows:

1. It applied to French persons.

2. It stated that for acts included in the list of war crimes in the 1944 Law, "when these crimes can be attributed to the collective action of a group or military formation belonging to an organization declared criminal by the international court [as the Waffen SS had been by the Nuremberg Tribunal]…then all individuals belonging to this formation or group may be considered co-authors, unless they can prove they were forcibly inducted <u>and</u> also prove that they did not participate in the said crime." (Emphasis added) The bill had originally used the disjunctive "or" but impassioned pleading especially by the Socialist Senator from Haute-Vienne, Gaston Charlet, resulted in the conjunctive, which the Alsatian representatives reluctantly accepted. The new law also required that there had to be at least one enemy defendant for a French defendant to be prosecuted under this statute otherwise the French defendant would go before the criminal courts.

To put the prosecution of the Oradour defendants in context, the number of war crimes committed in France by Germans was estimated by the *Service de recherche des crimes de guerre ennemis (*SRCGE, which was charged with studying the subject on a regional basis from 1944 to 1946) to be over 20,000. Of the nearly 19,000 war criminals involved, only 2,345 were actually tried in France, of whom over half were judged *in absentia*. While death sentences were pronounced over 800 times, only fifty-four Germans were actually executed—all between 1945 and 1951—primarily because most such penalties were imposed on defendants *in absentia*. The vast majority of the military war crimes' trials in France were extremely summary. For example, the Tulle trial by the Bordeaux Military Tribunal took only two days and it was longer than most.

No precise figure can be given for the number of SS soldiers involved at Oradour, although the number is generally thought to have been between 150 and 200. I think the lower figure is closer to the reality. Later, the Third Company was so badly mauled in Normandy that only eighteen of its members were still able to fight. Of the 28 Alsatian *malgré nous* (i.e. those forcibly inducted "against our will"), 15 were killed in the war and the 13 others were relatively easily found. One was serving in the French police in Saigon, one was in prison, and the rest had returned to Alsace.

The German defendants had been located in POW camps, identified as having been at Oradour, and brought to France. The rest had either been killed in the war or released from captivity without being identified as having been at Oradour. Because of limited resources, the French had expended little effort on locating wanted men who were not already in prisoner of war camps. Later, especially after 1951 there would be conflicts over extradition because the British and Americans were preoccupied with the Cold War and less interested in pursuing German war criminals (this is a subject to which I will return in the Epilogue, especially as related to General Lammerding).

The year leading up to the start of the Bordeaux trial had been an eventful one. In Korea, the U.S. waged a war on Communism; in Britain, Princess Elizabeth had been crowned following the death of George VI, and in Russia, Stalin lay ill, and he would die a month after the Oradour trial ended. The French, meanwhile, had launched an offensive against Hanoi in the Indo-China War. For the first time since 1945, there was a government of the right. The franc was in difficulty. One of the laws the government passed in furtherance of its efforts to put the war behind it was an amnesty for acts of collaboration, although it was not the first such act. In the arts, 1952 was the year in which Samuel Beckett's "Waiting for Godot" opened at the Babylone Theatre. The play was partly inspired by Beckett's experiences during the war, when he was aiding the Resistance and hiding in France mostly in Roussillon. In the cinema, the director Roger Vadim had just married eighteen-year-old Brigitte Bardot. In the world of *haute couture*, everyone was talking about a young man named Christian Dior.

As the 40s had become the 50s, the world had changed. In France, the violent score settling of the post-war period was over. Pétain and Laval, the former leaders of the Vichy government, had been tried and convicted, and Laval had been executed. The process of "purification" in France, relative to other collaborators had been swift and mainly extra-judicial. Of approximately 10,000 executions only about 15 percent had been were sanctioned by the courts. Women accused of fraternizing with the Nazis (so-called "horizontal collaboration") had their heads publicly shaved. In general, the punishment meted out to traitors and collaborators had been uneven, and this was a source of resentment. For years after the war, especially in small towns, people remembered who had collaborated or sold goods on the black-market. People would not patronize certain tradesmen or speak to certain other villagers. In general, people simply did not discuss the war. Today, many refer with pride to the Resistance activities of their relatives, but few confess to having collaborationist skeletons in their family closets.

The drama of Oradour was relatively well known, but the suffering of Alsace and Moselle under the Gauleiters (German governors) was not. France was reindustrializing with the help of U.S. aid and the Marshall Plan, and France and West Germany were already far advanced towards détente. During the Oradour trial the French Government would be authorized by the legislature to ratify the Common European Defense Treaty—albeit France later blocked it because many in France, especially the Communists, strongly opposed the rearming of Germany. Within little more than a year, however, full sovereignty would be returned to West Germany. In general, the Germans wanted to turn the page on the Nazi era and on the process of denazification. They were more concerned with the Cold War - the blockade of Berlin had lasted from June 1948 to September of the following year. Others, however--the survivors of the German excesses and their families, former Resistance fighters, the Communists --were not so willing to forgive and forget.

Almost nine years had elapsed since the Oradour massacre. The delay in beginning the trial had had a profound effect on all of those involved. For the survivors and the families of the victims, who could not believe that a crime of this magnitude could go unpunished for so long, the wait had been agonizing. For the defendants who had been held in prison since the war—seven Germans, an Alsatian volunteer named Georges René Boos, and an Alsatian named Paul G.—the time had passed no faster. For legal reasons that will be explained later, the French/Alsatian defendants, other than Boos, are identified in my book only by their first names and last name initial. The twelve other Alsatians, at liberty since the war, had established families and tried to forget about their service in the ranks of the SS and especially about the events at Oradour.

The summoning of the twelve to Bordeaux had touched a raw nerve in Alsace. There was great concern that men who had been forcibly conscripted into the SS were being prosecuted, especially given the region's past history.

A brief summary of the special history of the three eastern departments of France that comprised the border with Germany—Haut-Rhin and Bas-Rhin (Alsace) and Moselle (Lorraine) (Illustration 39), would help to explain why the trial set off such a strong reaction in those departments. These areas became part of France progressively from the seventeenth century until the French Revolution. Due to their cultural and linguistic characteristics—notably the German patois that was spoken there—France accorded these departments special political, religious and customs prerogatives; although these gradually diminished, especially in the Napoleonic era of centralization.

Following Napoleon III's capitulation in the Franco-Prussian War, Bismarck, pursuant to the Treaty of Frankfurt (May 1871), annexed these three departments. Over 125,000 people voluntarily quit them to live in France, but the vast majority stayed. Over the course of the half-century between 1871 and 1918 these departments were progressively integrated into Germany. After the turn of the century, however, the regime became more authoritarian and the army was

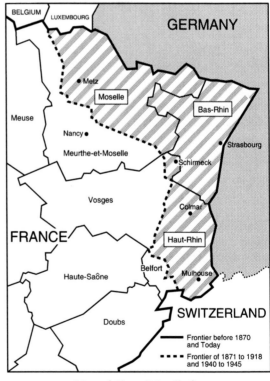

39. Map of Alsace/Moselle forming France's border with Germany.

in great evidence. This stimulated an autonomy movement, consisting primarily of elitists wishing to rejoin France, but including others who simply wanted to be independent. The fact that in the early 20th century Germany was more progressive than France on social matters—insurance for health, work accident and retirement—offset the effect of rigors of the regime and limited the broad appeal of autonomy.

The absorption by Germany of Alsace/Moselle was never really accepted psychologically by France. Thus, when WW I broke out, the provinces were one of the French army's first targets. However, nearly 400,000 Alsatians and Mosellans were mobilized in the German Army of Guillaume II. Most were sent to the Russian front, far from France, no doubt in part because of concerns as to their loyalty. Strict discipline was imposed on those left behind which caused much of the credit built up by the Germans over the years to be dissipated.

After the Allied victory, the Armistice was signed at Rethondes in the forest of Compiègne on November 11, 1918, and Alsace/Moselle once again became French. The Germans were expelled and the ranks of the civil service were purged of German speakers. In the period between the two world wars, the issues of preserving the German patois and other regional exceptions served to encourage diverse groups of people to advocate autonomy. Some wanted to again be part of Germany, others had a variety of reasons. Although some of the leaders of such groups were prosecuted for disloyalty, most of those condemned were amnestied.

During the Depression, some elements of the population were influenced by the rhetoric of National Socialism in Germany, especially those favoring a return to Germany. With the German invasion of Poland on September 1, 1939 and the resulting declarations of war by France and Great Britain, the French government evacuated nearly one-third of the population of Alsace/Moselle to the interior of France, mainly to the southwest. The move, whose logistics had been planned years before, took no more than a few days. While there were inevitably problems given the language and cultural differences, not to mention issues of housing, schooling, and employment, the move went relatively well.

For the two-thirds who stayed, the area seemed almost deserted. On the military front, little happened between September 1939 and

May 1940, the period of the so-called "phony war." However, on May 10, 1940, the Germans attacked France through neutral Belgium and the Ardennes. The vaunted Maginot Line proved to be paper-thin and France installed Marshall Petain to seek an Armistice which was affected on June 25, 1940.

While the Treaty of Frankfurt of 1871 had specifically sanctioned the annexation of Alsace/Moselle, the 1940 Armistice was silent on the subject. Notwithstanding earlier statements by Hitler that he had no territorial ambitions relative to France, he immediately effected the annexations which were memorialized by his state visit to Strasbourg three days later.

In accordance with the terms of the Armistice, Germany took back about 450,000 of the evacuees in the second half of 1940, while 150,000 chose to stay in France. They also freed prisoners of war from Alsace/Moselle since they had overnight become Germans, while over 1,800,000 French were held prisoner for the duration. The frontier was reset as before 1918. Some 50,000 Alsatians and 100,000 Mosellans were expelled to the unoccupied zone of France—essentially France below the Loire, except for the Atlantic coast and a part near the Italian border—because of their known French sympathies and/or ability to speak French. With them went the region's Jews, gypsies, homosexuals, Communists, unionists and others deemed "undesirables" by the Nazis.

At first a certain part of the population welcomed back the Germans, or was at least neutral in its sympathies. As the German Governors not only imposed German laws, language and culture, but put in place the whole apparatus of Nazi organizations such as the Hitler Youth, the Nazi Party, and the SD and SS, however, many became disillusioned and afraid. The establishment near Strasbourg of the "reeducation" camp at Schirmeck and the concentration camp at Struthof resolved the doubts of many others. During the occupation years, the people of Alsace bitterly resented the attitude of the Vichy Government, which in their view turned its back on the region and did little or nothing to protest the annexation.

Rather than elaborate on this summary, I will allow the witnesses called by the Alsatian defense to do so. These witnesses were presented specifically to educate the court as to the suffering of the people of

Alsace/Moselle under German occupation and the indoctrination of its youth including the *malgré nous*.

In consequence of this grim historical background, Alsatian politicians had done all in their power to dissuade the government from prosecuting *Les Douze*. Not only were *Les Douze* victims of a war crime—forcible induction—there were twice as many French/Alsatian defendants as German, and there were no officers on trial. When these pleas were ignored, pressure mounted to have the Alsatians tried separately from the Germans. All the demands for separate trials were refused. This was perhaps because the Alsatian politicians failed to raise a public outcry until it was too late; the issue was not widely publicized until a month before the trial, or perhaps because of the opposition of the ANFM representing the Oradour victims' families. The question of separation was left for the Tribunal to resolve. It is possible that a different decision might have been reached if the Alsatians could have counted on the unequivocal support of all the politicians and people of Moselle, whose sons were also *malgré nous*. They were not able to count on such support in part because forty-four victims of the massacre had been refugees from Moselle and only nine had been from Alsace.

When *Les Douze* learned that a trial was to take place (some had been given a full year's notice to attend), they were alarmed. They had thought that they had escaped criminal proceedings and were not going to be charged. They also knew they had been very fortunate to have survived the final months of the war. After the massacre at Oradour, the Third Company had joined the march north to Normandy, and in the fierce fighting which followed, the Division had been decimated. Major Diekmann was killed on June 29 by an artillery shell and succeeded by Captain Kahn. General Lammerding was wounded and temporarily replaced. Colonel Stadler was promoted, transferred, and replaced by Colonel Otto Weidinger. The Division had fought on through the Ardennes offensive, retreated to what remained of the Eastern Front, and surrendered in May 1945 in Czechoslovakia.

Oradour remained in mourning for several years. The survivors announced that they intended to preserve the ruin of the town as a memorial, and to build a new town alongside it. At first, the idea of preserving the ruins was dismissed by government experts as unworkable. It was impossible to make time stand still, the survivors were told.

Walls would fall down, trees and grass would grow, and cars would rust. The Oradour representatives persisted, and finally won the support of de Gaulle, who had visited the ruins on March 4, 1945 (Illustration 40). De Gaulle had made a point of visiting major cities after the Liberation. Limoges was one of these, and Oradour had been an important destination the same day.

40. General De Gaulle at Oradour March 4, 1945.

Chapter 10

The Setting

On Sunday, January 11, 1953, eleven Frenchmen from Alsace bade a somber farewell to their families and friends as they boarded a train in Strasbourg. They were on their way to Bordeaux to face trial by a Military Tribunal for their participation in the massacre at Oradour. The eleven men (and one who had missed the train) had all been forcibly inducted into the Waffen SS in early 1944, and attached to the Third Company of the Regiment Der Führer, 2nd SS Panzer Division Das Reich. The Germans had forcibly inducted over 130,000 Alsatians and 30,000 Mosellans into the German Army after the Armistice." These twelve Alsatian defendants had been dubbed *"Les Douze"* by the Alsatian press. None of them had been an officer or NCO. The men's ages at trial ranged from twenty-six to thirty-nine—several of them had only been seventeen years old at the time of the massacre. They were mostly married with families, and had taken up modest occupations. Some had become farm laborers, others were employed by the post office; one was a policeman in Saigon. They had been ordered by the Tribunal to present themselves at the Boudet Barracks in Bordeaux by 9:00 a.m. on Monday, January 12.

On the train, they talked, played cards and slept. They were allowed to travel unaccompanied by guards because they were not formally charged until they arrived for the trial. By the time the train pulled into the Gare de l'Est in Paris, a number of reporters and photographers met them and accompanied them to the Gare de Montparnasse on the city's Left Bank. There, they boarded the *"Rapide de Paris"* for Bordeaux, arriving the next morning at about 3:30 a.m. at the Gare St. Jean. Descending from the third class cars with their overnight bags, puffy-eyed with sleep, the men were disoriented and bewildered. Once again, reporters and photographers met them and blinded them with their magnesium flashes. Given the early hour, the Alsatians had no idea where to go, until one of the reporters told them that the defense team was staying at the Hotel Montre. Making their way to the hotel, the eleven roused one of their lawyers who arranged a couple of rooms for them to sleep in. Several who were, by now wide awake, opted for an early breakfast. At 8:00 a.m., they were loaded into police vans and taken to the Boudet barracks prison to await the proceedings which were to commence that afternoon. Meanwhile, the seven German defendants had been brought under armed guard from a prison in the southwest of France. All the defendants were incarcerated in the same prison, with the Germans separated from the Alsatian *malgré nous*.

The Bordeaux courthouse in which the Oradour trial was to take place had been specially selected for its size and location. It was small, so that demonstrations might be forestalled. Other less important war crime trials had been held in much larger courtrooms. It was located on a relatively narrow street, the rue Pessac, which, if necessary, could easily be barricaded against demonstrators. The building was known by the locals as the "Arab Tower" due to the rounded corner entrance topped by a sort of pyramid with a clock on its face (Illustration 41). When the trial began, the room was completely filled, except for three rows of empty benches borrowed from a nearby school. The place for each defendant was marked on the benches which had been arranged in a flat "V." Around them were chairs which had been set aside for their guards. The German defendants, it had been determined, were to sit on the right facing the judges. The Alsatian *malgré nous* were to sit on the left. In front of the defendants was the *barre* with its curved rail, where they would stand to testify (Illustration 42).

The witnesses, meanwhile, gave their evidence while seated between the judges' rostrum and the table of Colonel Gratien Gardon, the prosecutor on the left. Several reporters were placed on steps facing the *barre,* with their backs to the judges, while others were disposed at random

41. The Bordeaux courthouse exterior.

around the courtroom. A cluster of tricolor flags were hung high on the wall behind the judges, and several graphics had been tacked on the wall on the left above the prosecutor and on the right wall over the defense counsel. These included aerial photos, a map showing the route taken by the Division before and after the massacre, and a town plan of Oradour and its surroundings. The corners of the room were cut diagonally. It was lit with neon lights and had windows high up on the wall.

In addition to the defense counsel seated behind the defendants on the right hand side, there were the stenographers, one of them blind, who took turns transcribing the proceedings. The courtroom had speakers on the wall but the sound system worked only intermittently. The ANFM had been given exceptional permission by the Tribunal to have this transcript made. It would run to twenty-seven hundred pages. The ANFM had been formed in early 1945 by the merger of two committees fostering the interests of the survivors and their families that had started separately a few months earlier.

42. Courthouse interior. The President Nussy Saint-Säens and the six officer judges with their alternates behind; the prosecutor under the graphics to the left, counsel to the defendants to the right and behind the defendants and their guards in the middle. The *barre* where the defendants testify is in the middle; behind that on three low wide steps are some of the reporters. Note the three French flags on the wall over the judges and the speaker near the prosecutor (another one is out of sight on the right wall). The corners of the room are cut diagonally and there are windows high up on the walls.

Three of the defense lawyers were German, and more than two dozen were French. The German lawyers wore black robes with dress shirts and white bow ties. The French were dressed in black robes and white *jabots* (a kind of ascot). In the middle of the courtroom there was a low railing and metal chairs for the ANFM representatives and the families of the victims. Many of the latter had traveled by train from

Limoges on the same morning that the defendants had traveled from Alsace, and had been received at the city hall. Since no more than a dozen seats had been allocated to them, the ANFM representatives took turns attending. The little remaining space was divided among members of the public, most of who had been obliged to wait in line for hours to obtain entry. For most of the twenty-seven days of the trial, more than 200 people occupied the small courtroom.

In ordinary criminal trials in France, in 1953 as well as today, the representatives of the victims have the right to participate through their counsel as regular parties to the criminal proceedings. In effect, their civil case is attached to the criminal one. This right, however, did not extend to military trials, a fact that greatly distressed the ANFM. They were permitted neither to address the court nor to examine the extensive investigatory files available to the Tribunal. It is clear, however, that the president, the investigating magistrates and the prosecutor paid them considerable deference. In January 1949, for example, the investigating judge told the ANFM that, "My minister has decided that the Alsatians would be tried with the Germans." He noted that, "This decision conforms to the point of view that you have many times indicated that you wanted."

The extensive investigatory files referred to were based primarily on the work of the *juge d'instruction* (investigating magistrate) and judicial police working for him, especially in late 1944, 1946, and 1947. They interrogated witnesses, including the Alsatian defendants, and collected documents relating to the interrogation of certain defendants who had been in Allied prisoner of war camps. These files contained the details on the basis of which the Tribunal, and especially its President Marcel Nussy Saint-Saëns, would examine the defendants on their role in the massacre. The *juge d'instruction* had three options: 1) Determine that military justice did not have jurisdiction, 2) Declare there was insufficient evidence to bring charges (in French terms a *"non lieu"*), or 3) Send the accused to a military tribunal, which is what had been done in the Oradour trial.

Even before the session was formally opened, two incidents took place which dramatically illustrated the tension in the air. The first occurred shortly before the trial while the Alsatian defense team prepared its case in Bordeaux. Pierre Schreckenberg, the Alsatians' lead lawyer and a former head of the Strasbourg bar (1947-1949), received a message that Nussy Saint-Saëns, the civilian judge who was to preside at the trial, wanted to see him. When Schreckenberg returned, he told his confreres that Nussy Saint-Saëns had suggested that he plead his clients guilty and that if he did so, the Tribunal would consider imposing lighter sentences. While Schreckenberg was hesitant to reject the suggestion out of hand, Messrs. Lux, Moser and Schmidt, along with other members of the defense team, strongly opposed the suggestion. Such a plea, they said, would nullify what they viewed as the crime of the forced induction of their clients and of the other 130,000 Alsatians who had been impressed into the service of the enemy. That criminality had been clearly recognized after the war when Robert Wagner, the German *Gauletier* (Governor) of Alsace was executed for crimes including these forced inductions. So the Alsatian defense agreed that they would simply not respond to the president's suggestion. Plea-bargaining of this sort by the president of the Tribunal, however informal, was not legally authorized. However, the fact that Nussy Saint-Saëns was moved to take such an exceptional step shows the weight of the issues at stake.

The other incident also involved Schreckenberg. When he first entered the courtroom before the opening session, he walked over to present himself, and offered his hand to the prosecutor, Colonel Gardon. However, Gardon declined to shake it on the grounds that, as he said, "You represent war criminals." Schreckenberg was shocked, but characteristically not at a loss for words. He retorted, "For my part, I would not want to shake the hand of a government prosecutor who worked for Vichy while I was stagnating in a Nazi prison-camp." Schreckenberg had been arrested by the Germans for his Resistance activities in Alsace in April 1942 and held in Germany until the end of the war.

Chapter 11

The Trial Begins

At 2:10 p.m., the judges were announced, the audience stood and the president and the six military judges filed in (four officers and two NCOs plus an equal number of alternates). Marcel Nussy Saint-Saëns was the forty-five-year-old nephew of the composer Camille Saint-Saëns. A confident, broad-shouldered man with a ruddy face, he spoke with the southern accent of Béziers and would display a distinctly commanding manner throughout. Indeed, at times he seemed like an orchestra conductor (which his father was). He wore the traditional magistrate's red robe with white neckpiece and hat (he removed the hat while the court was in session) and several service medals. The other six judges all wore military uniforms.

As president of the Military Tribunal, Nussy Saint-Saëns would play a dominant role in the proceedings by conducting the examination of the defendants and witnesses, and by exercising his authority to keep order. In general, the prosecutor and defense counsel played more subordinate roles during the evidentiary part of the trial than they would have in an American criminal trial. They were required to ask the president to pose a question if they wanted it asked. All of this was normal under the French and Continental European inquisitorial system of criminal justice. Certain magistrates *(juge d'instruction)* participated in investigations and others such as Nussy Saint-Saëns conducted the court proceedings. The theory was that this level of involvement would make it easier for them to arrive at the truth. In the Anglo-Saxon adversarial tradition, by contrast, the prosecutor and the defense counsel play the most prominent roles, on the basis that truth is more likely to be arrived at through sharply contrasting points of view.

The judges other than the president did not speak at all, partly out of deference to the role and experience of the president, and partly because they were not required to have had legal training. The court sessions took place only in the afternoon. Thus, the judges, the prosecutor and defense counsel could prepare for each day's session.

Fixing his gaze on the spectators and the families of the victims, Nussy Saint-Saëns began by acknowledging that he was making an extraordinary statement in order to place the trial in its proper context. He said, "The real issue on trial here is Hitlerism…one needs the voice of Greek tragedy or that of a biblical prophet to describe the horrors… one cannot help asking…Why, why these deaths? Why this massacre, why?" Nussy Saint-Saëns then answered his own question by saying, "Because all elements of human dignity were lost, and all moral values were scorned, in an effort to establish by violence the regime of material force…I am certain, and I do not say this without emotion, that the victims of Oradour are present here, present and we hear them."

The president then turned the floor over to the prosecutor, Lieutenant Colonel Gratien Gardon (Illustration 43). A forty-three-year-old career officer, Gardon was a stocky and somewhat humorless individual with a receding hairline. As a young law graduate, he had attended the elite military academy at St. Cyr before serving three tours of duty in Indochina, which included stints as a prosecutor at the *Tribunals Militaires* in Saigon and Vientiane; in the year before the Oradour trial he had occupied a similar post in Tunisia. Significantly, especially for those, like the Communists who were against détente with Germany and its element of German rearmament, he was part of the official delegation to the European Common Defense organization negotiations. When he spoke at any length, he did so with extensive notes from which he only occasionally looked up. Associating himself with the remarks of the president, Gardon described Oradour as a "unique tragedy" in the annals of war. He assured the families of the victims that the trial would be concerned only with the truth. [Presumably an allusion to the political issues and hullabaloo involving the Alsatian *malgré nous*.]

Oradour-The Final Verdict

43. Prosecutor Gratien Gardon under the graphics.

44. Alsatian defense counsels Schreckenberg, Lux and others. Lux is standing at the right.

Not to be outdone, the gaunt and intense Schreckenberg also requested that he be associated with the president's statement (Illustration 44). He observed that the massacre of Oradour was well-known in Alsace, not only because two Alsatian refugee children were among the victims as well as fourteen children from the neighboring province of Lorraine, but because Oradour "has become the bloody symbol of the terror and of the madness of Hitlerism." He reminded the court that Alsace had been a victim of the same madness, and had lost thousands of its sons.

According to the transcript, Nussy Saint-Saëns then ordered: "*Chef d'escorte de la gendarmerie, veuillez faire introduire les accuses de l'affaire Kahn et autres*" ("Head of the police guards, would you bring in the defendants in the case Kahn et al."). However, *Franc-Tireur*, a Communist newspaper (January 13, 1953) claimed that the president made a serious slip of the tongue and said, "*Gardes, faites entrer les coupables*" ("Guards, bring in the guilty"). Neither of the major French dailies reported any such slip. If the Communist paper was the only one to note that alleged error, it could be attributed to the efforts before and during the trial of the Communists to find fault with Nussy Saint-Saëns. However, the *Franc-Tireur* version was confirmed by a reliable, if interested source in Louis Oster, Schreckenberg's young associate, who although not present in Bordeaux, heard about it from his employer.

The president noted that all of the expected defendants were present except two who were expected shortly. One was the *malgré nous* who had missed the train; the other was Georges René Boos, the only Alsatian defendant who had volunteered for the Waffen SS. In addition, forty-four defendants including Captain Kahn and Lieutenant Barth were being tried *in absentia*. Nussy Saint-Saëns then ordered the guards to seat the prisoners. He quickly ascertained that each was supplied with counsel, and then started the preliminary interrogation of the defendants, reading from dossiers that had been prepared for him by the investigating magistrates.

Karl Lenz, a German, was called to stand at the *barre* while the president read that he had been an adjutant (roughly the equivalent of a master sergeant) in the Third Company at Oradour. Lenz who had a receding hairline, was well turned out in a light striped double breasted suit (the German government had supplied each of the German prisoners with a suit), but had a distracted, uninteresting air (Illustration 45). He had been taken as a prisoner of war and since August 12, 1945, had been in prison awaiting trial for war crimes. Nussy Saint-Saëns remarked that it was scandalous that Lenz had been waiting in prison for so long, and inquired as to his family situation. Lenz replied, "I am married and have one child". The president complained to Gardon that the dossier did not contain that information. The prosecutor made no response. The president then ordered Lenz to sit down. When he discovered that another German defendant was married and had children, he remarked that if he had not intervened in the slow process of justice, "you would have been a grandfather by the time you were judged."

45. German Adjutant Lenz at the trial.

Nussy Saint-Saëns then called Albert D. to the *barre*. He was eighteen years of age at the time of the massacre. The defendant was fairly smartly dressed in a double-breasted suit. Noting with regret that Albert D. was designated in the indictment as Alsatian rather than French, Nussy Saint-Saëns asked if he was married. The response was affirmative; the defendant had a three-year-old child. The president said, "This shows again the lamentable effect of the slowness of this process; these people are married and have children."

With respect to another defendant, Albert L., Nussy Saint-Saëns then observed that the procedure applied to him had been "rather curious" in that in August 1948 he had benefited from a decision by a magistrate that he should not be prosecuted for the acts he was accused of today. The magistrate in question, said the president, had accepted that the defendant was under a moral constraint (or duress) as a result of being forcibly inducted into the SS and surrounded by German officers and NCOs. "But the curious thing is that a few weeks later the same magistrate decided that you could indeed be pursued for war crimes in Kahn et al." The issue, Nussy Saint-Saëns told the defendant, would be taken up later.

Chapter 12

The Issue of Separate Trials

After submitting each of the defendants to a similar ritual, and establishing their identities and basic histories, the president turned to the issue of the separation of the French-Alsatians from the Germans. Schreckenberg was asked to open this debate. It was well-known that the same issue was simultaneously being argued at a governmental level in the National Assembly. He started by informing the court that even before victory in Europe was assured, the Allies had invited each country to establish its own legislation to punish war crimes in its territory. France, accordingly, had passed the law of August 1944, which assigned the processing of such crimes to military tribunals. Schreckenberg noted that among the offences condemned by this law was recruitment by force into a foreign army—the precise crime to which the Alsatian *malgré nous* had been subjected.

A bill designated as the "Oradour Law" had been introduced in the National Assembly. After an unsuccessful attempt by an Alsatian member of the National Assembly to exclude those forcibly inducted into the German Army, Schreckenberg continued, it had been adopted on September 15, 1948, with the official title of the Law of Collective Responsibility.

Schreckenberg argued that the Law of Collective Responsibility was defective for several reasons, which at the very least should result in the motion for a separate trial being granted. His reasons were:

1. That the Law of Collective Responsibility substituted a concept of collective responsibility for one of individual accountability since the defendants had been in the Waffen SS and that organization had been found to be a criminal one.
2. The burden was on the defendant to prove his innocence as a non-participant in the war crime and not on the prosecutor to prove guilt. Thus, the normal presumption of innocence embedded in both the French Constitution and the European Convention on Human Rights, of which France was a signatory, was reversed.
3. That the Law of Collective Responsibility was retroactive legislation, in that it was passed in September 1948 and the crime in question had occurred in June 1944; that the concept of retroactive legislation had been considered to run counter to the basic principles of criminal law since at least Roman times.

[At another point in the trial, it was noted that the "Law of Collective Responsibility" had been applied only once before by a military tribunal, namely in Lille in 1949 against certain SS soldiers who had murdered eighty-six civilians of Ascq. The murders had been carried out in reprisal for the sabotaging by the Resistance of the rail line between Lille and Tournai at the beginning of April 1944.]

Returning to the "curious" issue that Nussy Saint-Saëns had raised relative to Albert L., Schreckenberg noted that in the cases of eight of "Les Douze," the original investigating magistrates had treated them as witnesses to the events in Oradour rather than targets, and assured them that they were only being questioned to clarify those events. The other four, including Albert L., had been officially informed in August 1948 that there was no adequate basis for prosecution. It was also pointed out by other counsel for the Alsatians, that if their clients had refused to obey the orders of their superiors, the result would simply have been that twelve more bodies would have been added to those of the Oradour victims.

M. Richard Lux, one of the Alsatian lawyers, talked emphatically about the absence from the court of Captain Kahn, commander of the Third Company at Oradour. Lux claimed that he had information that Kahn was hiding in Sweden and that the Minister of Defense [who was an Alsatian] believed that the Ministry of Justice knew his whereabouts. The Alsatian members of parliament, he continued, had questioned the government and found that no demand for extradition had been made—a discovery which had upset them. The government's failure in this area had had incalculable consequences, Lux said.

The prosecutor, Gardon, resisted the concept of a separate trial as a matter of principle. His main concern, however, was to ensure that any ruling on the procedural issue of separation did not imply a determination that being forcibly inducted was an absolute defense to the charges. Around 8:00 p.m., while the session was still in progress, the Alsatian defendant who missed the train arrived and joined the other defendants on the benches. The first session did not conclude until 10:00 p.m. Most of the time had been taken up by arguments related to the separation issue. At times, there had even been arguments between the French lawyers defending the Germans and the French counsel for the Alsatian *malgré nous*.

On the second day, proceedings opened with a speech by M. de Guardia, the Parisian lawyer who was acting as lead counsel for the Germans. De Guardia said that he also opposed the motion for separate trials—presumably in the hope that a joint trial would spread the blame more evenly, and the German defendants would be concomitantly less severely judged. De Guardia also made the point that Alsace was not on trial here. As he said, a handful of men are not a province. Nor was Germany on trial—every nation has its executioners and its heroes. In an apparent allusion to the Communists (especially those of Limousin who had adopted the cause of the Oradour victims as their own), he said that there were those who wanted to politicize the trial but he added, "We do not have the right to evoke the martyrs of Oradour next to a political flag." President Nussy Saint-Saëns interjected that he hoped he had demonstrated that he had no intention of letting politics be introduced into the trial.

On a more tenuous tack, de Guardia observed that the German defendants had not volunteered for SS duty either, although he conceded that their circumstances were somewhat different from that of the Alsatians. M. Touzet, another French counsel for the Germans, then pointed out that while the legislators from Alsace were now trying to obtain a change in the Law of Collective Responsibility, that law had been adopted unanimously in the National Assembly during a semi-holiday period by only seventeen legislators—no quorum was required. On the key issue of obedience to orders, he argued that a soldier is not free to revolt against his officers. That would violate "the grand principle of military obedience in time of war in a military operation." Thus, for the Germans, the key defense was obedience to orders notwithstanding such obedience was excluded as a defense in the 1944 Law.

M. Touzet also pointed out that the "real monsters" of Oradour were not the defendants, but the officers who organized the massacre. "What do we really want?" he demanded, warming to his theme. "That the parliament modifies the Law of Collective Responsibility and the Alsatian defendants leave here acquitted? If they were discharged," he continued, "they would then be sent to the ordinary criminal court in Limoges." He doubted that they would welcome that. Indeed, it was the Limoges criminal court, which in 1946 had summarily convicted one of the Alsatian defendants, Paul G. and sentenced him to death. The judgment had been annulled on appeal; Paul G. had thereafter been held in prison until the start of the present trial.

At this point, M. Moser for the Alsatians stood up and demanded to be heard. Did M. Touzet really want to put all of the accused in the same camp, he asked, namely that of Hitler? He made it clear that he did not want counsel for the Germans insinuating themselves into matters uniquely relating to the Alsatians. That, he said, would be to chain the victim to his executioner. At this juncture, the president felt obliged to act as peacemaker, assuring counsel that the Tribunal had listened to all of their arguments with care. Moreover, he said, while at the beginning of the trial, he had evoked the invisible presence of the martyrs of Oradour, he was also conscious of the valiant example set by Alphonse Adam, head of the Alsatian student Resistance, who was shot on the banks of the Rhine for refusing to wear a Nazi uniform.

Much procedural wrangling followed, in response to which Nussy Saint-Saëns stated: "Without prejudging the issue, it is certain that most of the defendants...can be judged under the penal law of France...without invoking [the Law of Collective Responsibility which] only complicates things." On another tack, counsel for the defense pointed out that one German and three Alsatian defendants were minors at the time of Oradour (they were seventeen years old) and thus should not be prosecuted. The prosecutor responded that criminal law provisions for minors did not apply to military tribunals.

Finally, as military protocol demanded, the president instructed the captain of the guards to post a sentry in front of the room where the judges would deliberate. Two and one-half hours later, the judges returned to the courtroom. After requesting that everyone present stand, the president announced that it had been decided by majority vote that no separation of the defendants would take place until at least the evidentiary part of the trial was concluded.

After this announcement was made public, the Alsatian politicians renewed their efforts to have the Law of Collective Responsibility amended in such a way that separation of the German and Alsatian defendants would become compulsory. Consequently, as the trial unfolded, serious parliamentary efforts were made to interfere with its procedures. These efforts inevitably pitted the province of Alsace against the families of the Oradour victims and their supporters, the Limousin Communists, the Socialists and others.

During the first two days of the trial, which were largely taken up with the "separate trials" debate, the faces of the victims' families betrayed puzzlement and impatience. The defendants, both German and French were from equally simple backgrounds. Most had had only an elementary school education, i.e., to the age of fourteen. They appeared to be having difficulty following the arguments, but seemed relieved not to be testifying. Nussy Saint-Saëns, for his part, appeared satisfied with the decision not to conduct separate trials at this stage. This was probably because, as he had said earlier, he intended to conduct the trial essentially as if the Tribunal was hearing a case under the criminal law, rather than relying on the law's concept of collective responsibility or on any presumption of guilt.

By an ironic coincidence, on the third day of the Oradour trial, another trial started in Metz, the capital of Lorraine. The defendants were Karl Buck and his two deputies who had run the Nazi "re-education" camp at Schirmeck, thirty-two miles from Strasbourg. That camp and its equally sinister neighbor, Struthof (where the grandmother of my son-in-law was executed), were the only Nazi concentration camps on French soil. Buck was a convinced Nazi even after Germany lost the war. He said the Nazi party was the only means by which Germany could have been saved.

Georges René Boos, the former SS sergeant, joined the defendants on that Wednesday, January 14. Since he had volunteered in 1941 to serve in the Waffen SS, he was seated on the benches with the German defendants. Boos had been a prisoner of war in the UK until April 1947 before being transferred to prison in France. Although France had earlier charged him with treason and war crimes, for technical reasons, some of those charges had not been pursued. Further procedural issues were dealt with before the session terminated.

Chapter 13

The Defendants Interrogated

On the fourth day, the trial began with the reading of the indictment (*acte d'accusation*") by the clerks. This took over two hours—the indictment was a forty-seven page, single-spaced document. It classified the defendants as forty-four *in absentia* (including Captain Kahn and Lieutenant Barth) eight in jail (seven Germans plus Paul G. but not mentioning Boos), and thirteen Alsatians formerly at liberty. It did not name either Lammerding or Stadler. The courtroom listened in silence as the details of the tragedy were delivered in a dry monotone. When the clerks were finished, the president ordered the captain of the guards to bring his men to attention. He then requested that the defendants and the rest of those in the courtroom rise while the clerk read the names of each of the 642 victims of the massacre. Once again, there was a deathly silence. Due to the extensive media coverage of the trial, this reminder of the horrors of Oradour was reported throughout France and elsewhere in the world, which was no doubt what the president intended.

When all were once again seated, the president called each of the defendants (Germans and French mixed) in turn, to the witness *barre* and read aloud the charges against each of them. He then advised them that French law gave them the right to say anything that might assist in their defense. Most of the defendants responded that they had nothing special to say, although a few said that they regretted being involved in the affair. What Nussy Saint-Saëns did not need to tell the defendants was that they were obliged to testify. French law did not provide an equivalent of the U.S. Fifth Amendment Constitutional protection against self-incrimination.

The president then asked counsel if they intended to offer obedience to orders as an absolute defense, and received an affirmative response. He cautioned the lawyers (including the Germans) that they were under an obligation to say nothing against their conscience or the law, and that they were required to express themselves with decency and moderation. He made it clear that if there was any infringement of this requirement, he could and would withdraw his authorization for them to participate. He then asked whether there was anyone among the spectators who had been called as a witness. One or two responded in the affirmative and were told that until they had testified, they were not permitted to attend as spectators, in case their testimony would be influenced by other witnesses (in the U.S. this is called sequestering the witnesses).

Over the course of the next few days, in an attempt to elicit information about their specific roles in the massacre, the president examined each of the defendants in turn. It was clear from his questions that he had studied the files closely. First, however, he announced that he wished to satisfy himself as to certain facts: who had been in which section (similar to a squad) of the Third Company, who had been in the firing squads, and what weapons they had carried. The ensuing cross-examination was more frustrating than enlightening.

The president began with the highest-ranking defendant, the German adjutant Karl Lenz. Born in 1914, he had become a gardener in his early teens but had lost his job during the depression. In 1935, he had joined the army and later the Luftwaffe. When the president observed that the defendant had been awarded a medal for the Sudetenland campaign (the annexation in 1938 of German-speaking territories in Czechoslovakia), Lenz volunteered that his unit had not actually participated in that campaign. Nussy Saint-Saëns wryly rejoined that it was not only France that handed out decorations for doing nothing.

After the invasion of Russia, Lenz had served as a technician with the Luftwaffe on the Eastern Front until April 1943. He had been transferred to the Division Das Reich as part of an inter-service exchange organized by Himmler. He had been wounded in August 1943, and had rejoined his unit in France in March 1944.

The president established from his files that the Third Company consisted of three sections, armed with eighteen light machine guns, four heavy machine guns and two mortars. In addition to the rifles that the men carried, the officers had automatic pistols, and the junior officers and NCOs had submachine guns.

When asked if they carried grenades, Lenz said, "I didn't notice. I was not interested in the question. Most of the time I was absent from the Company." Noting this uncommunicative response, the president explained that he was asking about grenades because he thought that they had been used to blow up the church. Finally, the Alsatian SS volunteer, Georges Boos, supplied the information that they had carried both hand-grenades (American style, pineapple-shaped) and so-called "hip grenades" (German-style, long-handled). When the president asked how a bomb could be made from such grenades, Boos explained, "We put some hand grenades in the middle and we take off the handles of some other [hip] grenades and wire them all together."

Returning to Lenz, the president tried to determine why he did not appear to have had any set responsibilities within the Third Company. Lenz explained that this was a consequence of his poor relationship with Captain Kahn, the company commander, following an episode when he (Lenz) had been put in charge of instructing one of the company's sections. He had based his teaching on his experiences in Russia, rather than on the manual of instruction as Kahn had wished. From then on Kahn had victimized him and made him his scapegoat. On his arrival in France, he had requested a transfer back to the Luftwaffe, and in consequence, Kahn had withheld all responsibility from him. Lenz's counsel observed that his client had no military competence, and that his fellow defendants had recognized this fact. Lenz repeated that he did not remember or notice prominent events at Oradour, which caused the president to suggest that perhaps he was suffering from amnesia. He attempted to lead Lenz through the events of the massacre, minute-by-minute, but the defendant continually fell back on the formulaic response, "Because of the passage of time, that fact has escaped me," To that, Nussy Saint-Saëns eventually responded: "Because of the passage of time, I am here to refresh your memory." When that jibe failed to elicit more information, the president looked Lenz in the face and told him that he was certain that he was not telling the whole truth. "I invite you to tell the truth because...in this horrible drama there are some defendants who have been very frank about what they did; but some other ones...have attempted to play innocent..." He added that there were going to be no scapegoats.

In a further attempt to prime the pump of this very dry well, the president pointed to a map hanging on the wall. "If the Third Company came from St. Junien [about eight miles away] and entered Oradour from the south," he asked, "how could Lenz not have seen what was going on?" Lenz said the map did not refresh his memory, and besides, they had driven through Oradour in trucks which had had their camouflage tarpaulins in place, and he had seen nothing. He had only alighted from the truck after they had passed through the town and pulled up on the north side of it. After that, he had been ordered to climb a tree as a lookout, and there is where he had stayed. The president's blunt response was that Lenz had clearly spent his years in prison polishing his story.

Eventually, Lenz admitted that he went into the village around the time that Kahn gave the signal to the execution squads and that afterwards he went into the Beaulieu shed and saw twenty bodies. Several of his fellow soldiers had also been there. Nussy Saint-Saëns asked him if one of these was his co-defendant Blaeschke, as Lenz had told the British when they interrogated him as a prisoner of war. Lenz denied that he had told the British any such thing. The British had concluded that Blaeschke was at the garage because Lenz had told them that a medical officer was present, but in fact Blaeschke had not been there—he claimed it was another medic. The president commented that it was the first time that he had heard the British police accused of a lack of thoroughness; usually they were considered superior to their French counterparts in this respect. Lenz claimed that he had signed his deposition without reading it. What he did remember clearly was that when he had encountered Kahn, the Captain had reprimanded him because his trousers were not tucked into his boots, his handkerchief was missing, and his watch was dangling from his pocket. It was for that reason that Lieutenant Barth had told him to climb a tree and be a lookout.

Trying another tack, the president observed that in 1947 Albert L., one of the French/Alsatian defendants, had told the investigators that he had seen Lenz fire a submachine gun and throw grenades into the church. Then the following year, Nussy Saint-Saëns continued, Albert L. had told the *juge d'instruction* (the investigating magistrate in charge of the judicial military police) that he had made a mistake and had confused Lenz with Topfer (who was now dead). This change of story, the president told Albert L., was particularly infuriating. "The best way to obtain the indulgence of a Tribunal composed of soldiers is to be truthful," he said, "and in this particular case, I believe that it is in your interest to be very direct and very frank." The president asked why he had said that Lenz had been present. "To tell the truth," Albert L. started only to be interrupted, "Ah, to tell the truth—Nussy Saint-Saëns interjected wearily, "Listen, there is an extremely painful scene that I remind you of, that took place in a Commissariat of Police in Strasbourg…where several of your comrades decided to deceive justice by telling lies. We have proof in the files. Do you want to continue in that vein? I tell you it will be the worse for you."

At this point, Albert L.'s defense counsel interrupted, asking to know what possible motive his client might have for helping Lenz. Albert L. himself then confirmed that he had no motive other than to correct a mistake. Later, when asked why Oradour-sur-Glane had been targeted, Lenz said that he did not know. However, he had heard after the event that it was because Major Kämpfe had been killed in an ambush at Oradour.

The other defendants were called to testify. Fritz Pfeuffer, a German, stepped up to the *barre*. A heavily built, twenty-seven-year-old man with the pallor and docile aspect of a long-term prisoner, he had been incarcerated since the war. He told the court that at the age of seventeen, following seven years in the Hitler Youth, he had joined the SS Deutschland Division in Prague in January 1944. Soon afterwards he had been transferred to the Third Company of the Division Das Reich in the southwest of France. He admitted that he had participated in patrols in the Lot and Lot-Garonne Departments in which houses had been burned and blood spilt, but he claimed that he had not personally been involved in any reprisals or engagements with the *maquis*.

President Nussy Saint-Saëns asked Pfeuffer if he had received any specific orders in respect to Oradour. Pfeuffer replied that he had not, although he remembered arriving in St. Junien the day before, because it had been his eighteenth birthday. Also, he said, there had been a rumor going around that the maquis had captured Captain Gerlach. He and his colleagues had been told that they would be leaving early in the morning. When they left St. Junien, he had had the impression that they were heading for some sort of active duty. In the lead truck, Lieutenant Barth had told him that it was not Gerlach but Major Kämpfe, the commandant of the Third Battalion, who had been captured. Nussy Saint-Saëns asked if Major Kämpfe's capture had been given as the reason that they were going to Oradour, but Pfeuffer replied in the negative.

When the president asked what he had actually done in Oradour, Pfeuffer said that he had been part of a group which had gone to the north end of town to round up outlying farmers and to ensure that no one entered or left the village. He insisted that he personally had neither shot anyone nor heard any shots there. Then he and the rest of the group had been summoned to the village, where Captain Kahn had directed them to the Beaulieu shed. While there, fifteen to twenty men were waiting anxiously. Kahn explained that the men were terrorists, and were to be shot when he gave the signal. He ordered two light machine guns to be placed at the door facing the victims, with the rifle squad behind. Pfeuffer acknowledged that he had manned a machine gun and had fired when the signal was given. When asked whether all the men in the garage had been killed, he answered that it was difficult to say. He confirmed that he had aimed at the men's chests, and said that the firing squad had withdrawn after the execution. The president asked who had finished off the wounded, and Pfeuffer said that NCO Baïer had asked him for his pistol before going into the garage with Captain Kahn for this purpose. He, himself, had not been involved with the burning of the victims because for reasons of safety, his machine gun had to be kept away from fire.

At this point in the trial, the president turned to the spectators, and said, "I see that there is a child present who must be seven, eight, or nine years old. Is she accompanied by someone here?"

"Yes, M. President," a woman replied.

"You are her mother?"

"Yes."

"Listen, Madame, I understand that you are following the proceedings with great interest, but permit me to pose a question. Do you believe that this is a suitable place for a child of that age? As a father, I tell you frankly that I do not."

The mother replied, "Maybe not, but my daughter will not leave. She wants to find out who executed her father and her grandfather."

They were allowed to stay.

In general, the German defendants were very unforthcoming and it was clear that their responses had been well rehearsed. Given that they had spent years in prison and had probably also been carefully counseled by their lawyers, this was unsurprising. With the exception of a few who admitted being in firing squads, the Germans erected a wall of denial around themselves, and without their uniforms and weapons, it was hard to envision them as murderers.

The Friday session of the first week ended late in the afternoon. The defendants filed out as they did each day to board police vans for the short trip back to the prison. Until that moment, the families of the victims and their supporters had remained silent before the Alsatians and Germans. However, two busloads of protestors from Limoges and the Oradour area had arrived earlier that day. For the first time since the trial began, there was an organized demonstration outside the courthouse with shouts of "murderers!" Given the heavy police presence, it was not likely that there was any real danger, but the incident provided unambiguous evidence of how high feelings were running.

President Nussy Saint-Saëns opened the final session of the first week on Saturday by quashing rumors concerning the issue of non-separation of the forcibly inducted Alsatians and the Germans. It was time, he said, to stop debating the procedure and move on to the trial proper. He concluded by saying that so long as he was in the chair there would be no judicial scandal about Oradour. Presumably, he referred to the fact that he was determined to prevent the political and emotional maelstrom the trial was in, to result in any impropriety.

After Nussy Saint-Saëns had completed his questioning of Pfeuffer, the next witness to testify was Paul G., an Alsatian. Unlike the rest of Alsatian defendants (other than the volunteer Boos), Paul G. had been in prison since the war, but his counsel argued that he had been forcibly impressed into the SS, just as they had. Born in 1926 as a "natural child" (i.e. illegitimate), Paul G. was brought up by his grandparents in the Bas-Rhin Department of Alsace. Although never a member of the

Hitler youth, he was a victim of a forced labor decree in October 1943. He had been sent to work for three months in a factory in Mayence, Germany. When he came of age, he was conscripted.

The SS sergeants who interviewed him saw his blond hair, blue eyes, and strong build, and decided that he was the perfect Aryan type for the SS. To see him in court so thin, pallid and wearing a black patch over one eye, this was hard to imagine. Soon, he was wearing the uniform of the Third Company of the Division Das Reich, and by March 1944, he was with the company in the southwest of France. The president noted at this point that the mayor and priest of his home village had attested that Paul G. had been distressed by his service in the SS. He had sent a letter to his former teacher saying that he hated the company of such brutal murderers. So why didn't he desert, Nussy Saint-Saëns demanded? Paul G. responded that his family had remained in Alsace, and the Germans had made it clear that if any Alsatian deserted, his family would be sent to re-education or concentration camps.

The examination continued. When Paul G. was quartered near Montauban, the court heard, there had been a *résistant* named Julien Vigneau who lived and operated in the region. In May 1944, Paul G. had overheard some officers saying that the Gestapo was going after Vigneau. At great personal risk, he had had managed to warn the *résistant*. As a result, Vigneau had avoided arrest. Later, in Normandy, Paul G. had been wounded by an exploding shell and lost his right eye. His lawyer reminded the court that after he had recovered from his wounds, he had returned to his village in Alsace and had never concealed the fact that he had been at Oradour-sur-Glane. This openness had facilitated his arrest. In 1946, after a whirlwind trial by a criminal court in Limoges, he had been condemned to death for his admitted killing of a woman at Oradour and participating in the destruction of the village. The decision was reversed on appeal because of his youth, and the fact that he had been forcibly inducted. The appeals court had remanded his case to the military courts, and that process had continued through various appeals until this current trial. That is why he had spent seven years in prison while his *malgré nous* co-defendants were at liberty. None of the other Alsatian defendants had been tried before for what they did at Oradour.

When the president indicated that he wanted him to go into detail about the events of June 10, Paul G. testified in a straightforward manner. He said that after they passed through the village, they were divided into groups of two or three by Lieutenant Barth and ordered to prevent people from entering or leaving the village. He, himself, had been put with a German and a Russian soldier. They had come across two women, one about sixteen years old, and the other an older woman. There was also a man hiding behind a hedge when the Russian and the German had opened fire. One of the women was hit and began to scream, holding her stomach (Paul G. demonstrated for emphasis). "To my surprise I opened fire," he said. "Under orders from Lieutenant Barth they transported the bodies to a burning farm nearby and put them in." Nussy Saint-Saëns noted the irony of the fact that it was now established that one of their victims, Octavie Dahlstein, age 67, was a refugee expelled from Moselle, Lorraine by the Germans for being "too French."

After this incident, Paul G. testified that he had been ordered to the church. There, he found Diekmann and Kahn dispatching soldiers for firewood and supervising the burning of the bodies. He also saw Genari (one of the absent defendants) smashing up the confessional. "What else did you see?" he was asked. Paul G. wrung his hands and paused for several moments before answering. He then saw Lieutenant Gnug light the charges he had placed between the vault of the nave and the roof which brought down the bell tower. One of the stones from the explosion fell and cracked Gnug's skull and after Normandy they had been in the same hospital. Paul G. admitted that he had heard the groans of the women beneath the firewood. He had also talked to an SS soldier who described administering the *coup de grace* to a women and a baby whom he had found hiding in the toilet of the rectory. [This was presumably Mme Henriette Joyeux, who was shot after she had jumped out of the broken stained-glass window with her baby, following Mme Rouffranche. Apparently, Mme Joyeux had managed to crawl to the W.C. with her baby, before being finished off].

Before the SS soldiers left Oradour, Paul G. continued, Barth had forbidden them to volunteer anything about what had happened. "But if asked, you should say that *maquisards* shot [at us] when we entered the village and afterwards the townspeople fled into the woods." Finally, the president asked the defendant what role Lenz had played in the Third Company. "He did absolutely nothing...He was considered a joke by everyone," said Paul G.

Next it was the turn of Albert D., another Alsatian, who had been twenty-six years old at the time of the massacre. He testified that he had been part of the cordon around the village. He had turned away a young girl, a woman, and a man, but one other man, a music professor [apparently it was Jean Baptiste Tournier, age fifty-one], had insisted that the soldiers let him through. He had proceeded to the village and to his death. Albert D. began to weep. Nussy Saint-Saëns said, "I see you crying. There is finally a human gesture." After Oradour, Albert D. had deserted. As the Germans had threatened, his father was sent to the re-education camp at Schirmeck. Albert D. said his brother was also a *malgré nous* and never returned from Russia. When accused by the president of having been the instigator of an agreement among himself and his comrades to deny they had shot anyone at Oradour, Albert D. denied it.

Jean-Pierre E., another Alsatian, succeeded Albert D. at the *barre*. The president acknowledged that not only had this man refused to join the Hitler Youth when Alsace was annexed, but that he had actually accomplished several acts of minor resistance. For example, he had smashed the window of a store featuring a photograph of Hitler. The Alsace authorities had been aware of his French sympathies and this was one possible reason why he was forced into the SS Division instead of the Wehrmacht. Jean-Pierre E. had been seventeen at the time of the massacre. One part of his testimony about what had happened the next day adds a useful piece to the puzzle as to why Oradour was selected for annihilation. He said that on Sunday, he and the Third Company had made an attack on the Chateau de Morcheval, which was near Nieul where they had been billeted on Saturday and Sunday nights. The Chateau had been a Resistance headquarters, but the *résistants* had managed to escape. If that target was the reason Nieul was chosen as the company billet on the 9th when Gerlach was sent out to confirm the arrangements, it provides some support for the theory that Oradour was chosen as a target because it was conveniently located on the way between St. Junien (the billet on the 9th) and Nieul (the billet on the 10th and 11th).

Jean-Pierre E. and Albert D. had been together on sentry duty and both told the story of the young girl, the woman, and the man that they had turned back, as well as the music teacher who had insisted on going through the cordon into the village. At one point, Jean-Pierre E. had seen about twenty village men, both old and young, in a garage surrounded by SS men [presumably the Desourteaux garage]. They had tried to be freed by waving their identity cards, but Kahn had rejected their pleas. Kahn had then ordered a machine gun to be turned on them. They had all fallen to the ground, and two NCOs (one of whom was Boos) had administered *coups de grace*. Afterwards, kindling and straw had been brought in by means of a human chain, heaped on top of the victims, and lit.

Jean-Pierre E. also testified that he had seen Boos give explosives to Kahn. Kahn had taken those into the church (presumably with Gnug) after which Jean-Pierre E. had heard an explosion and the church had begun to burn. The testimony is unclear, but it is possible that this was a second attempt to blow up the church and its bell tower. The first attempt had been the detonation that Mme Rouffranche described, and that it was in this second explosion that Gnug was injured by falling stones. The president, however, did not pursue the matter.

From time to time, Jean-Pierre E. went into houses that were not burning strongly and threw alcohol on the furniture and floor to speed the fire along. He had seen Boos enter the church and throw grenades. Later, he carried firewood in, but it had been Captain Kahn, he said, who actually lit the fire. Most of the men had gone to the church and heaped kindling onto the bodies there. As he had been ordered to stand by his machine gun, he had taken no part in that job. He had heard the cries of those still alive inside the church, however. Also, another Alsatian told him that a woman had been weeping and begging Kahn in German to let her out. She was probably from Alsace or Moselle. Kahn had refused, informing her that, "We do not want witnesses for later on."

Chapter 14

The Alsatian Political Position

On Saturday afternoon, January 17, while the president of the Tribunal interrogated the defendants, the political leadership of Alsace was meeting in Strasbourg. At issue was how they might reverse the Tribunal's decision not to grant separate trials for the French-Alsatians at that time. At the end of the day, they issued a statement expressing disappointment that determination of the separate trials issue had been postponed by the Tribunal. The statement said that while its authors expressed confidence in the Tribunal, they condemned the fact there was no separation of the *malgré nous* from the Germans. The statement also drew attention to the government's failure to obtain the extradition of the real architects of the massacre—the SS officers who had planned it. Throughout the Alsace region on the following day, demonstrations were mounted demanding the separation of the Alsatian and German defendants.

That same Sunday the veterans' association of Lorraine issued their own quite different statement. They requested that the Bordeaux trial be permitted to run its course without any separation of the defendants. They deplored the tendency to paint the Alsatian defendants as victims of the SS, and demanded to know why they had not tried to desert, given the length of time that the Division had been in France. The Lorraine statement particularly stung the people of Alsace.

On Monday, January 19, while the Tribunal was in session in Bordeaux, a delegation of Alsatian politicians and members of the National Assembly held a meeting with René Pleven, the Minister of Defense. Their intention was to gain his support for a bill modifying the 1948 Law of Collective Responsibility. Pleven was sympathetic and promised to present the proposal to the Council of Ministers which would meet the next day, and to introduce the bill to the legislators as soon as possible. Some Alsatians conceded that changing the law while the trial was underway was unusual, and could prove problematic for certain members of the Assembly. This, in fact, turned out to be the case.

Chapter 15

Further Interrogation

In Bordeaux, President Nussy Saint-Saëns pressed ahead with the questioning. He made it clear as he did so that he was investigating the defendants as individuals, rather than pursuing the idea of their "collective responsibility," as the Law of Collective Responsibility permitted. The *malgré nous* defendant, Louis H., had been born in Lyon, but had lived in Alsace from the age of ten. In 1939, just before the German invasion, he and his family had been evacuated to the Paris region. The following year after the Armistice, they returned to Strasbourg to collect their furniture but had been refused permission to leave. Louis H. had been sent to work in Germany for three months before being forcibly inducted into the Division Das Reich and sent to Montauban in March 1944.

Describing the departure of the Third Company for Oradour from St. Junien on June 10 of that year, Louis H. testified that a German soldier had told him that, "Things are going to get hot." There had been a brief hiatus outside Oradour while the officers and NCOs were briefed, and then he and his colleagues were ordered to establish a cordon around the village. The testimony which followed included an anecdote about a cow trapped in a burning barn. Louis H. had put on his gas mask and tried to help save the animal, but the smoke had been too thick and the fire too intense. The tale prompted the observation from Nussy Saint-Saëns that rather more concern had been shown for the cow than for the village's human inhabitants.

When the Third Company reached Normandy, Louis H. and two other Alsatians had attempted to desert. On June 26, near Caen, they were discovered by a German patrol and escorted back to the company command post where Captain Kahn castigated them. He ordered them to be taken to the front line, and on July 1, under heavy bombardment, Louis H. was wounded in the face and arm. Continuing to advance, despite his wounds, he found himself face-to-face with a Canadian soldier who would have shot him had not an officer intervened. Louis H. was sent to a local field hospital and later to England for treatment. After his recovery, he was sent to a prison camp in Edinburgh, where he was visited and questioned by a French officer. At that point, he had volunteered the information that he had been at Oradour. Shortly afterwards, he was asked whether he wished to complete his education or join the Free French army. He chose the latter, and took part in the Allied invasion of Germany under General de Lattre de Tassigny. Later, he served in Indo-China and then joined the French police force in Saigon; it was from there that he had been recalled to stand trial.

The next witness, Herbert Daab, was German. He had joined the Hitler Youth and had been conscripted into the SS, and at the time of the massacre had been eighteen years old. Although only twenty-six years old at the time of the trial, he looked much older. He had a receding hairline and the same prison pallor that he shared with the other German defendants. He admitted to the president that he had participated in the Frayssinet operation in which civilian men had been shot and women hanged, but he insisted that he had merely guarded a truck throughout. "It is very curious how many cooks and vehicle guards seem to have been involved in these operations," Nussy Saint Saëns observed dryly.

As regards Oradour, Daab admitted that he had been one of about eight members of the firing squad under Sgt. Boos which had executed twenty men of the village in the Desourteaux garage. Daab testified that they had been told that the villagers were partisans and that he and his colleagues had been ordered to shoot them on Captain Kahn's signal (a burst from his automatic pistol). Daab said that he had fed the machine gun, and that he and his fellow gunner had fired about 100 rounds. Although later wounded in Normandy, he had fought on, and had finally been captured by the French shortly before the war ended in May 1945. He had spent the next eight years in prison awaiting trial.

Thirty-nine-year-old Albert O., the father of four children, had the pinched and weather-beaten look of a poor farmer. He had served in the French army from 1934 to 1935 and been re-mobilized in 1939 until the surrender, only to be forcibly inducted by the Germans into the Division Das Reich in February 1944. Although he had been a free man since the war, he seemed more outwardly disturbed by the events that he was being forced to re-live, than any of the other defendants.

Initially, Albert O. had been involved in assembling the villagers on the village green. Sgt. Staeger instructed the men, "When you go in the houses, you see a child, man or woman, or anyone who is sick, they must be shot in their bed." Albert O. had been very scared, he said, and when they reached the first house he had asked to stay outside. Ordered inside by Staeger, he had remained in the front hall. A German soldier had passed him, harassing an old woman who could only walk with the aid of two canes. Albert O. had told the soldier to leave the woman alone; Staeger, overhearing him, had ordered Albert O. to shut his mouth or be shot. When the woman started to descend the steps, Staeger had directed a burst of submachine gun fire at her. She had fallen and two of the bullets had ricocheted and hit Albert O. in the legs. Crying out that he was hit, he had been ordered by Staeger to report to a medical orderly on the village green, but not to describe how he had come by the wound. Albert O. had replied that he did not wish to lie. Staeger had replied, "Well you work it out."

The orderly had looked at the wound, and told him that it was not grave. He proceeded to extract one of the bullets on the spot. Albert O. had begged him not to take out the other bullet straight away because of the pain, and had been told to wait while the orderly consulted Major Diekmann. On his return, the orderly asked him what country he came from, and when he told him that it was Alsace, he ordered Albert O. back to his section. Albert O. had walked about thirty yards and fallen down. Blaeschke (one of the German defendants), helped him to the truck where he remained for the rest of the afternoon. The president, looking at his file, asked, "Is it true that you were in tears?" Albert O. paused a moment, began to sob, and mumbled "yes."

It later transpired that Albert O.'s brother-in-law had been conscripted in Alsace but had refused to wear a German uniform, declaring that he was French. Three days later, he had been executed without a trial. His mother had shown similar courage, hiding two other conscripted men until the Liberation.

Another Alsatian witness, Auguste Anthoine L. (called "Albert L.") provided a contrast to the other defendants—especially the Germans—with his open expressions of regret. He began by saying that he was ashamed to have been at Oradour. He had seen great horrors there, he said, and was still haunted by the cries of the victims. His strained features confirmed that he had been deeply affected by the experience. Aged thirty at the time of the massacre, Albert L. had no love for Germany. His father had been drafted into the German Army in WW I when Alsace had officially been part of Germany, but he had deserted, and only escaped execution because two of his brothers had been killed fighting for Germany. Like Albert O., Albert L. had served in the French Army in 1934 and again in 1939. In 1940, he had been awarded the *Croix de Guerre* while fighting the Germans, only to be forcibly inducted by them in February 1944. As an example of the way that the SS behaved, he testified that while traveling by truck from Montauban to Limoges, he and his fellow soldiers had passed an old man reading a newspaper by the side of the road. For no reason at all, the man had been shot dead. Such things, Albert L. said, happened all the time.

Recalling his experiences at Oradour, he told the court that Staeger had primed them for action with the words: "Now we are going to see what you Alsatians are capable of." Standing guard outside the village, Albert L. had seen a girl of about eighteen years old walking towards the village with a bag of groceries under her arm. Knowing how trigger-happy Staeger was, he had told her to turn back, or risk being shot. She had done as he had told her, and Albert L. expressed the hope that she was still alive today. Subsequently, Staeger and his section had marched about thirty of the village men including an elderly priest, Jean-Baptiste Chapelle, age seventy-one to the Denis wine store [one of three priests killed]. There, they got the captives to drag several carts out of the Denis storehouse before herding them inside. When Kahn fired the signal, Albert L. and the others in the firing squad shot the men as they had been ordered. Then they piled kindling and straw on top of the bodies and set them on fire.

The unit then proceeded to the church, where they were ordered to collect flammable material from the nearby barns. President Nussy Saint-Saëns asked who had issued this order. "Boos," replied Albert L. Nussy Saint-Saëns asked Boos if he had heard what Albert L. had said, and Boos acknowledged that he had. Albert L. recalled that he had returned to the church twice with combustible material and that on returning to one of the barns, he had found two women there, one of about forty years old, and the other of about twenty. "If I had been a minute quicker, I could have told them to hide. It was just at that moment that Boos came in, passed by me and shot the two women." He testified that he had also seen Boos and Staeger throw grenades into the church.

Albert L. had left Oradour in the truck at about 9:00 p.m. The company had quartered in Nieul, and Kahn had distributed wine and liquor which they had pillaged from Oradour. On Sunday morning, at about 4:00 a.m., a detail of about thirty men, including Albert L., had returned to Oradour with two sergeants. There, they had dug burial ditches, interring a number of the bodies. They were ordered by one of the company cooks to collect all the chickens, pigs and other livestock that they could find in the village. Since he had trouble understanding Nussy Saint-Saëns, Albert L.'s lawyer asked for the questions to be translated into Alsatian, which was done. Albert L. went on to tell how the company had taken appalling losses in Normandy. At one point, all but eighteen of the normal complement of 150 of them had been either killed or wounded, and they had had to relocate to await replacements. Eventually, he was able to desert, and had been taken prisoner by the Americans. They had turned him over to the French, to whom he had described what had happened at Oradour.

On the following day (January 20), the president announced that he intended to interrogate Boos, but would first question Joseph B., an Alsatian from Boos's section. Joseph B.'s father, a laborer, had joined the fanatically Nazi SA (the *Sturmabteilung*, or Storm Troops) "…without conviction, but out of necessity" because he had ten children and SA members got extra rations. Now a mason and married with three children, Joseph B. had been forcibly inducted into the SS in February 1944. He had been eighteen years old at the time of the massacre.

Joseph B. testified that he had been in the section under Sgt. Boos which was responsible for assembling the people of Oradour at the village green. Along with a dozen other SS soldiers, he had then marched twenty men to the Desourteaux barn. When Kahn had given the signal, he had shot them, as Boos had ordered. He had carried a rifle, and had fired it at the men in the barn three or four times. He noted that the other execution squads had fired at the same time. The squad had then been ordered by Boos to get firewood from the bakery opposite the barn. They had formed a chain and piled wood on the bodies, and then they had been ordered to take cover as Kahn was about to blow up the church.

Joseph B. recounted how he had seen two women approaching the church after the slaughter had begun inside it. They had come to the village, they had told him, to get their children. Joseph B. and the others warned them that if they came into the village, they would be shot, but then Boos and another soldier appeared. Shots were heard. Joseph B. was unable to say if they had come from that particular building because there was shooting going on all around him. He did testify that the two SS men had come out of the barn alone. On this grim note, Nussy Saint-Saëns summoned the key defendant to the *barre*.

Georges René Boos, the only Alsatian defendant who had volunteered for the SS, was a stocky man with light brown hair. In court, after his long incarceration, his gray tweed suit looked a couple of sizes too large for him (Illustration 46). Born in Bas-Rhin in 1923, he had been sixteen years old when the war started in 1939. He and his parents were evacuated by the French government but had returned after the 1940 Armistice. His father, who had strong Nazi sympathies, took German citizenship, and became a member of the SA. In March 1941, Boos volunteered for the Waffen SS. Although raised a Protestant, he resigned from his church, as the Nazi Party encouraged its members to do. Individuals who took this step were known as *"Gottgläubig"* or Believers in God, indicating that they retained Christian beliefs rather than subscribing to atheism, which had Communist connotations.

After training as a medical orderly, Boos had served two tours with the SS on the Eastern Front, where he met Captain Kahn. They had both been assigned to a field police unit, whose principal task was the "cleansing" of the front line of partisans and civilians. Boos's second

Oradour-The Final Verdict

46. Sgt. Boos, the Alsatian SS volunteer, at the *barre*. The prosecutor is seated behind the microphone. There is a guard posted at the exit.

tour included the battle of Kharkov. Unlike many of his colleagues, he survived this engagement. He was awarded the Iron Cross (Second Class), promoted to sergeant, and sent with the Division Das Reich to France in April 1944 as a combat soldier.

With an evident hardening of his attitude, the president addressed the defendant. "Boos. You know the facts of which you stand accused. I do not hide the fact that they are grave, because I'm in the habit of laying my cards on the table and speaking in good faith. I think it is in your best interest to tell us the whole truth. Do you have any statement to make?" Boos said, "I sincerely regret my involvement in this whole sad affair."

Nussy Saint-Saëns asked him about Captain Kahn, and Boos replied that Kahn had been a very tough officer who had reprimanded him several times.

The president pointed out that when one of Boos's Alsatian co-defendants, Jean-Pierre E., had given a deposition in January 1947, he said you were extremely tough yourself. As an example, referring to his file, he described how Kahn had once ordered five company members who came from Alsace to sing *'La Strasbourgeoise'* (an Alsatian song) to the rest of the men. Jean-Pierre E. had claimed Boos was the only one who had actually sung. When the officers and NCOs laughed at him, "You took your revenge on the five Alsatians by forcing them to put on their gas masks and drill in the mud and water until they dropped. Is that true?" Boos denied it.

Nussy Saint-Saëns then turned to Jean-Pierre E. The defendant confirmed that the story was substantially true, and that Boos had treated the other Alsatians brutally. The president informed the court that Fernand G., an Alsatian soldier, had spoken about Boos in a police interview shortly after the war. He had said that Boos despised the Alsatians who had been forcibly inducted because at heart they were not Nazis; their sympathies were for France. In response, Fernand G. had stated, the Alsatians had considered Boos more Nazi than the Germans.

The president asked Boos if Kahn had explained why they were going to Oradour. Boos replied, "As far as I remember, the objective of the mission was to search for Major Kämpfe. He told me as a group leader, 'we have to expect some fierce combat.'" It emerged that Boos's section had remained a short distance to the southwest of Oradour, on the other side of the Glane River. After awhile, a group had conducted the women and children to the church led by Lieutenant Gnug. The remaining men were divided by Kahn into groups of varying sizes. Boos had found himself in charge of about twenty of them. By then, he told the Tribunal, Diekmann, Kahn and Barth had already decided upon the locations in which the executions would take place.

A dispute then ensued as to where the executions by Boos's firing squad had taken place. Joseph B. (who was in Boos's group) insisted it was in the Desourteaux barn facing the Bouchoule bakery, but Boos maintained that it was some thirty or forty yards from there. Wearily, the president explained that when the bodies had been recovered after the massacre, they had been removed from the Desourteaux barn. He said that, in his view, the real reason that Boos was making this claim, and appeared so uncomfortable, was that the Desourteaux garage was directly opposite the Bouchoule bakery. That bakery was where a child had been put inside a brazier (a metal bucket into which hot embers are drawn from the bread oven to make room for the dough) and burned alive. The president then ordered the brazier brought in and placed in front of Boos. He asked Boos what he had to say. Boos did not reply.

The president then asked Boos if after the execution, he had administered *coups de grace*. Boos acknowledged that he had done so on Kahn's orders, and afterwards covered the bodies with flammable material. Half an hour later, he said, he and his men had been ordered to the church. The president interjected that Joseph B., had testified earlier in the day that Boos had shot two women near the church. A statement made in June 1945 by Albert L confirmed this testimony. He said to Boos, "Don't you think you have killed enough?" Albert L. said that after the women were shot Boos had replied, "Shut up or I will shoot you next." "That isn't true" Boos replied. "I never shot women at Oradour." "I saw him do it with my own eyes," Albert L. confirmed emphatically. "So did I," said Joseph B.

President Nussy Saint-Saëns once again leaned on the Alsatian volunteer for the SS, saying, "I tell you, Boos, the Tribunal has come to observe that Albert L. has always been frank, even when it was to his detriment. Why don't you tell the truth when it concerns you?" Boos lashed back at the *malgré nous*, "I don't understand why my Alsatian comrades are attacking me at every turn?"

The president changed tack. "I am obliged to stress, there is a witness, the mechanic Beaubreuil, who was hiding [with his brother] under the floor boards of the kitchen of his aunt, Mme Mercier. Her house is situated precisely facing the church, and while he was hiding [there], he heard a young girl talking to another woman in the garden of the house. When he went out after the massacre, he discovered two bodies under the debris. You see Boos, as I said earlier; I'm prepared to put my cards on the table." Nussy Saint-Saëns once more pressed him to be frank. Boos replied, "Concerning these matters, I have always been frank. I have hidden nothing. I am prepared to take responsibility where necessary." "Ah," said the president ironically. "You are prepared to take responsibility!"

Boos continued with his account of events. After the firing squad had finished its work, he said, he was told to get his men under cover because the church was to be blown up. A little later, he had heard the explosion in the church, and then the firing of weapons. Captain Kahn, who was standing with Diekmann near the church, summoned him. "It was at that moment that I heard the moans and the cries," Boos said. "I saw soldiers firing machine guns in the church. I also saw Gnug, who had been wounded and was being carried by two soldiers."

The president informed the court that in his 1947 deposition to the investigators in Alsace, Jean-Pierre E. had stated that he saw Boos firing into the church. From the defendants' bench, Jean-Pierre E. confirmed that he had seen Boos do this. In testimony given immediately after the war, President Nussy Saint-Saëns continued, Albert L. had stated that Boos had also thrown grenades into the church among the women and children. From the bench, Albert L. confirmed that he had seen this. Boos denied it.

The president then asked about events at the command post that Diekmann had established at the Masset house just outside the village. Boos answered that there had been some French civilians there when, at around 9:00 p.m., he had returned from taking Gnug to the hospital in Limoges. He had been chosen for this task, he explained, because he had once been a paramedic. The civilians had arrived on the 7:30 p.m. tram, and had apparently been held, because Diekmann and Kahn had gone to Limoges to report to Colonel Stadler, and no one else knew what to do with them. He had checked the civilians' papers, Boos said, and later told Kahn that they were from villages other than Oradour. He knew that this was not the case, but he had been trying to save their lives, and as a result Kahn had let them go.

When the president questioned Boos about what had taken place at the house of the fabric merchant, Dupic, where a large number of empty wine and champagne bottles had been found, Boos said that he did not know. Nussy Saint-Saëns did not pursue the matter, although testimony from the police investigation strongly suggested that some sort of sexual violence had taken place in Oradour, probably at the Dupic house. Witnesses who had visited the church on Sunday had testified that they had seen the partially disrobed body of a young woman there. The body appeared to have been violated but was unburned; indicating that it had been put there after the inferno in the church had died down.

The president then interrogated Boos about the events in Normandy. The defendant, the court learned, had been captured by the Americans near Aix-la-Chapelle in October 1944 and then transferred to a prison camp in England, where the British interrogated him. "I'd like to say that at that time, I was beaten so severely over the course of four weeks, that I could not be transferred to a prison camp," Boos claimed. "You were beaten?" asked Nussy Saint-Saëns skeptically. "That is very surprising, because as I was saying relative to another deposition, we are used to hearing criticism of the French judicial police, but we have always held up the British judicial police as an example." "It wasn't the police. It was the military," responded Boos. "All the more surprising," said the president. "The [British] military are not in the habit of beating people while interrogating them."

It is noteworthy that the defense lawyers did not raise any specific objection to the introduction of evidence that was allegedly obtained by torture. It was probably apparent to them that President Nussy Saint-Saëns was extremely skeptical about Boos's evidence, and it was unlikely that they had any proof to support the claim that he had been beaten.

On the following day, a Wednesday, three Alsatians and three Germans testified. One of the Alsatian defendants stated that after he deserted in Normandy, the Germans had carried out their threat and sent his parents to the re-education camp at Schirmeck. He also said that at the end of the war, his father had emerged looking like a skeleton. Another Alsatian described how his cousin had fled to England. Two days after the cousin's departure, he said, his parents had been sent to a camp in Silesia. None of these Alsatians had been involved in the action at Oradour, except as sentries.

The next three German witnesses were all from the Headquarters' Company of the Regiment, rather than from the Third Company itself. Blaeschke was the medical orderly who had taken Albert O. to the truck after he was "accidentally" shot by Sgt. Staeger. He had played only a minor role at Oradour, but the president pressed him on his participation in the hanging of the three women in Frayssinet in May. Albert O. testified that Blaeschke had brought one of the women out of her house to be hanged, but had not carried out the hanging himself. Another German, Bœhme, had played only a marginal role at Oradour, and appeared to have had difficulty recalling what had happened there. His lawyer claimed that he suffered from memory-loss because as a motorcyclist, he had taken several falls. The third German, Degenhardt, explained that he and two fellow soldiers had become separated from their unit on their way to Limoges from the south. They had been attacked, had abandoned their vehicle, and had hitched rides in passing

German trucks. He said they arrived at headquarters in Limoges in the middle of the day on Saturday, June 10. In the late afternoon, they had been ordered to go to Oradour in two half-tracks with Diekmann in the lead vehicle. They then found the village in flames. Diekmann had stopped a few minutes to talk to Kahn, and he had ordered Degenhardt and the others to proceed to Nieul for the night.

By the end of the ninth day of the trial, the interrogation of the defendants by the president was complete. On balance, very little information had been elicited beyond that which the investigating magistrates had already compiled. In general, the accused had spoken little and revealed less, while the presiding officer had said much and made much public—particularly the details extracted from the defendants by the military and judicial police in the two or three years after the massacre. The only defendants who had been genuinely forthcoming were Paul G, who of all the *malgré nous* had suffered the most, since he had spent most of his adult life in prison, and Albert L., who seemed deeply affected by what had happened. Boos's testimony had been a curious mix of stubborn denial, convenient forgetfulness, and damning confessions of guilt. None of the defendants had asked forgiveness for what they had done. Perhaps they had been advised by their lawyers that to ask forgiveness would imply guilt.

A little over 400 miles away on that day in Metz, Lorraine, another military tribunal was in the process of convicting Karl Buck and his two deputies. They were sentenced to death for their atrocities at the "re-education" camp at Schirmeck.

In Paris, meanwhile, the amendment to the Law of Collective Responsibility proposed by the Alsatian deputies had been approved by the Justice Committee of the National Assembly with mainly the Communist members voting against the motion. Its proponents, racing against time, were desperate to pass the law before the Tribunal finished the trial—which they were under great pressure to do from the ANFM and the Communists.

Aware that the Alsatian politicians had a good chance of seeing the amendment made law, the ANFM began to think in terms of a consolation prize, namely an increased role for itself in the trial. Their champion was Gaston Charlet, a lawyer and senator from Haute-Vienne—the Department of which Limoges is the capital—and a senior member of the ANFM. Charlet and his followers wished to see the law changed so that civil parties could formally participate in military justice proceedings.

In Bordeaux, on Thursday, January 23, the tenth day of the trial, the Alsatian defense counsel M. Richard Lux moved to reopen the question of a separate trial. The denial of the earlier motion, he claimed, had caused so many demonstrations in Alsace that for the good of justice, the question should be revisited. Unexpectedly, the prosecutor changed his position and supported this request. Gardon, it seemed, had discussed the issue with his superiors in Paris who had been lobbied by politicians from Alsace. Counsel for the Germans, for their part, said that they would trust the wisdom of the Tribunal rather than mounting more arguments against separation. In the end, despite the prosecutor's change of position and the public and political pressure from Alsace, the Tribunal denied the motion, saying that they saw nothing new that would cause them to change their earlier decision. The ruling was greeted with applause from the ANFM and its supporters in the courtroom.

Chapter 16

The Survivors Arrive to Testify

As the president's examination of the defendants was drawing to a close in Bordeaux, Robert Hébras and several other survivors who had been called as witnesses for the prosecution boarded a train in Limoges. Hébras was deeply apprehensive at the thought of the trial, and of coming face-to-face with the men who had tried to kill him. On a more mundane level, he was also concerned about the cost of his coming, for while the government was paying his train fare, it was not going to reimburse him for hotel or meal expenses. He tried to sleep, climbing into the overhead luggage rack so that he could stretch out properly. He was promptly hauled down and reprimanded by the conductor.

Thursday morning, on their arrival at the courthouse, the survivors were shown into a small room behind the judges' rostrum where they were told to wait until called. Robert Hébras was now twenty-eight years old and married. He lived in the 'new' Oradour where he had just opened his own garage. Dressed in his Sunday suit with a white shirt and tie, he was visibly nervous. A week after the massacre, Hébras had felt well enough to visit the ruined village with his father, Jean. The two men had stood silently in front of the ruin of the house in which they had lived with Mme Marie Hébras and Robert's two sisters, Georgette and Denise—all now dead. Hébras stayed with his third sister, Odette, until late June when representatives of the Resistance came to recruit him and his friends, André Desourteaux and Pierre Dupic. The three went about ten miles north to the Monts de Blond hills near Cieux to await the arrival of weapons, which were delivered on or about Bastille Day (July 14). On August 7, the Germans attacked Hébras and twenty-nine other maquisards; nine of his comrades were killed but Hébras once again escaped. After Limoges was liberated a fortnight later, he joined the Free French army in which he served out the war.

The first prosecution witness was forty-year-old Hubert Desourteaux, the son of the late mayor, Dr. Paul Desourteaux and brother of, Jacques, Emile and Etienne, all pf whom were victims of the massacre. Still wearing his coat and scarf, he described seeing the arrival of the Germans in full battle gear (Illustration 47). At first he had tried to flee through the fields to the south of the village, but upon hearing shots, he had returned and hidden in his father's house. From there, he had seen a group of men walking along with an escort of soldiers. Then "…suddenly I heard a noise of machine guns everywhere…and I asked myself what had happened…" Later, he found out that men had been executed in his garage next door.

Shortly thereafter, the SS set fire to the house he was hiding in and he fled into the garden. He heard the explosion from the church, and then he heard a cry from a woman, which was followed by three shots. "The next day" he told the court, "I found the body [of Mme Hyvernaud] covered with the entrails of animals." In addition to the explosion in the church, Desourteaux heard constant machine gun fire and other explosions. He also heard a series of crashes which he later discovered to have been caused by slates falling from the roof of the burning church.

The following day, at about 9:00 a.m., the trucks carrying the German burial detail departed. Hearing cries, some survivors discovered a burned-out car and an injured SS man. The car had been stolen from the village, and the driver had missed the turn. It was thought that he might have been drunk, perhaps as a result of the orgy which many believed to have taken place at the Dupic house.

When Hubert Desourteaux went to the village at around 11:00 a.m., he found it still smoldering. He recognized several of the corpses, but most were too badly burned. He saw the bodies of the men in the Laudy barn and in front of the Bouchoule bakery. Then as the witness painfully recalled, when he went inside the church, "I saw a pile of ashes,

47. Hubert Desourteaux testifying.

48. Yvon Roby testifying.

Oradour-The Final Verdict

49. Robert Hébras testifying.

50. Marcel Darthout, testifying.

bodies and stones. In the corner of the confessional there were two children who were curled up together; one of the corpses still had dried blood at the mouth." He thought they were eight or nine years old.

At this point, the president asked the interpreter to find out if the defendants had anything to say. There was silence from the benches of the defendants. Desourteaux added that later in the afternoon, the deputy Prefect of Rochechouart, Belloc de Chamboran, had arrived and Desourteaux and some others had taken him to the church. He had been unable to believe what they showed him there. The picture taken by Ecto O. Munn in early October 1944 of Hubert standing at the rear door of his destroyed garage shows much of the understandable sadness that gripped him (Illustration 34 at the end of Part I The Massacre). Even in his testimony, he had an air of inconsolability. He never did recover from the experience as his later suicide perhaps attested.

Desourteaux was followed to the witness table by thirty-eight-year-old Aimé Renaud, who had also hidden in the Desourteaux garden. Renaud leaned forward in the witness chair as he testified. The machine-gunning by the firing squad that they had heard, he said, lasted at least ten minutes. Regarding their visit to the church on the following day, he said simply, *"Monsieur le President,* it was horrible." As well as the incinerated bodies of women and children, they had discovered makeshift burial areas with body parts protruding from the ground.

The next witness, Aimé Renaud's thirty-two-year-old wife, Janine, kept her hat and coat on, and clutched a handkerchief in her right hand as she spoke. She had been able to see the church from her hiding-place. After the explosion, she had seen dense fumes coming out of the windows and had heard 'unimaginable' cries. When she finished her account, she wept, saying, "I did not find a single member of my family."

Clement Broussaudier, the first of the Laudy barn survivors to testify, was thirty-four years old at the trial and a deliveryman in Limoges. He wore a light-colored suit and his scarf was tucked inside his jacket. He recounted the story of the execution in the Laudy barn and of his survival and escape. The president asked him if he had noticed any of the SS speaking in French, but Broussaudier said that he had not. He was followed by Yvon Roby, a twenty-seven-year-old postal clerk in Paris (Illustration 48). After Roby had completed his testimony, along much the same lines as Broussaudier, the prosecutor asked the president if he could clarify a point. The defendants had said that the signal to start shooting was when Kahn fired his automatic pistol, but witnesses had testified that the firing started after an explosion. In response to a request from the president, Boos gave a possible reason for this: "It must have been the echoes, because Kahn was just a dozen yards from me when he fired in the air."

Mathieu Borie, another survivor of the Laudy barn, was a thirty-two-year-old mason who worked in St. Junien. At the time of the massacre, he had been waiting to be called up by the Resistance. He largely confirmed Broussaudier's testimony. When it was Hébras's turn to testify, he recounted the story of his escape from the Laudy barn (Illustration 49). It took him less than twenty minutes to do so, and while the president listened intently, he did not ask him any questions. Afterwards, he thanked Hébras, who went to sit with the ANFM group to listen to the rest of the testimony.

He was followed by Marcel Darthout, the fifth of the Laudy barn survivors, who at the time of the trial was working in Paris (Illustration 50). A few weeks after the massacre, Darthout had had another narrow escape. He had been in a hospital in Confolens and was transferred to another one in Chabanais. The day after he left, the Gestapo came to the hospital in Confolens looking for him. The woman in charge regretfully reported that Darthout had died the day before.

Looking almost scholarly in his horn-rimmed glasses, Darthout described what had happened in the barn in essentially the same manner as the others. However, he added the details of his four bullet wounds, his garments catching fire, and the pain that he suffered. At the end, the president asked him if he had anything else to add. He said he would like to mention the uniforms of the SS, "They all looked the same," he said. "I did not notice any difference that day between the Alsatians and the Germans. They were all the same; equally aggressive…All did their job."

The next day, a Friday, January 23, Nussy Saint-Saëns announced that the first witnesses to be heard would be police investigators who would testify about the origins of the massacre and the possible motives of the SS. The first witness was fifty-five-year-old Pierre Arnet, who was now the chief of police in Strasbourg in Alsace. In September

1944, while serving in the Limoges police, he had been charged with the investigation of the massacre. Introducing Arnet, President Nussy Saint-Saëns asked him to summarize his investigation, with particular regard to the possible motive for the massacre.

After identifying the Third Company, Arnet recounted the story of the blowing up of the St. Junien Bridge the night of June 7-8 and the attack on the Wehrmacht soldiers. He noted that the train that was subsequently sent from Limoges the next morning, June 8, to pick up the stranded passengers was armored. It brought more Wehrmacht soldiers and a lieutenant of the Gestapo named Wickers, who quickly summoned the mayor and the chief of police of St. Junien. At the conference that ensued, the Germans decided to erect roadblocks in the town and take civilian hostages. The mayor of St. Junien responded by ordering a large meal for the German officers. After they ate and drank, they went to sleep and the hostage idea was dropped.

On the morning of June 9, an officer of the Limoges Gestapo telephoned Wickers and told him that the Division Das Reich was coming to relieve the Wehrmacht in St. Junien. Around 4:00 p.m., the First Battalion began to arrive in force and the Wehrmacht and the Gestapo went back to Limoges. During the night a curfew was enforced and a number of patrols were sent out.

On the following morning, the Saturday of the massacre, there was a meeting of the SS police in Limoges, which the Milice claimed they did not attend. Thereafter, Lieutenant Kleist of the Gestapo, along with an interpreter named Patry, and four members of the Milice, including Camille Davoine, in charge of Jewish Questions, left Limoges for St. Junien. When the SS police arrived, they spent an hour in conference with Major Diekmann. Afterwards, as they returned to the car, Kleist told Patry that forty hostages were to be executed at Oradour-sur-Glane. There was going to be "a lot of blood," he said. For that reason, rather than going to Oradour, Kleist and the four *miliciens* would accompany a unit from the First Company to Saillat-Chassenon to check out a factory where there were a number of non-French workers.

The president requested that Arnet elaborate on the details because he said they strongly indicated that the massacre had been premeditated. Was it true, he asked, that Kleist, a Gestapo lieutenant not known for his squeamishness, had elected not to accompany the Third Company to Oradour that day? Arnet confirmed that this had indeed been the case. His source for the story had been Patry himself, and although Patry was executed shortly after the war as a collaborator, Arnet believed his story. I note that at the time of the trial, Davoine was still in prison, but for reasons unknown was not called as a witness.

The activity of the local Milice also strongly suggests premeditation. I have interviewed a former Limoges police officer, Herve Machefer (post-war son of Martial Machefer, the Communist who testified at the Oradour trial). He told me that according to his study of the subject, there was a meeting of the Limoges Milice called by Jean Filliol, the head of the notorious second section (intelligence and action) at the Milice headquarters in Limoges on June 9. Filliol had announced that the Division Das Reich was on its way to Limoges to engage in an "operation," and ordered four *miliciens* to accompany elements of Diekmann's First Battalion the next day.

Arnet summarized his findings concerning *maquis* activity in or around Oradour as follows: "It is absolutely certain that the rumors about *maquis* activity in or near Oradour were pure fantasy. It was a quiet place; the calmest in the world; there were no *maquis*." As noted, Borie was a résistant, but was being held in reserve. The president observed that Oradour was something of an island in that respect…because fifteen or twenty miles away the *maquis* were extremely active. Arnet confirmed there was some activity in Cieux and in Oradour-sur-Vayres, but Oradour-sur-Glane was "*tranquille*".

In June 1944, Hubert Massiera was attached to the *Renseignements Généraux*, a sort of internal intelligence group (somewhat similar to the CIA). At the time, he said, the German authorities in Limoges were claiming that an officer and two German soldiers had been killed in the area. Other versions of this story were more specific, describing how a three-man medical team had been found dead just outside Oradour. Having investigated these claims, however, Massiera had found them to be baseless. He went on to tell the court that he had been on the Angoulême-Limoges train on June 8 that was halted because the St. Junien *maquis* had blown up the bridge the night before. The two Germans who were walking towards St. Junien had been shot right in front of him. In Massiera's opinion, the massacre at Oradour was a direct consequence of the killing of those two Germans outside the railway station. [I suggest that this begs the question as to whether he was of that view because he had witnessed the attack, or because he had been in the Vichy administration when he undertook the investigation, and was trying to find excuses for the massacre.]

Masiera was one of the first outsiders to see the ruined town, and he said, "In the whole village there was not a house that was not a burned-out skeleton. Doors and windows were blown out and floors had collapsed. Inside the church, we found ourselves staring at the charred human remains on the right-hand side of the church, just in front of the little door. They were nearly a foot high. In the ashes we found various metal objects—women's costume jewelry, bracelets, toecaps, and eyelets for shoelaces. In the same part of the church on the right in the Ste. Anne chapel, you could see the point of impact [of bullets] marked on the walls and in particular on the plaque commemorating the dead [of the First World War]. I also saw the burned bodies in the Laudy barn and Beaulieu shed. There, the main point of impact was at about five feet three inches. The holes were much more numerous at the level of the head and the chest."

Massiera concluded his testimony with this observation: "It was out of the question for the Germans to annihilate St. Junien because it was a town of 10,000 people, but they wanted to make an example. I believe they chose Oradour because it had only about 800 inhabitants [the actual figure was about 1600, including refugees]."

For the victims' families and their supporters, the suggestion of a link between local Resistance operations and the massacre was unwelcome. They insisted that the massacre was a completely gratuitous act against an innocent village, and criticized the fact that the Tribunal was giving prominence to police officials who had been Vichy functionaries at the time of the massacre.

The investigation by Chief of Police Felix Hugonnaud, in Limoges, also sought to identify a motive for the massacre. According to Hugonnaud, Major Diekmann went back to Limoges from St. Junien sometime during the night of June 9-10. There, he learned that Kämpfe had disappeared and that Gerlach had been captured but had escaped. The Germans reported to the police investigators that Kämpfe's personal papers had been found on a street in Limoges. He had probably thrown them out of the truck himself, they told the investigators, in the hope it would help his comrades to follow his trail. In fact, it is more likely that the Germans simply invented that story along with many others. According to Hugonnaud, Kämpfe was captured just outside of Saint-Léonard-de Noblat thirteen miles east of Limoges on the way back from Guéret as he rode down the N141. He was then taken another eighteen miles farther east to Cheissoux, Guingouin's headquarters. At the German headquarters in Limoges, a rumor circulated that thirty *maquisard* prisoners were offered in exchange for Kämpfe. A witness, M. Vigneron, claimed that he had seen a car bearing a white flag driving around St. Leonard de Noblat announcing the Germans' willingness to ransom the missing major, but that nothing had come of this initiative.

Hugonnaud reiterated that Diekmann was in Limoges on Saturday morning and was aware of Kämpfe's capture, and the fact that despite a wide-ranging search, the missing officer had not been found. He claimed that Diekmann had talked in general terms about reprisals.

Hugonnaud's view was that while there were many stories about what happened to Kämpfe, it was clear he was not dead on the June 10. A witness from St, Leonard had seen Kämpfe on June 11 "very much alive." Moreover, Hugonnaud said the Germans continued to search for him after the massacre. Hugonnaud did not identify this witness at the trial, but Guingouin (who was neither interrogated by the police investigators after the war nor called as a witness in the trial) later stated that he had ordered Kämpfe's execution only after he learned about the Oradour massacre. Oddly, the president asserted without providing any source for his statement that Kämpfe had not been executed but had been killed trying to escape. That was the somewhat euphemistic formula used by both sides in the terror war, but significantly one not taken advantage of by the person most concerned—Georges Guingouin.

Forty-five-year-old René Pasquet, a former head of the *maquis* in Oradour-sur-Vayres, thirty miles southwest of Oradour-sur-Glane, testified that because of a denunciation, the Milice and Gestapo were aware that Oradour-sur-Vayres was a center of Resistance activity. Accordingly, he believed that the Germans had simply made a mistake and gone to the wrong Oradour.

Pierre Poitevin, who followed Pasquet, was the first journalist to visit Oradour-sur-Glane after the massacre. He had written a book describing what he saw, and at Nussy Saint-Saëns' request, recounted the main points, "I went to Oradour on Sunday morning, when I heard that the village was burning. I went by bicycle and arrived about 11:15 a.m. It was still burning." He cycled past the church and then turned around and left, not really appreciating the full extent of the massacre. He was not able to go back until Thursday. By that time, the seminarians had finished their work [burying the dead] and had left. He went there on the tram with some investigators. He was wearing a Red Cross armband, but it was known that he was a journalist, and there were some objections. In the end, though, the head of the investigators said that he could accompany them.

"Our first stop was the church. There, I saw bullet casings all over the ground near the door, the melted bell and all the debris. The left-hand side, with the confessional, altar and chapel, was practically intact. There were no bodies there. At the back on the right, though, it was horrible. I saw children's hands hanging from a piece of iron, skulls, perhaps ten of them; the small skulls of infants with their brains coming out. In a chapel, there was a mass of hardened flesh."

The Germans had posted guards outside the village on Sunday and Monday and no one had been allowed in. For the next two weeks, entry was confined to those with a pass from German occupation authorities. It was only after Monday that the emergency aid people found the ditches containing the bodies that the Germans had removed from the church and elsewhere, and buried on Sunday and Monday. Poitevin said, "I saw and photographed the bodies of Mme Joyeux and her baby boy [René]." They had been shot after jumping out the window behind Mme Rouffranche. "I also saw the body of Dr. [Paul] Desourteaux, next to a barn with his small white beard; he had been cut to pieces. We found bodies in wells on the village green, near the church and elsewhere where they had been dumped. As for the brazier, I saw it before the authorities even opened it; there were embers and they said there were human remains. On Tuesday or Wednesday, two bodies were found in a wheelbarrow near the bakery."

Poitevin quoted a German lieutenant as saying: "There are the victims of Oradour but the Allied bombings have killed more people." In response, according to the stenographer and the newspaper reports, there were murmurings of disapproval in the audience. The president immediately explained that the witness was merely repeating what a German had said.

Poitevin continued, saying that he believed that the massacre had been an act of madness. The stenographer did not note any reaction to this statement; but it was not a point of view which the victims' families and supporters welcomed, given their opinion that the massacre had been a calculated act of terror. Indeed, some, especially the Communists, regarded Poitevin as an apologist for Vichy.

M. Moser, one of the lawyers for René Camille G., requested details about the sentries who had deterred people from entering Oradour during the massacre. A villager, Louis Compain, described how he had been turned away near the hamlet of Les Bordes. One SS had said "*tous kaput*," while another had been sitting on a rock crying. Moser asked about the two young Jewish girls and their brother. The witness said that they had been members of the Pinède family, from Bayonne, and that one of the SS sentries had allowed them to escape.

Poitevin then told the court that Monsignor Rastouil (Bishop of Limoges) had had problems with the Gestapo and the Milice because of his preparedness to confront the Germans about Oradour. When a high-ranking *milicien* [Philippe Henriot] had been assassinated in Paris around that time, for example, the Vichy secretary of the interior had ordered that a mass be said for him; Rastouil had refused. As a result, he had been arrested and held at Chateauroux. He had only been released following the intervention of the Papal Nuncio.

[Ecto O. Munn, from the SHAEF Special Staff, obtained a statement from Msg. Rastouil which recounted what had happened subsequently. The Bishop had written a letter of protest about Oradour on Wednesday, June 14 to General Gleininger, the head of the local Wehrmacht garrison. On Friday, June 16, the Bishop announced that he would hold a funeral service for the dead of Oradour on Wednesday, June 21. The Gestapo tried indirectly to prevent the ceremony. First, they circulated a rumor that he had been arrested and later that bombs had been placed under the cathedral. On the night of June 20-21, they had a work crew in the cave with shovels and pickaxes to give credence to the bomb rumor. Just as the bishop reached the point in the ceremony when he was going to give the general absolution, the Prefect sent word that he should curtail the ceremony as the Gestapo was getting agitated. The bishop was ready to comply but then he considered the possibility that there would be a riot among those attending if he failed to complete the ceremony. He decided to go ahead, albeit with brevity. When he finished, he left after making a slight bow in the direction of the Prefect.

He concluded his statement to Munn by saying, "There had been no placing of bombs, but it was a trick, a pretense, designed to sabotage the funeral service in memory of the victims of Oradour-sur-Glane."]

Poitevin ended his testimony by saying that when the first explosives had been detonated in the church, all the windows were blown out. Had this not happened, everyone inside would have been asphyxiated. However, since the windows were blown out, the SS had gone into the church to finish the job.

Anna Coudert-Brun, who lived near the crossroads of the route to Saint-Victurnien and Limoges, testified she had seen the SS column arrive around 2:00 p.m. When they departed in the early evening, she said some of the troops had been shouting rowdily and causing a commotion.

Marcel Bélivier, twenty seven years old at the time of the trial, had been hiding in a barn outside the village in the hamlet of les Brégères. He had seen the cyclists who had been stopped by the SS near the bridge. They were taken to the Beaulieu forge where they had been executed. He had also seen the SS pursuing a woman whom they shot. She was later identified as Mme Milord. At the end of his testimony, he caused a sensation by saying he recognized among the defendants the SS who had taken his mother into the barn and killed her.

He identified Henri W., one of the Alsatian defendants, and shouted, "That is the man who killed my mother". Henri W responded that he was not on that side of the village. Nussy Saint-Saëns asked Bélivier if he was sure of this identification, given how many years had passed. Bélivier replied that when the SS were rounding everyone up, he had hidden in a cowshed, but had seen his mother being led away. He was certain that the soldier in question had been Henri W. The matter remained unresolved.

When asked whether he knew which soldiers had conducted the cyclists to the village green, Boos demanded to know whether he had the right to refuse to answer. As a defendant, the president told him, you are free to speak or remain silent. The stenographer noted that seconds then passed, with the audience attentive. In fact, there was some uncertainty as to whether a defendant had the right to remain silent in a case such as this (i.e. subject to both military law and the European declaration of Human Rights; as noted there is no French constitutional provision similar to the U.S. Fifth Amendment). After a long pause, Boos confirmed that Albert D. had been there. The latter immediately denied it. Boos described how he had seen the cyclists' execution in front of the Beaulieu forge (which was just a few yards south of the Beaulieu shed on the main street). Albert D., Boos said, had been among the soldiers who had led them there. Albert D. again denied this.

The following day, Saturday, January 24, other survivors told their stories. For the most part, these were peasants and farmers who had come to court dressed in their Sunday best. In several respects, they resembled the Alsatian defendants, many of whom worked on the land. Those who had lost family members were close to tears as they described their experiences. Jean Lamige, a farmer living in the nearby hamlet of La Brande, had hidden in the woods when the SS arrived and saw the SS beating an elderly cripple who was not moving fast enough towards the village green.

Another farmer, 45-year-old Maria Demery, from the nearby village of Bel-Air, said, "I lost thirteen of my children and grandchildren." The stenographer noted that the witness burst out sobbing. When she was able to compose herself she told of entering the village in the late stages of the massacre where she had found the school in flames, with an abandoned exercise on the blackboard. The children's bags and berets were still hanging from their hooks.

President Nussy Saint-Saëns asked the defendants if the sentries posted around the town had been killing people gratuitously. Paul G. responded that his group had been ordered by Lieutenant Barth to shoot anyone who tried to go into the village. Nussy Saint-Saëns asked Lenz if he had questioned that order and he replied in the negative. At this point Paul G. started weeping, and the president asked whether the other defendants had tears to shed. Jean N. rose and said that nothing compared to losing one's family. Henri W. said his father had been sent to Schirmeck reeducation camp. Lenz's counsel pointed out that Lenz had had regrets because he had a wife and child, and Lenz himself then began to weep. Albert D. said that he had lost a brother in the war and regretted Oradour, but added that the massacre was not his fault. With that, the last session of the second week ended.

At the start of the following week, on January 26, a succession of witnesses from the northern outskirts of Oradour were called to the stand. They had escaped the SS by hiding in outlying buildings or in the fields and woods. Most of them had lost their relatives, and had been among the first to return to the village. Searching for their loved ones, they had discovered the horrors there. In one of the more curious incidents reported by these witnesses, the attractive looking Mme Blanche Taillandier, who was forty three years old in 1953 (Illustration 51), told how the SS had caught her in the house of a friend (Mme Sage) a quarter of a mile northwest of the village. Someone who appeared to be an officer had been present and had demanded food. She was told she would be released but that the officer wished to be served lunch first. He had been interested to hear she was from Paris and was probably impressed by her beauty and sophistication. "Everything is going to be burned in an hour," she was told. When she asked why, an SS soldier

51. Mme Blanche Taillandier testifying.

52. Martial Machefer testifying.

replied that "terrorists have killed a German officer, so we have to kill everyone in Oradour," she noted that the half-tracks were constantly moving around, presumably bringing people to the village green from outlying hamlets and farms and patrolling. She had personally seen Dr. Jacques Desourteaux leave to go back to the village because he said it was his duty since it was in danger. .

Pierre Tarnaud, a forty-four-year-old farmer, had been rounded up by the SS, but had managed to escape. Tarnaud testified that he had three children, the oldest of whom was Lissette, then six years old. When Lissette's friends had come to their house on the way to school, his wife had told them that Lissette was not ready. The friends had left, saying *au revoir*, and had never been seen again. Tarnaud had seen the SS troops leave Oradour between 9:00 and 10:00 p.m. A burial detail had returned the next morning, singing loudly. They had left around 10:00 a.m. and he had decided to go back into the village.

"I arrived at the north end of the village. There were bodies everywhere. I could not look. Finally I saw the Denis storehouse. I could see only charred and burned corpses. I went farther down and arrived at the church. It was an unimaginable scene since everything was burned including women and children. There was nothing left except heaps of ashes. I cannot say exactly the depth of the bodies, but there were ashes everywhere. I saw the body of a woman in the middle of the church. Her legs were twisted by the heat, and the bottoms of her feet were completely burned. I saw the legs of children, and two children were in the confessional."

Tarnaud was unable to contain his anger, "These men," he insisted, "merit severe punishment." He was cut off by Nussy Saint-Saëns who reminded him that the question of punishment was for the Tribunal to decide.

The two Beaubrieul brothers were the day's final witnesses. They were the ones who had hidden in the floor of their aunt's house during the massacre, and had heard two women being shot. Although Boos denied shooting the women, insisting that he was not there, the president pointed out that Albert L had testified to Boos's guilt. The testimony of the brothers helped to confirm it.

Boos, apparently exasperated by these accusations, interjected a suggestion. Maybe, he said, Albert D. could tell the court whether a certain execution had taken place." Perhaps he was alluding again to the cyclists at the Beaulieu forge. The president commented ironically, "It seems that you have a particular friendship for Albert D." Boos responded, "I just want to know the truth and only the truth."

Moser, counsel to René Camille G., asked if Boos had talked to Albert D., and told him that he had an account to settle with him. Boos replied, "It is not true. I told him I admire him because he tells the truth and he does not incriminate me. And today was the first time he incriminated me. Someone speaking on behalf of the Alsatians also told me to be careful about what I say here because they are going to attack my family." Who told you that? asked the president sharply. "An Alsatian lawyer" said Boos. Cautioning Boos that he should speak carefully, as this was a serious accusation, Nussy Saint-Saëns asked him for the name of the lawyer who threatened him in this way. Boos said it had been a tall, fair-haired man who was not in court at the moment. An Alsatian lawyer said that he must be referring to Mr. Lux.

By the following morning, Tuesday, January 27, flu had swept the courtroom, and handkerchiefs and medicine were in evidence. *Le Figaro* recorded a statement by the *Fédération Régionale des réseaux de Forces Françaises Combattantes du Sud Ouest* (a group of former *résistants*) to the effect that that the *maquis* had been numerous in the Dordogne-Perigord region, and that there had been every opportunity for the Alsatians to desert. They were making the point that the *malgré nous* were not really under duress.

While President Nussy Saint-Saëns did not allude to it, most everyone in the courtroom was aware that earlier in the day parliament had debated the modification of the Law of Collective Responsibility. Indeed, some key lawyers and journalists had been absent attending the debate.

The next witnesses described what had happened when they had arrived at the tramway-stop at Puy Gaillard on the late afternoon tramway. After they had been escorted to the Masset house, they were ordered to wait until an officer arrived to determine their fate. The SS troops, meanwhile, were eating *rillettes* (a kind of pate) and fresh bread that they had stolen from the bakery. They were also drinking fresh milk from a ladle, and killing chickens. They seemed to have a plentiful supply of cigarettes, perhaps because it was tobacco-ration day in Oradour.

Oradour–The Final Verdict

More disturbing, several of them were digging a ditch near the house. Others were meaningfully cocking and brandishing their weapons. One of the passengers understood some German and whispered that the SS were going to separate those who lived in Oradour from the rest. No one, he told them, should admit that he was from the village. When a woman passenger tried to explain to the SS that she was not from Oradour, however, the soldiers ignored her, saying that they did not understand French.

The villagers and the other passengers were separated after a fashion. A woman who lived in Oradour but worked in Limoges was allowed to join the outsider-group when she showed an identity card with her work address on it. One passenger asked what the people of Oradour had done, and was told by a soldier that they had killed a much-decorated officer—presumably Kämpfe. The soldier also said that a cache of arms and munitions had been found in the village, and that 'terrorists' had caused the fires. "The people of Oradour, all are kaput, all dead," he told them.

Finally, an officer arrived around 10:00 p.m. and was briefed on the situation. A witness described the officer as being about five foot eight, slight in build, and about forty years old. He had a severe air, and spoke only a little heavily accented French. The witness was then shown a photo and said that was the one. Nussy Saint-Saëns confirmed it was Captain Kahn she had seen but the President later announced that the photograph in question was not actually Kahn but of someone who supposedly resembled him. Eventually, the officer had decided to let all the passengers go, and they were marched west to the Les Bordes road, where they saw the body of the miller, Marie-Leon (André) Foussat, 39, in a ditch beside the road. After they were released, an armored vehicle zigzagged after them for awhile. Many were afraid that they would be shot in the back.

A twenty-seven-year-old passenger, Marguerite Senon, addressed Nussy Saint-Saëns, "M. President, I lost my father, my grandparents, my uncles, aunts, and numerous cousins. For me, these are terrible memories. What we want is not vengeance but justice. I do not hate those Alsatians who proved their patriotism and made a heroic resistance against Nazism. They honor Alsace, but the men who had the cowardice …" Nussy Saint-Saëns told her, "That is a question for the

Tribunal. Just tell us just what you saw." "When the SS took us to the Masset farm," she said, "their faces were neither sad nor repentant. On the contrary, they were roaring with laughter."

When the freed passengers arrived in Les Bordes a short distance away, the witness continued, the people there were waiting in the street, wanting to know what had happened. The mothers in particular demanded to know what had happened to their children, saying that they had heard shooting but couldn't imagine that the children had been hurt. The passengers did not have the heart to tell them what they knew.

After the passengers left the Masset house, the SS burned it, along with the neighboring Thomas house. The passengers had not dared leave Les Bordes for Oradour. The following morning, at about 6:00 a.m., they had heard the SS return. They had seen more flames and heard more shooting. Around 11:00 a.m., a woman left Les Bordes and went through Oradour toward Le Repaire, about a mile south, where her parents lived. On the way, she passed her uncle's house. All that remained of it was a vase with flowers in it and her uncle's dog howling at the dead. A few hours had been sufficient to annihilate the village.

"They killed all the people," she said, "and saved the animals."

M Courivaud told how on June 10 he had left Oradour to visit an aunt in Les Bordes. He had decided to return to the village around 7:00 p.m. to see what had happened to his family. Miraculously, several had been among the surviving tram passengers. The next day, searching for his twenty-four-year-old son, Maurice, a butcher, he had found destroyed houses, looted safes, and burned and half-buried corpses. Near the bridge over the Glane River, he saw the body of a man. "His head had been crushed and his brains had leaked out," he said.

Picking his way through the ruins, he had been stopped by two Germans, and had explained why he was there. "Raus!" (Get out!) He was told. He had finally found his son among the bodies at the Desourteaux garage. He remembered seeing an aircraft circling the ruins, and at one point strafing them. No other witness mentioned seeing such a thing, so Courivaud was probably conflating two separate incidents.

President Nussy Saint-Saëns announced that the next witnesses would testify about looting. Thirty-one-year-old Mme Lamothe, told how she had been away from her home and had returned to find the farm ransacked. The SS had ransacked the house taking everything in the kitchen and the gold from the safe.

Justin Darthout lived near the crossroads on the Nieul road. The SS had put up a hand-lettered arrow in front of his house pointing the way to Nieul with "K 3 1" written on it (K for company in German, 3 for Third Company, and 1 for First Battalion). Darthout testified that when their trucks had passed by in the evening, the men had been singing at the tops of their voices, accompanied by an accordionist. Many had bicycles and bulging sacks with them. Darthout also noted two Oradour trucks in the convoy, one marked "Tissues Depic" (the fabric merchants in Oradour) and the other "Denis Wines." Another stolen car contained several civilians. It was suggested that these might have been members of the Milice, although no witness recalled seeing any civilians moving about during the massacre.

Two drivers from St. Junien, forty-eight-year-old Emile Démery and fifty-eight-year-old Jean Nadaud, testified that around 6:00 p.m. on June 10, two SS men and an employee of the town hall had requisitioned their trucks and made them drive to Nieul with a load of bread and baggage. The witnesses observed that the SS must have been short of vehicles to need these slow, coal-burning civilian trucks. En route to Nieul, they had seen flames over Oradour. The SS men had explained that these were caused by the *maquis*. One of the drivers was a volunteer fireman, and thought it strange that he could hear no sirens. They arrived at Nieul about 11:00 p.m. but the SS would not let them go home. Around 3:00 a.m., two SS soldiers asked them for a cork screw. "Do you know Oradour?" one of the soldiers asked the drivers in French. The drivers nodded after which the soldier went on. "We came to do a massacre. We killed the women and all the children in the church." The soldier knew St. Junien, he said with tears in his eyes, because he had lived there and made his first communion there (presumably as a refugee from Alsace). The SS finally released the two drivers early the next morning. On their way back to St. Junien, they passed through Oradour and saw the destruction there.

Residents of Nieul testified that around mid-day on the June 9, a number of SS men—presumably led by Lieutenant Gerlach who later that day was captured by the *maquis*, but escaped—had arrived to arrange for the Third Company to be billeted in the school and in some of the houses. The following evening, vehicles had come and gone throughout the night. There had been much drinking and carousing. One of the SS-men had been wounded. [Probably Albert O. who had been hit by Sgt. Staeger.] When the soldiers had left on June 12, some of their grenades were found in a schoolroom.

The president closed the session of Tuesday, January 27 at 5:30 p.m. On the legislative front, meanwhile, the Alsatian Deputies were making a last-ditch effort to secure the repeal of the Law of Collective Responsibility. They used two principal arguments to support their case: 1) That the Law was a departure from the normal conventions of criminal law in not being based on individual responsibility, and in placing the burden of proof on the defendant rather than the prosecution; and 2) That trying the French/Alsatians alongside the Germans in effect ratified the annexation of Alsace. Those from Limousin argued that the massacre of Oradour cried out for justice, and that concern for the feelings of the people of Alsace should not further delay the rendering of the judgments.

In the end, the National Assembly voted by 372 votes to 279 to abrogate the Law of Collective Responsibility. Politicians from Lorraine had mostly voted against their Alsatian neighbors, partly because there were no soldiers from Lorraine in the Third Company (although thousands had been forcibly inducted in the Wehrmacht), partly because of the forty-four Oradour victims from Moselle.

M. Brouillaud, the president of the ANFM, had missed the last two days of the trial in order to follow the legislative debate in Paris. Now at the opening of the session on January 28 he rose to speak, although he was not technically authorized to do so. "Last night, more than 350 deputies approved the massacre of Oradour. Our dead have been dishonored. In a few days, the executioners of Oradour will be set free. For that reason, the ANFM is leaving." As the ANFM supporters rose to their feet, there was an uproar. The president ordered the guards to expel those responsible but M Brouillaud reiterated his protest. A journalist called out "the press is with them; we're [expletive] leaving, too".

Seeking to maintain order, Nussy Saint-Saëns addressed himself to M. Brouillaud, explaining that even if the text voted by the National Assembly was also adopted by the Council of Ministers, it would have no immediate effect. Ultimately, if the Council approved the bill, the president of the Republic would have to sign the bill and it would have to be published in the official journal, and make its way to Bordeaux before it could take effect. Apologizing for delivering what was in effect a law lecture, the president said that he hoped that this explanation would reassure the ANFM, and that the trial could continue in calm and with dignity. M. Brouillaud responded that the ANFM reserved their position. Later, he and his supporters, and several members of the press, did in fact leave, and M. Brouillaud gave an impromptu press conference outside the courthouse.

The president called the first witness of the day, the redheaded sixteen-year-old Roger Godfrin, who had been a child at the time of the massacre and had managed to escape across the river. Godfrin had been taken by a road worker to the village of Laplaud. Thus, he was there on Sunday night when they had brought in the badly-wounded Mme Rouffranche after she had been found in the garden of the rectory. It was from her that he learned what had happened in the church, and that he had lost his entire family.

Godfrin began to protest the National Assembly's decision concerning the Law of Collective Responsibility, but was diverted to the subject at hand. "On June 10, 1944, I was seven years old. We were from Lorraine, and because we were patriotic Frenchmen, the Germans expelled us. At Oradour, I lost my father, mother, three sisters, and a brother. My youngest sister was three years old, and these Boches put her in the flames. I call them 'Boches' because…" Nussy Saint-Saëns interrupted Godfrin to caution him that he had sworn to tell the truth without hate." In France, witnesses swear to testify, "…without hate and without fear, to speak the complete truth and nothing but the truth". [Note that because of French church/state separation strictures no Bible was or is used.]."

Godfrin then recounted his vain efforts to persuade his sisters to flee with him from school, and that he ran through the fields and discovered M. Thomas, the baker, who employed his (Godfrin's) father. "I hid behind a hedge. There was Mme Octavie Dalstein of Lorraine, her niece Françoise and me…He must remember, Paul G.…!"

The president reminded Paul G. that he had admitted being present, and then, mindful of the fact that he was addressing a teenager who had lost his whole family, congratulated Godfrin on his courage. Ignoring Nussy Saint-Saëns' words, Godfrin said that he had been following the trial in the newspapers and had read that the Alsatian SS soldiers were considered less at fault than the Germans. Before he could say more, the president cut him off.

Other witnesses described returning to Oradour a few days after the massacre to find out what had happened and to help bury the victims. Corpses were laid in rows on makeshift biers for eventual identification by relatives. The body of a woman was discovered down a well, but no one was able to remove it. Dr. Robert Bapt, then medical inspector of health in Limoges, had disobeyed German orders not to take photographs. He now showed the pictures that he had taken to the Tribunal. Nussy Saint-Saëns ordered that they be passed to the defendants. The photographs were passed from hand-to-hand by the defendants who regarded them with bowed heads. Only one, the Alsatian, Albert D., showed any emotion, shuddering visibly when he saw them. Blaeschke, the German medical orderly announced that he refused to look. The photographs showed horribly mutilated corpses, many of them cut in half. The bullet wounds suggested that in many cases the SS had aimed for their victims' legs, and that in consequence many had been burned alive.

René Hyvernaud, had gone into Oradour on that Sunday morning looking for members of his family, and had discovered the horrors in the church. He saw the body of a woman completely undressed but intact lying on top of the pile of others and the corpses of two children in the confessional. Outside the rectory in the W.C., he found the bullet-ridden body of his sister, Henriette Joyeux, who had jumped out the window with her baby after Mme Rouffranche. Hyvernaud had lost his entire family, and concluded with the words, "I regret one thing—that I will not come face-to-face with the executioners who did this." The president quietly intervened to say that the trial had so far been dignified and calm and that he wished it to remain that way. He gave special thanks to the witness and excused him.

After a recess, the president announced that he had resolved the issue concerning the Strasbourg lawyer Richard Lux and Boos. He reported that there had been a misunderstanding stemming from a conversation in the Alsatian dialect and that no threat had been made.

He said he was personally satisfied that there was no incident for which to reproach the lawyer, and he was invited to continue to participate in the trial.

Andre Petit had been a policeman in Limoges at the time of the massacre, and described the events in Tulle and other incidents involving the murder of civilians. In general, he said, there had been a heightened nervousness among the Germans after the landing in Normandy. This had expressed itself in violent incidents and in greater activity by the Milice who had more or less taken over from the French police. He had had the impression that worse was to come.

Petit had visited Oradour on the Wednesday after the massacre. He had found "horror on a gigantic scale." He did not see a single body whole. He sensed an operation executed at speed, and with a clear intent to destroy evidence. "We brought coffins with us, but too few."

Jean Hyvernaud, a forty-six-year-old farmer, gave the day's final testimony. Hyvernaud had gone to the church on Sunday at around 4:30 p.m. looking for his two children. He had found the body of one of them, his mouth open, lying on his side, and badly burned. He had a wooden clog on one foot but the other was badly twisted. His neck was also twisted out of shape. "I leaned over and kissed his poor face. Some friends came and they took him away. I made a small coffin and the next day I put him in the garden, where I kept him for eight days until we had permission to take him to the family grave." Hyvernaud never found the body of his second child.

On Thursday, January 29, the sixteenth day of the trial, the first witness to testify was twenty-five-year-old Yvonne Hyvernaud (née Gaudy). She wore a hat and had a scarf wrapped around her shoulders. At times, she had to stop talking long enough to hold her head in her hands. On the day of the massacre, she said, she had been stopped by three different patrols but released each time. On one of these occasions she had seen an officer distributing papers to the other officers and NCOs, probably plans of the village. When questioned, Boos denied ever being given such a plan.

Forty-four-year-old Martial Machefer, lost his wife and two children at Oradour. One child had been eleven years old and the other only fifteen months old. He wore a striped suit and kept a cane within reach because of his war wound (Illustration 52). On the day of the massacre, he had seen Mme Ducharlet approach one of the SS sentries. The SS man shot her, protesting in French that she should not have come so close to him. When Machefer had returned to the village the next day, he had discovered Pierre Dupic, seventy-seven years old, buried in his garden. Dupic's body had been covered lightly with soil but his left hand had been left sticking out. The Germans had even replanted beans over him. He had also encountered two women who had told him that they had gone to the school. They found children's jackets, hats and school bags there, but no children.

Looking into the church, Machefer was dumbfounded. "The scene was indescribable. It was unbelievable. There were piles of bodies. Two children were riddled with bullets were holding hands in the confessional; a child of four or five years old held onto the plaque with the roster of the dead from the 1914-1918 war." He said that in the church he had seen the nude body of a woman he did not know lying on top of the burned corpses. She did not have any wounds or marks of fire. In his deposition for Ecto O. Munn, he further stated it was his impression that she had been violated, killed, and placed with the others.

The Communists were eager to exploit the massacre and the trial for political ends. They wished to emphasize their support for the Limousin area, and to distance themselves from the much more prosperous and conservative region of Alsace. More broadly, they wanted to sabotage the détente with Germany. Aware of this, and observing the witness's emotional state, Nussy Saint-Saëns was anxious that the line between testimony and polemic should not be crossed. So when Machefer, whom he knew to be a Communist, stood up after delivering his testimony and declared that he was the sole advocate for the dead, President Nussy Saint-Saëns stopped him. Machefer countered that he had sworn to say what was in his heart. With some firmness, Nussy Saint-Saëns excused the witness.

Alphonse Lévignac, a fifty-five-year-old insurance agent living in Nieul, lost two sons at Oradour. The family had been living in Avignon, but because of Allied bombing raids, Lévignac had decided to bring his two sons, Jean, sixteen years old, and Charles, eleven years old, to Oradour. They arrived on June 6. On the afternoon of the massacre, at around 3:00 p.m., the two boys had gone out with a cart to find firewood. The SS had stopped them by the river and made them take the cart to the church, where they were ordered inside with the others. On Sunday, when he went looking for his sons, Lévignac had encountered Mme Rouffranche. She had been covered with dirt and he had thought that she was an African. Regarding the accused men, Lévignac said that he only hoped that their remorse was as great as his pain. He asked them if any of them remembered seeing his sons—the ones who arrived with the wood cart. A few murmured, "No." As he left the courtroom, he muttered that the defendants were all liars.

René Touch had been a seminarian in Lorraine, but in 1944 had moved to Limoges to avoid being conscripted into the German Army. On the Monday night after the massacre, he had been sent to Oradour with the Red Cross. He and other seminarians had recovered the body of the tramway company employee, Chalaud, and that of Octavie Dahlstein, the Lorraine refugee shot by Paul G. When he had reached Oradour, he said, there were still carts containing firewood outside the church. Inside, the church bell had melted onto the floor, as had several bodies which the SS had not been able to remove. The seminarians were forced to scrape these from the floor. Behind the altar, they found the bodies of a dozen or so children. The fact that no women's bodies were found here suggested that the women had tried to leave what little air there was to these children.

The left side of the church was not burned. The altar cloth and the national flag were untouched. There was even a paper on the altar listing those from Oradour who had become prisoners of war or had been sent to Germany under the STO program. The statue of Saint Victurnien, however, was charred and all but unrecognizable. On the right side of the church, the altar of Ste. Anne was piled with ashes, corpses, and chairs. Outside the small door leading out of it, they found a burial pit covered with branches and metal shutters—its presence betrayed by swarms of bluebottle flies. Behind the church, in the WC, they found the bodies of a young woman (Mme Joyeux) and her baby. There was a large bloodstain on the wall. In one of the barns, they measured the height of the bullet holes, and discovered that they were less than a yard from the ground. These men, it appeared, had been shot in the legs and then burned alive.

René Touch also had a collection of photos. The president said, "Show them these photos so that they may contemplate the work of the valiant Regiment Der Führer and its mighty warriors." Touch described the burial process, "They took bodies out of the communal pits near the church and put them on shutters. People came, and identified the dead. When the bodies were buried in the cemetery, flowers were put on them. I think for us it was an extremely moving moment. We sang 'It is just *au revoir*, my brothers.' [To the same tune as Auld Lang Syne]" The president asked about the tabernacle [the cabinet in the church where the goblets and other objects used for Mass were kept] and Touch confirmed that it had been broken open and everything inside had been stolen.

Guy Pauchou, from Rochechouart, about sixteen miles from Oradour, had been a clandestine member of the Resistance. He had seen elements of the Division Das Reich arrive in Rochechouart, where they had attempted to provoke the population. The SS had commandeered people's vehicles, he said, and had demanded that the mayor identify any Resistance members. Having arrested two young men, they had tried to force them to admit to being terrorists. They had situated machine gun nests at a number of strategic points and opened fire at random intervals, on one occasion shooting a sixty-four-year-old woman.

The Germans had also asked him about a sign showing the direction to Oradour-sur-Vayres. That is where the *maquis* were, they had been told. Pauchou also observed that one of the Das Reich Alsatians (Dieboldt, from the Second Company) had defected to the *maquis* on June 9, demonstrating that such a thing was possible. The president, referring to his files, noted that Dieboldt had joined the Hunters Battalion of the FFI, and had died fighting the Germans.

The witness said that he had not heard about Oradour until late Sunday. The Deputy Prefect, for whom Pauchou worked, was asked to investigate the massacre, because the Milice was watching the Prefecture in Limoges too carefully. When the Deputy Prefect's report came back, Pauchou was able to pass it directly to the Resistance. "Eight days later," he continued, "the Milice, pretending to be *résistants*, went to St. Junien and asked to contact *maquisards*. Eight came forward, and were lined up against a wall and shot." As a former *résistant* himself, Pauchou confirmed that there had been no *maquis* within a dozen miles of Oradour. He explained that this was largely because the mayor (Dr.

Paul Desourteaux) was a Vichy appointee, and unsympathetic to the Resistance.

"In general," Pauchou said, "the SS attacked defenseless civilians rather than the *maquis*, and because there had been no arms or *résistants* in Oradour, it had been very easy to exterminate."

The next witness was Pierre Masfrand, a seventy-year-old doctor, who had been practicing at Rochechouart at the time of the massacre. Later, he had been appointed conservator of the ruins of Oradour. He testified that many of the objects that had been found, like cigarette and glasses cases, were shot through with bullet holes. He displayed a bottle which had been melted by the heat. He quoted the Bishop of Limoges who said of the Oradour church bells that, "They fell in tears of bronze on the stone floor of the church." Masfrand concluded his testimony with the observation that Oradour had been a relatively prosperous village with plenty to eat, and thus [to the SS] well worth looting. "Oradour had been more favorable to the ideas of Pétain than to those of the Resistance," he said, "and if the Germans had wanted to mount an operation against the *maquis* there were plenty of other places they could have gone." SS documents and maps discovered after the war had shown that they knew quite well where the *maquis* were.

Chapter 17

Witnesses for the Alsatians

On the following day, Friday, January 30, it was the defense's turn to present its witnesses. The Germans and the French/Alsatian volunteer, Boos, had none to present. Counsel for the other French/Alsatian defendants—*Les Douze*—had prepared a defense primarily based on the fact that their clients had been forcibly inducted into the Waffen SS. Then, as a result of indoctrination by the Hitler Youth and other influences, they had been deprived of the ability to make genuine moral choices. In this connection, the defense wished to show the unique trauma that Alsace had suffered as a result of its annexation and nazification.

Before the first witness could be called, however, Nussy Saint-Saëns reported that he had learned that demonstrations were being held outside the courthouse, and elsewhere in Bordeaux. He said that he knew from meeting with representatives of the ANFM that they did not organize these demonstrations. Indeed, he commented, the ANFM had kept a very dignified attitude during the proceedings, and he concluded that the demonstrations must have been organized by "uncontrolled elements," by which he clearly meant the Limousin Communists. President Nussy Saint-Saëns further explained that such demonstrations were actually detrimental to the cause of the victims and benefited the enemies of France. He suggested to the radio representatives present in the court that his views be broadcast.

The Communist paper, *L'Humanité*, took a different view. It claimed that a delegation of elected officials, representatives of Resistance organizations and parents of victims, all from the Limoges area, had gone to Bordeaux to support the families who were at the trial. That delegation, the paper said, had suffered various humiliations; in particular that Nussy Saint-Saëns had agreed to meet only a handful of their representatives rather than the delegation en bloc. *L'Humanité* went on to protest what it called "maneuvers inside and outside the courtroom that tend toward the acquittal of the guilty."

As a further preliminary to the defense's submission, Nussy Saint-Saëns ordered that a number of German weapons be brought into the courtroom to show what the Oradour villagers had faced. Unfortunately, as several newspapers pointed out, many of the weapons on display were either not in use at the time of the massacre, or were different from those issued to the Division Das Reich. If nothing else, however, they provided Boos with the opportunity to show off his knowledge of rates of fire and other technical matters pertaining to firearms.

After this display had been viewed, M. Schreckenberg was invited to present witnesses on behalf of *Les Douze*. First to testify was Georges Clément, a sixty-four-year-old director of the Bank of France, who uniquely among his colleagues, had remained in Alsace during the annexation. He had served in the Resistance until his arrest in 1943 and after the war had testified at the Nuremberg trial. Clément's testimony bore heavily on the case because there was considerable skepticism on the Limousin side as to whether the French/Alsatian defendants were really forcibly inducted, as they claimed, or merely volunteers. If the latter, the Limousin witnesses suggested, the defense had no right to claim moral constraint or duress.

Clément told the court that as soon as German governors had been appointed—Turquel for Lorraine/Moselle and Wagner for Alsace—German civil and racial laws had been instituted. All civil servants suspected of French sympathies had been discharged from employment and expelled. The 1918 frontier was reinstated, German banks and commercial enterprises replaced French ones, the German language was made compulsory, and all French flags and books were destroyed.

Even people's names were Germanized. The few Jews ("Israelites") who remained were summarily expelled alongside the thousands of

Alsatians who were in any way suspected. The assets of all those expelled or evacuated were confiscated or sold. Those who protested the new regime were imprisoned, sent to the camps at Schirmeck and Struthof, or deported to Germany. Active *résistants* were executed. In April 1942, a German court condemned two eighteen-year-old Alsatians to death for putting a grenade in the empty car of the governor. Records indicated that one of them was beheaded.

In August 1942, military conscription was established in Alsace for young men born between 1920 and 1924. This caused an immense outcry, and security measures at the border were reinforced to avoid wholesale defections. Parents were warned that if their sons left, their assets would be confiscated and they themselves interned. Those aiding young men to hide or escape were also subjected to severe punishment.

The Wehrmacht draft papers started by using the word "volunteer." Many young Alsatians declined to "enlist," however, and others attempted to show their loyalty to France by carrying French flags and singing *la Marseillaise* when they reported for duty. The usual German response was a beating so severe that victims had to be hospitalized, followed by forcible induction, often into the SS. The word "volunteer" soon vanished from the draft papers, although it would re-appear towards the end of the war. Despite German efforts to prevent Alsatians from fleeing the country, especially to nearby Switzerland, a number attempted this. Some were successful but many were not. The latter were either summarily executed or sent to forced labor camps.

The next witness, fifty-eight-year-old Emile Cremer, had been condemned to death in March 1943 as a *résistant*, but as a wounded WW I veteran his sentence had been commuted and he had been sent to a concentration camp. He later became the president of the *Union Nationale de l'Association des Déportés*. He opened his testimony by recounting what had happened to him in the corridor of the courthouse, an incident which, he said, had prompted tears—tears that he had not even shed on the day that he was condemned to death. He had encountered M. Brouillaud, president of the ANFM, and had offered him his hand. Brouillaud, however, had refused it, describing Cremer as the defender of 'twelve little murderers." The president quickly responded, "Everyone deplores this incident, you may be sure."

Among more general issues relating to the repressive climate in Alsace, Cremer told the court about the network that he had organized in 1940 with M. Kalb, the vice president of the Senate and a lawyer representing Les Douze. This network had enabled nearly 3,000 young people to escape from Alsace, and had helped escaped prisoners from Germany to reach unoccupied France or England. The network had been seriously compromised by arrests in 1941 and he had been arrested and condemned to death two years later.

Cremer gave specific examples of German atrocities inflicted on those caught attempting to escape, and on their families. One group of young men had been denounced by a mayor in the occupied zone and then conscripted forcibly into the SS. Such men could easily have ended up in the Third Company at Oradour. They had been dispossessed of their personalities and had become robots, unable to apply any morality to their actions, Cremer said. That is the point that Cremer said he wanted to make about life in Alsace. "I cannot really communicate the horrible atmosphere of the concentration camps. When I returned, I tried to make my friends understand it, but I couldn't because it was unthinkable—a veritable fourth dimension. One also cannot understand what the atmosphere was like in Alsace."

Joseph Rey was arrested for Resistance activities in April 1942 and sent to the nearby "re-education" camp of Schirmeck. Now the mayor of Colmar in Alsace, he was asked by counsel to describe how Nazism was imposed on the young men of the province after the annexation. "When forcible conscription was introduced in 1942," Rey said, "young men were given the choice of signing up or being shot, and their parents were sent to the camps in Poland or Silesia. "They asked me what they should do. I asked them, 'Do you have the courage to choose death?' I told them to sign! I could not ask seventeen year olds to choose death, I could not."

Rey used the example of his mother, who lived at Metz, to illustrate the unique history of Alsace/Lorraine. She had been born French, became German in 1871 after the Franco-Prussian War, and then became French in 1918 following the Allied victory, and then German again in 1940, and French again in 1945. This case history clearly delineated the fragile relationship of the people of Alsace and Moselle with France (especially the France of Vichy), and the sensitivities with which the present trial had to contend.

Returning to the question of the pressure on the *malgré nous*, Rey described how two Alsatians who deserted near Toulouse were captured and executed in front of the other Alsatians in their company. He observed that the father of the defendant, Alfred L., had been a German soldier. Alfred L.'s father had returned home, but Rey's had not. Of the 130,000 Alsatians forcibly conscripted in the German military, any one of them could have been at Oradour.

"What would I have done if threatened with death," he asked rhetorically. "I cannot say. When you have a family at home, you think of that family."

Edouard Richard, from Colmar, had been a refugee in the southwest of France during the war. Now sixty-eight years old and a retired journalist, he testified that in August 1942, after the forcible induction decree, a delegation of former Alsace officials (then refugees like himself) had met Marshall Pétain in Vichy. On that occasion, Pétain had assured them that he had sent a delegation headed by Pierre Laval to protest the decree to the Gauleiter in Alsace. When the delegation had asked the Vichy government to publish this protest, however, it had been refused.

Richard outlined the problems that Alsatians in the SS had faced when they wanted to desert. If a uniformed SS soldier had presented himself, he told the Tribunal, Richard would not have helped him for fear that it was a trap. For this reason, it had been almost impossible for the Alsatians to desert. As far as the French were concerned, the SS had been made up of volunteers. After his testimony, the president remarked, "It is certain that all those who were subjected to German occupation believed that the SS were all volunteers. From that point of view, the details presented today in the testimony are extremely interesting."

The next witness was Paul Winter, a fifty-five-year-old industrialist who had led the Resistance in the Haut-Rhin Department of Alsace. He had also been involved in the escape of General Hénri-Honoré Giraud from a German prison-camp in Kaliningrad. That incident had provoked the Germans to execute between 100 and 200 people in Alsace, because as Winter put it ironically "*ici, Messieurs, le sacrifice était payant"* ('here, Gentlemen, sacrifice was rewarded')." The worst part of the annexation, Winter testified, had been the imposition of National Socialism (Nazism). The Nazis had wanted Alsace to serve as a model of a Germanized state after the war, and in consequence were much more severe in the application of the German laws than in Germany itself. It was not illegal to speak French in Germany, for example, but anyone speaking French in Alsace was likely to be sent to Schirmeck.

Winter provided the following statistics concerning the suffering of the Alsatians under the Germans: 140,000-150,000 men conscripted, 40,000 dead or disappeared, 10,000 imprisoned, 10,000-20,000 tortured. These figures, he said, did not count those who died in concentration camps or as a result of forced labor. Moser asked Winter what an eighteen-year-old member of a firing squad should have done. Laid down his rifle? "I cannot tell you," replied Winter.

Another witness, a fifty-eight-year-old farmer named Joseph Zimmerman, told of how the small town of Ballersdorf in Alsace was martyred after 18 of its young men fled to Switzerland. The Gestapo surrounded the village and searched every house. The young men they captured were sent to Schirmeck and executed, while their families were sent to work in Germany. After that, there were very few escape attempts from that area.

Albert Martin, twenty-six years old, was the last witness of the day. He was an Alsatian who had been conscripted into the SS (although not into the Division Das Reich) and sent to Italy. He said he and several others had consulted their schoolteachers when they were called up, to ask them what to do.

Remarkably, Martin said, they were told that they should obey because if they did not, it would certainly be held against them after the war, in which it was assumed the Germans would be victorious.

In July 1944, after the failed assassination attempt on Hitler, Martin recounted how some Alsatians and Germans had been discussing the news and one of the Alsatians had remarked, "It would have been better if he had died."

His words were reported. Two of the Alsatians were arrested and kept in a pig sty for a week, after which the company was assembled in dress uniform to watch the pair being hanged.

Some commentators have questioned whether the testimony of the Alsatian witnesses constituted a valid defense. Could those Alsatians who refused to be conscripted and were sent to Schirmeck and Struthof, really be compared to those who joined the Waffen SS and carried out the June 10 massacre? Was the suffering of Alsace really any excuse for the behavior of the *malgré nous*?

Chapter 18

Schedule Interrupted to Hear Mme Rouffranche

On Saturday, January 31, Mme Rouffranche, who had been too ill to testify earlier, had made the trip from Oradour where she was living in the new town. After being found late Sunday afternoon June 11, 1944 and taken to the Chateau Laplaud, she was transferred to a hospital in Limoges. As long as the Germans occupied Limoges, she was not allowed any visitors except for her father and mother. The Germans never came themselves, but as a precaution, the hospital changed her room on several occasions. She was interviewed by Ecto O. Munn on October 4, 1944 (Illustration 37 at the end of Part I The Massacre). Her testimony to him contained a number of details used in my description of the massacre that were not in her court testimony or in other later accounts. As the only survivor of the 450 or so women and children who had been subjected to the horrors in the church, and the only person able to testify to the key fact that the SS had detonated explosives there, she was a unique witness.

Walking with the aid of a cane, and dressed entirely in black, she appeared frail and older than her fifty-five years—she was born December 19, 1897. She testified with quiet solemnity, and Nussy Saint-Saëns informed her that the Tribunal was most sympathetic to her situation. "If you get tired," he said, "you need only say, and we will suspend your testimony." Mme Rouffranche told her story. After she had finished, the president asked her if she wished to add anything. "I ask only that, with God's help, justice be done. I ask as one wounded, and as a true witness of what happened in the church, as a survivor of that crematorium, and as a mother."

Apologizing for the painful memories which the trial was undoubtedly stirring up, the president continued to question Mme Rouffranche. He explained that if the Tribunal was to understand how events unraveled on that terrible day, it needed the facts. After the judges all crowded around her (Illustration 53), Nussy Saint-Saëns showed her a plan of the church (Illustration 20) and asked where she had been. She put on her glasses and said that to begin with, everyone had congregated in the center and she had been on the left side of them. "As we moved forward towards the altar we were separated…one group, I do not know how many, were pushed towards the little door on the right…it was there that they found a mass of bodies…and at this time we took refuge in the sacristy. Nobody pushed us and nothing was said. The box exploded

53. Mme Rouffranche testifying on January 31, 1953, surrounded by the judges while she responds to the President's request that she show on a diagram of the church where certain actions took place.

by itself. The explosion was delayed because [the Germans] needed time to get away. After the smoke had dispersed, they came back into the church, and that was when they machine-gunned us (the witness demonstrated their motions)."

With gentle encouragement from the president Mme Rouffranche described how the floor of the sacristy had ignited, burning alive all those inside, including her other daughter, Amélie.

The president then told the interpreter to ask the defendants if they had anything to say. Fritz Pfeuffer, a German, said that he did. "In Oradour, I was part of a firing squad. It was the first time that I was obliged to shoot men. Believe me, M. president being only eighteen years old at that time [his birthday was the day before]; it was not easy for me. The officers were standing behind us. I believed that as far as they were concerned that they had very good reasons to do this, but when I learned later what happened to the women and children, I was upset and deeply troubled. I understood that the officers had exceeded their authority. I am ashamed for them and especially for the fact that they lack the courage to come here today to settle their account."

"Was it not the NCOs who were in charge of such jobs in the SS organization?" Nussy Saint-Saëns asked. Pfeuffer said that he didn't know as he had not been there, and Boos also denied having been in the church. At this point, the president allowed his incredulity to show. "Remember that it was not the first time that the SS behaved in this way," he said. "We know that similar things happened in Poland and Yugoslavia—they had their own Oradours. Your organization specialized in such operations, and the generals and SS officers who have left you to face criminal charges are cowards. These ex-generals of yours make speeches when they are beyond the reach of French justice, but now that the account finally has to be settled, there are no more generals to be seen, only simple soldiers."

[This may well have been an allusion to the letter sent by General Lammerding to the Tribunal on October 29, 1952. In it, Lammerding had laid the blame for Oradour at the feet of Diekmann, whom he said had exceeded his orders which were just to take hostages. Moreover, Lammerding claimed that he had initiated a court-martial investigation which was terminated by the death of Diekmann. The letter was neither read nor otherwise referred to at the trial.]

At this point, having listened to Mme Rouffranche, M. Broulliard and the other ANFM members left the courtroom. Broulliard held a press conference outside, saying that the families of the victims had decided to leave so as not to have to listen to the testimony of any more of the Alsatian witnesses. He particularly criticized the fact that several of the defense lawyers and witnesses were simultaneously participating in the trial and working to undermine it in the legislature. He reminded those listening that the trial was of a handful of Alsatian executioners, rather than of Alsace itself.

A last-minute witness for the defense was inserted. In 1944, Julian Vigneau had worked in a café in a small village near Montauban where the Third Company was stationed before moving north. Vigneau was a clandestine *résistant* who provided the *maquis* with false identity cards and allowed the café to be used as a message drop. The defendant, Paul G. had been a regular customer there, as had several of his colleagues. One day, Paul G. had come round to warn Vigneau that he was going to be pulled in and questioned. The Gestapo searched his house a week later, but by then Vigneau had disposed of any incriminating evidence.

Chapter 19

Alsatian Witnesses Resume

The next Alsatian witness was Georges Bourgeois, a thirty-nine-year-old member of the National Assembly from Haut-Rhin and the head of ADEIF (*l'Association des Évadés et Incorporés de Force*, formed in 1946). Bourgeois had deserted from the German Army and been condemned to death *in absentia*. Before testifying, Bourgeois announced he wished to tell the court what had happened to him the previous day. M. Brouillaud, president of the ANFM, had asked to see him. "We had a frank discussion, but M. Brouillaud demanded that I inform the Tribunal that I would not support the Alsatian defendants who had been forcibly conscripted. I have come here to tell the truth, and I want to ensure that other witnesses will not be harassed [by Brouillard]." In response, Nussy Saint-Saëns observed that the incident had been a regrettable one, and said that he did not wish to hear that anything of the sort had happened again. Brouillaud's statement was arguably subornation of perjury, but for obvious reasons the President Nussy Saint-Saëns chose to ignore this.

Bourgeois recounted how he had been forced into the Wehrmacht in Austria where, at age thirty-five, he had been bossed around by eighteen-year-old corporals. The discipline had been hard to endure, especially for the older recruits. For Bourgeois, in his German uniform, it had been impossible to contact the Resistance. He was then posted to Moselle, in Lorraine. Before being forced into the German Army, he had promised his wife he would never bear arms against France, but now he was at risk of breaking that promise. He asked his wife if she was prepared to accept the consequences if he deserted. She said that she was, and proceeded to distribute her children among relatives and friends. Bourgeois deserted in August 1944. His wife was visited soon afterwards by the Gestapo, but by then France was in the throes of liberation, and she escaped deportation.

When the Americans liberated Moselle, they did not understand the history and situation of the Department, and despite the fact that the Germans had condemned Bourgeois to death for desertion, the Americans put him in a prisoner of war camp in Marseille with 35,000 other prisoners, mostly Germans. Fortunately he was eventually able to explain his situation to a French officer and was freed. He returned to Mulhouse, in Alsace.

The Tribunal reconvened on Monday, February 2 to hear from the defense witness, René Paira, who was made Prefect of Bas-Rhin in 1945 after the Germans departed. Paira testified as to the despair in Alsace after the annexation. Surveillance, he said, was constant. You could not listen to the BBC or you would be sent to the camps or deported whereas in the rest of France you would only get fined for such activity. Due to the costly German defeats on the Eastern Front, Paira continued, the need for recruits had been great and volunteers had been few. In August 1942, Hitler had announced that forcible induction in the German Army was to be implemented. In all, as many as 20,000 Alsatians had escaped to Switzerland and elsewhere, but many of their families were deported in consequence and these punishments were widely publicized by the Germans to discourage others. A family that he knew, Paira said, had a young child of Lycée age who after only six months of Nazi indoctrination had announced that he was going to have to denounce his parents for speaking French at home. Given the circumstances, this was not unusual. "It is impossible to judge the young of that generation without taking into consideration the pressure from the German authorities and the incessant propaganda that they were subjected to. Inevitably, those things left their mark on them."

Paira said that he knew a young man from Lorraine who had lost his wife and children in the Oradour massacre, but were nevertheless unprepared to see the region of Alsace put on trial. "It would be criminal to set the suffering of Oradour against the suffering of Alsace," the young man said. "Both stem from the brutal oppression of the same enemy."

Camille Wolff, a rotund forty-five-year-old deputy from Bas-Rhin (Illustration 54), had been arrested by the Gestapo in August 1940 and personally condemned to death by Himmler. Later, however, he had been pardoned and forcibly inducted. When a group of Russians had escaped from a German prison, the Germans had executed twenty other Russian prisoners.

54. Camille Wolff, condemned to death by Himmler for Resistance activities but later pardoned, and then a Deputy in the National Assembly, testifying for the Alsatians.

"If they had given us Alsatians the order to be in a firing squad," Wolff wondered, "would we have laid down our weapons and not fired at those Russians?"

M. Hetzel, age twenty-eight, the same age as Albert D. and Jean-Pierre E., two of the Alsatian defendants, was from Strasbourg in Alsace, and had been forcibly inducted after several years in the Hitler Youth. He testified to the psychological skill of the leaders of the Hitler Youth, and described how they had used those skills to destroy the natural instincts of the young people in their charge. They had succeeded in killing individuality before it even emerged, he said. The president concurred, "Is such an education not precisely the reverse of Christian education?" he demanded. "Is it not founded on a systematic contempt for the sentiment of pity?" In response, Hetzel stated that meetings of the youth and other organizations were invariably scheduled for Sunday mornings, in order to conflict with religious services.

When Hetzel was mobilized in June 1944, just before he turned eighteen, he was told that because they had been forcibly inducted, the Alsatians were always suspected of planning to desert. Eight days earlier, an Alsatian had deserted, but had been captured. His fellow Alsatians were ordered to execute him. Alsatians generally were subjected to hard punishment. "I remember fainting during a training exercise in which I was wearing a gas mask and helmet. As a reflex action, and to make sure that I had really fainted, the NCO took my knife and threw it straight at me from a range of fifteen yards. I was hit in the knee, but it could have hit me anywhere. They tried to turn us from human beings into machines."

Twenty-six-year-old M. Edmond Schiltnescht, another witness from Alsace, told how he had been forcibly inducted into the Deutschland Regiment of the Division Das Reich. Two Alsatians had deserted but had been caught by the French police and returned to the Regiment, where they had been court-martialed in front of all the Alsatians in the Regiment. Their condemnation to death had made a serious impression on the witness and the other seventeen- and eighteen-year-olds who realized that asking for help from the French population, was likely to be pointless.

On Tuesday, February 3, Robert Latzarus gave evidence. An officer of the judicial police in Strasbourg and president of a veterans association, thirty-six-year-old Latzarus had been responsible in 1945 for compiling a dossier on the Germanization of Alsace in connection with the trial of Wagner, the Governor appointed by the Germans in 1940. Latzarus had also represented France on the Nuremberg Tribunal.

Latzarus told the court that he had found a memo from Wagner detailing a conversation that he had had with Hitler. A few days after the Armistice was signed on June 1940, Wagner had been summoned to the Black Forest to receive his instructions from the Führer. With him were Turkel and Simon (who became the Governors of Lorraine and Luxembourg); Wagner's orders had been to re-Germanize Alsace as swiftly as possible.

He opened the "re-education" camp at Schirmeck and in May 1942 introduced *"service obligatoire du travail"* (not to be confused with STO) which involved the mobilization of young men into paramilitary outfits preparatory to military service. When Wagner had suggested introducing compulsory military service, however, the German General Staff had objected, saying that the Alsatians were unreliable and could even be dangerous in the Wehrmacht.

So Wagner had attempted to attract volunteers, posting notices suggesting that young Alsatians "join the German Army and fight the Bolsheviks." The attempt failed. Wagner had claimed that he, recruited 2,000 men, Latzarus said, but the real number was half that. "These Alsatians were really dangerous people, because they were fanatics, and universally condemned by their compatriots."

Previously, Latzarus explained, the SS had only accepted volunteers—blond, blue-eyed "Aryans" with good teeth, ideally—but the losses in Russia had changed everything. Wagner had decided to induct young Alsatians into the SS because he knew that it was harder to desert from that unit than from the Wehrmacht. SS soldiers were tattooed with their number and blood type, greatly facilitating identification.

At Nuremberg, General Keitel had confirmed to Latzarus (who cross-examined him), that he had had deep reservations concerning forcible conscription. When Wagner had persisted with the notion, (and according to Keitel, made a private accord with Hitler) Keitel had washed his hands of the matter. Inevitably, there had been many desertions. An Alsatian named Albert Reidemier had jumped from a train near the border, but had been denounced by a railroad worker and arrested. In judging him, the German court stated that, "The death penalty is absolutely necessary in this case, because others might be tempted to desert, and they must be intimidated."

Some Alsatians, Latzarus reported, had attempted to escape military service by mutilating themselves or by scalding themselves with boiling water. Wagner had considered the punishments meted out in these cases too lenient, and insisted that the death penalty be prescribed. Latzarus ended his testimony by informing the court that he had attended the execution of Wagner and his two deputies by a firing squad at the military prison in Strasbourg on August 14, 1946.

One of the most important and moving witnesses for the Alsatian defense was Marie-Louise Neumeyer. A thirty-one-year-old teacher from Schiltigheim in Alsace, still dressed in mourning clothes, she described how she had lost her sister and brother, who were refugees from Alsace, in the massacre. She had received news of their deaths at the same time she discovered that another brother and sister had, quite separately, died of disease.

"The drama of Oradour was extremely painful for us. We felt with the whole population of Oradour, the horror of the crime. Unfortunately, alongside the tragedy of Oradour, I lived through another, that of Alsace and of those forcibly inducted. A woman told us that she had seen the German police bringing back young Alsatians who had tried to cross the frontier. They were taken to the concentration camp of Schirmeck where death awaited them after tortures that one can only imagine." The parents of those who succeeded in escaping were also sent to Schirmeck, Mme Neumeyer said.

"I was asked if I knew any of the defendants. I had known the mother of Albert D. for several years and my mother had known her for even longer. I met the mother of Albert D. several days before the trial, and she told me that her son was among the defendants. I did not know this and I did not know her son. However, this mother's pain has touched me and has distressed me. I hoped that it can be assuaged because she also has a son who was declared lost in Russia." On his bench, as Neumeyer spoke, Albert D. wept silently, his face buried in his hands.

The concluding witness for this session was the Vicar General of the diocese of Strasbourg, Monsignor Neppel fifty-six years old (Illustration 55). Some of his parishioners who had been evacuated to Oradour had been among the victims. He knew the families of Alfred D. and Jean-Pierre E. He said that they were honorable and brave, as were their children. To think of them brought before this Tribunal as criminals, he said, gave him great pain.

Later that day, the court went into private session. The issue was the application of the law of January 30, 1953, modifying the Law of Collective Responsibility. Colonel Gardon asked for a division of the trial, and after only twenty minutes of discussion, it was ruled that such a

55. Monsignor Neppel, Vicar General of Strasbourg testifying for the Alsatians.

division would start the next day. The German defendants would attend the pleading relative to them, but the Alsatians would not be present, and thereafter the reverse would apply. In effect, it had been decided that the separate trial sought (so far unsuccessfully) by the Alsatians would now come into effect. Rather than beginning again with separate trials, however, the defendants would simply be divided. It had been clear that Nussy Saint-Saëns wanted to have at least the evidentiary part of the trial include both the Germans and the Alsatians, so that they could be cross-questioned and conflicting accounts reconciled. Due to the delays in the legislature, that goal had been achieved, and the presence or absence of German or Alsatian defendants during the pleading stages of the trial was essentially irrelevant.

The last session of the evidentiary part of the trial ended at 6:30 p.m. as tens of thousands of demonstrators orchestrated by the Communists of Limousin massed in front of Limoges town hall. They were demonstrating against the abrogation of the Law of Collective Responsibility, and the consequent division of the trial. They were also demanding the extradition of General Lammerding, who had been seen in Bonn, where he was receiving advice about how to avoid being extradited. As usual, the relationship between the ANFM and the Communists was strained. The ANFM appreciated the Communists' support but were suspicious of their political motivation.

Chapter 20

The Case Against the Germans

When the trial opened on the afternoon of Wednesday, February 4, the benches of the Alsatian defendants were empty. President Nussy Saint-Saëns explained to the audience that because of the modification of the Law of Collective Responsibility by the legislature there would be a division of the trial between the Germans and the French/Alsatians. If a full separation ("disjunction") had been put into effect, it would have necessitated a full new trial for both groups. Additionally, there was no longer a presumption of guilt attaching to any of the defendants. Not surprisingly, not only were the benches of the Alsatians empty, the places reserved for the representatives of the ANFM had nearly all been vacated after the demonstration of Tuesday afternoon.

The president invited Colonel Gardon, the prosecutor, to present his case against the German defendants. Gardon arose and stood behind the lectern. He spoke softly and without much emphasis.

Within moments, however, M. de Guardia of the Paris bar asked leave to intervene. He said that because of the abrogation of Articles 1 and 2 of the Law of Collective Responsibility, four of the Germans could now be accused only of criminal association. For technical reasons, the Tribunal could no longer charge them with murder, pillage, or arson. De Guardia acknowledged that the legislature was probably unaware that the abrogation would have this effect, but added that it was the duty of the defense to seize any advantage it could. Perhaps he also intended to make a point vis-à-vis the Alsatian defense, which had participated in the judicial process while simultaneously attacking the same process in the Parliament.

"So the defense requests the dismissal of four of the accused," Colonel Gardon retorted. "Can that really be what the legislature intended? I don't think so." He argued that while the modification the Law of Collective Responsibility changed the burden of proof, it did not eliminate the facts set forth in the indictment. The Tribunal retired to deliberate and returned shortly afterwards rejecting de Guardia's plea.

Colonel Gardon then commenced his main summary against the German defendants which he said would be divided into four parts: (1) the facts relative to the activities of the Division and the defendants, (2) the applicable law, (3) the invalidity of their counsel's defense, and (4) the view of the prosecutor as to each defendant's responsibility.

The prosecutor began by stating that for centuries there had been efforts to civilize the rules of war perhaps in echo of the chivalric code; and that these efforts had eventually given rise to international agreements such as the Geneva and Hague Conventions. All soldiers know, he said, that they cannot violate these agreements with impunity, and it was with just such a violation that the defendants were charged in this trial. For this reason, it weighed on the Tribunal to examine the precise responsibility of each defendant. At the same time he wished to examine the broader historical context of the events that preceded Oradour. The Division Das Reich, he said, "was an enterprise of systematic terrorism."

After summarizing these events, and those at Frayssinet, Gardon came to Oradour. He asserted that the whole Third Company had gone to Oradour and had participated in the massacre except the administrative section, which had remained behind, but was supplemented by men from Diekmann's Battalion Headquarters' Company. Remember, Gardon said, that the Alsatians had been told that they "must behave during this operation as if they were in combat" and that "we are going to see now what you Alsatians are capable of." Continuing this line of reasoning, he argued that everyone in the unit had been involved in the encirclement and round up. Even the sentries had been there to prevent people from escaping and they had also killed. All had been at the church except for one group, and everyone had participated in the burning and pillaging.

Although relatively little attention had been paid in the trial to the forty-four men charged *in absentia*, the prosecutor did devote some time to two officers so charged, namely Captain Kahn and Lieutenant Barth. Essentially, he blamed the officers for the organization and execution of the operation. His references to the other NCOs and privates (presumed to be still living but not accounted for) were extremely summary.

Gardon then came to the Adjutant Lenz. Seeing him now, he said, it was hard to imagine him over nine years ago in his helmet and boots—armed, hideous, grotesque, dedicated—setting out to ruin and terrorize. Rebutting Lenz's claim that he had done nothing and seen nothing, Gardon observed that NCOs don't generally keep their rank by doing nothing.

Three of the German defendants, the prosecutor said, had been members of firing squads, and had participated in burning buildings. Three others from the Headquarters' Company, namely Bœhme, Degenhardt, and Blaeschke (the medical orderly, who had ministered to Albert O. and Gnug), had had lesser roles. Gardon said that under the circumstances he would not ask for the death penalty in their cases.

In the German Army, Gardon said, every soldier was given a paper containing the "Ten commandments" to be followed by them in war. They read as follows:

"1. The German soldier fights chivalrously. Acts of cruelty and acts of destruction are unworthy of him.
2. The German soldier must be in uniform and wear a distinctive insignia.
3. An enemy who surrenders must not be killed, even if he is a franctireur [sniper] or a spy; they will receive a just punishment from a Tribunal.
4. Prisoners of war must not be maltreated or injured. We take their arms, their maps, their [military] drawings but nothing else of theirs must be taken.
5. Dum-dum bullets are prohibited.
6. The Red Cross is inviolate. Wounded adversaries are treated with humanity. We must not hinder the medical personnel or chaplains to exercise their medical and spiritual functions.

7. The civilian population is inviolable. A soldier does not have the right to pillage or destroy, or to harm historic monuments. Buildings consecrated to religion, the arts, the sciences and charity must be especially respected. Neither foodstuffs nor services can be claimed from the population except under superior orders with compensation.
8. A neutral territory must not be violated in the course of war operations; it should neither be over-flown, nor be bombarded.
9. If a German soldier is made prisoner, he must give his name and grade if asked.
10. All infractions are governed hereunder and are punishable."

The acts committed at Oradour, Gardon argued, not only violated French and international law; they were in breach of the Germans' own instructions to their soldiery. He further argued that there were aggravating circumstances, including premeditation, which had been established by the meetings, the comments on the way to Oradour, and the signal by Kahn. Was premeditation established in the case of Kahn's subordinates? Yes. When they set out for Oradour, everyone knew what was going to happen. Blaeschke, Bœhme and Degenhardt were part of the Division Das Reich before Oradour and so were guilty of abetting a criminal organization.

Continuing his litany, Gardon reminded the Tribunal that pillage and arson accompanied or followed by murder was punishable by death. Other aggravating circumstances included the commission of barbarous acts (the church massacre), and of reprisals. As to Bœhme, Gardon noted that the Bordeaux Military Tribunal had investigated the Frayssinet murders in February 1949, and Captain Kahn had been condemned to death for them *in absentia*. From Bœhme's deposition to the British, as well as from evidence given at the present trial on January 27, his participation was clear. Having originally claimed that he did not remember being at Frayssinet, he later admitted that he had brought the women to the hanging squad. One man who had been present in court on January 27 and had been upset with Bœhme's testimony concerning the hangings in Frayssinet was Jean Badour of Bordeaux, the son and nephew of the three women hung. He claimed that, "No German was shot. The whole thing was faked to give a pretext." The president did not comment. [I think it is unlikely that the SS would have bothered faking such a death given how many civilians they gratuitously put to death.] The pleading of Gardon was interrupted as the session ended at 7:30 p.m.

The next day, Thursday, February 5, after further legal wrangling concerning Bœhme, Gardon turned to the issue of the defense which he assumed would be employed on behalf of some or all of the German defendants, namely, obedience to orders. The horrors committed at Oradour," he said, "were not carried out by an undisciplined rabble which had escaped the control of its officers, but by a troop of fanatics. That begged certain questions. There were no armies anywhere in the world, he admitted, in which prompt and rigorous obedience were not required. So should these men have disobeyed orders which were incontestably criminal? The question was a complex one, given the hierarchical and disciplinary nature of military life. Was it possible to imagine an army in which orders were subject to debate, and discipline was reduced to a vague obligation of subordination? The answer was clearly no. He cited the basic regulation of the French army: orders must be executed "without hesitation or complaint." Furthermore, it is neither a crime nor a misdemeanor if the act is sanctioned by law and—there is a conjunction—ordered by a legitimate authority. Naturally, the authority that gives the orders is responsible for their consequences.

However, argued Gardon, a critical qualification came into play at that point: that discipline in the French army was subject to the general context of conformity to the law. An officer could not take advantage of his position to commit a crime. But what should a soldier do if ordered to commit an illegal act? Was the carrying out of such an act justified by the requirement of obedience? Gardon conceded that if an order had the appearance of legality and related to behavior normal in war, disobedience was not justified. On the other hand, and here he gave his key argument of the trial, if the order was manifestly illegal and concerned acts generally viewed as reprehensible (like the killing of the women and children in the Oradour church for example), disobedience was not only justified but required.

A corollary of the obedience issue which Gardon acknowledged was Article 327 of the Criminal Code. Article 327 provided that a homicide was not a crime if it was "authorized by law and ordered by a [competent] authority." That said, Gardon contended, Kahn had not been authorized under German or French law to order the burning and killing in the church, and Article 327 makes clear that a crime is not justified merely because it is ordered by an authority. Gardon reiterated that an act committed in obedience to an order is only considered a war crime if the illegality of the order is manifest, or put another way, if no justification is conceivable. Thus Article 327—like similar laws in Belgium, Holland, Italy and Germany—concedes that there are limits to the requirement that a subordinate should obey an order.

In German law, Gardon explained, if a violation of criminal law was committed, the individual giving the order was responsible for the violation, but a subordinate was also culpable as an accomplice. "if he knows that the order of a superior concerns an act which would constitute a crime under military or penal law." Gardon conceded that while most orders benefit from a presumption of legality and regularity, that presumption did not apply in the case of a manifestly illegal act like the extermination of the village of Oradour.

There remained another issue, Article 64 of the Criminal Code states that an act is not a crime if the actor, "is constrained by a force which he cannot resist." Did the rigorous discipline of the SS and the particular circumstances of the war (including the fact that the soldiers risked being shot if they disobeyed) constitute an irresistible force? Had the defendants committed criminal acts under duress? Had they killed in order to avoid being killed? Gardon was sure that defense counsel would so argue.

The prosecutor's rebuttal was that the comportment of the defendants, before, during and after the crime—as described by a number of witnesses—told its own story. Do not forget the testimony of M. Bélivier, he reminded the Tribunal, who saw the SS fall like wolves on an innocent woman in a field. Or the testimony of M. Lamige who saw other SS brutalizing a crippled veteran of the 1914-1918 war. Or that of the escapees from the Laudy barn, themselves the objects of the cruelest treatment, who saw the SS escorting weeping women and children to their deaths. Or that of Mme Demery, who saw the SS laughing and yelling as they descended from their trucks. And then, there was the radio music during the executions, the many bottles stolen and emptied, the visits to the grocery store, the firing-squad member eating a sugar-lump as he waited to execute the men at the Laudy barn, the behavior at the Masset farm, the singing and accordion-playing, the hysteria at Nieul, and the joking and the party atmosphere on the Sunday morning. In short, the idea that the soldiers' behavior was a consequence of the sort of duress for which Article 64 made allowances simply did not conform to the facts.

[I would note that the problem with this line of reasoning is that no individual defendant could be tied to any one of these gratuitous types of behavior; Gardon was relying on a kind of collective responsibility. However, this idea of collective responsibility was dependent upon a false syllogism, as follows: (1) There were many acts showing the enthusiasm of those in the Third Company, (2) The defendants were in the Third Company, and (3) Therefore, each defendant was enthusiastic and not constrained.]

Gardon then moved from the general to the particular. He noted that even the German authorities considered Oradour a blot on the honor of the German Army. Rommel was said to have told Hitler in person that "This kind of thing dishonors Germany." Gardon quoted a German writer, M. Hans, who in 1950 described Oradour as, "a case of cruelty that so exceeded human understanding as to be diabolic." Gardon said that the responsibility of Kahn, Barth and the others *in absentia* was total and terrible. He demanded the death penalty for all of them.

He continued, "For those who acted according to orders, and I talk here about the defendants here present: Frenzel, Pfeuffer and Daab [all of whom were in firing squads], they took part knowingly in these monstrous crimes that were inexcusable and I do not hesitate to proclaim that they are undeniably guilty. But I have to recognize also that they acted according to their assignment. There are here, gentlemen, incontestably extenuating circumstances that you will have in the quiet of your conscience to appreciate how far they extend." Gardon then stated that he requested a sentence of hard labor for those three. "For Blaeschke, Bœhme and Degenhardt, because of the general comportment of the First Battalion and in particular the events of Frayssinet, I would also request a sentence of hard labor for the crime of association with criminals."

"As to Lenz, the adjutant, his defense is that he knew nothing, did nothing, and saw nothing. The truth, however, is certainly otherwise, notwithstanding the conspiracy of silence to which this defendant's former subordinates are adhering. I have not forgotten the first statements by Boos to the British authorities (as a prisoner of war). These were made before the defendants were able to talk together and agree on a plausible common defense. Boos declared then on April 24, 1947, that Lenz was head of a firing squad. Here is his statement, which I consider vitally important in that it was made to individuals who had no direct interest in the trial."

Gardon noted also Albert O.'s declaration to the Strasbourg police that Lenz had thrown grenades in the church. Albert O. then changed his testimony to say that he had confused Lenz with Töpfer; but Töpfer was much taller than Lenz, so he could hardly have confused them. Given that this was the SS, the prosecutor's main point was, "It is inconceivable that Lenz played no role in the operation." Gardon requested the death penalty for Lenz.

It was not sufficient to just stigmatize the crime, Gardon said in conclusion. It was also necessary to judge those who took part.

Chapter 21

The German Response

Fortunately for the German defendants, the French tradition of providing a strong defense for unpopular clients was a well-established one. The reality, nevertheless, was that these defendants had participated in an atrocity committed on French soil. They were being tried in France, and they were the former enemy.

M. de Guardia of the Paris bar made a considerable impression in the courtroom according to several journalists. He was representing all the German defendants and was thus charged with addressing the broader issues, leaving to his colleagues the various arguments specific to their clients. Accordingly, he moved straight to the main question at issue: can a soldier disobey an order? De Guardia acknowledged that he found the prosecutor's argument in this respect "admirable" but was uncertain as to whether he found it intellectually watertight. The answer, he agreed, was yes, in principle, a soldier was required to obey an order without discussion. But there were exceptions. If the order was monstrous, the soldier had to refuse to obey. But things were never quite that simple.

M. de Guardia said that the soldier, whether a general or private soldier, can ask, "How do I execute that order?" But he can never ask, "Why?" The private cannot ask why he must sweep an already spotless room twice, and the general cannot ask whether the war he is entering into is just. It is not his problem. The civilians have decided for him.

The army does not need philosophers. It needs technicians and heroes. The issue of obedience to orders had often been dealt with before by military tribunals, de Guardia said, and in his view, it had never been analyzed with greater clarity than by the Belgian tribunal at Liege in 1950. He summarized that decision as follows:

When we oblige a soldier (who has not the means to do it) to understand clearly the orders he is given and to refuse in time of war, under the threat of criminal penalties, to execute an order that apparently violates in a flagrant manner the law and customs of war, we risk gravely disrupting military discipline.

When a soldier received an order to act in a way which apparently violated the laws of war, de Guardia continued, he was faced with a terrible dilemma: if he obeyed the order he would violate the law; if he disobeyed, he would be punished. As the Belgian Tribunal said, it would only be human under those circumstances to obey the order, because if he refused, he would have no way of justifying his choice, and the sanction for disobedience was certain, immediate and dire. If he obeyed the order, however, and his action constituted a war crime, the sanction was random, eventual, and uncertain.

De Guardia suggested that war crimes should go before an international tribunal composed of the vanquishers, the vanquished and the neutrals. Here perhaps, the generals of the various armies could be brought; the International Red Cross could open its files. "How many of the great generals of war would leave that courtroom free?" de Guardia asked. "It is a question I dare not pose."

A succession of lawyers presented both general and specific defenses for the German defendants. As to whether they were volunteers or conscripts, the defense pointed out that as well as often being very young and unsophisticated at the time—seventeen was not an uncommon age to join—many were also misled by being promised a six-week holiday if they enlisted, which in the event, it goes without saying, they did not get. More to the point, counsel raised the question of *when* the Waffen SS became a criminal organization. It was identified as such in October 1946 at Nuremberg, but was it definable in those terms in January 1944, when these defendants joined it? Could they have deserted? Hardly. That in itself would have been a criminal act. Counsel also pointed out that these German defendants had already been in prison for over nine years. For those who were seventeen or eighteen years old at the time that they were captured, those nine years represented one third of their lives to date. Some of their lawyers referred to them as scapegoats, given that their officers were not before the Tribunal.

The next day, Friday, February 6, Lenz's counsel, M. Lafeuillée-Viellard, began by pointing out that his client, Lenz, was the man the company ridiculed; he did not embrace Hitlerism, and considered it facile. If officers like Diekmann and Kahn—those responsible for the massacre—were here on the defendants' benches, he argued, Lenz would be regarded as of no importance. With the officers absent, however, there appeared to be a distinction between Lenz and the other defendants, namely his rank. Counsel opined that it was only Lenz's rank that had led the prosecutor to demand the death penalty for him.

Lafeuillée-Viellard then argued that the massacre was premeditated by the officers but not the other ranks. The men, he said, did not know what was going to happen, and if there were odd references to the probability of bloodshed, a fire fight with the Resistance was an ever-present possibility. What is more, the defendants had been told that the execution of Resistance members and the burning of their homes were covered by the general orders. Most of the company had not known what was happening in the church, and the worst excesses there were probably carried out by an inner circle.

Lenz's counsel repeated that his client was neither intelligent, nor rabid, nor a Nazi. Originally, he had joined the Luftwaffe; Göring, however, had needed 3,000 men to guard stolen artifacts, so he had had 3,000 Luftwaffe soldiers (including Lenz) transferred to the SS, and had received 3,000 Waffen SS soldiers [presumed by Göring to be better as guard troops] in return. The testimony of his fellow defendants indicated that Lenz counted for nothing in the Third Company. As Paul G. said, everyone mocked Lenz. There were misfits like him in every army in the world. He had asked to be transferred back to the Luftwaffe, but the transfer had been in suspension.

The prosecutor, Lafeuillée-Viellard continued, claimed that Lenz lied, but he had produced no proof of any acts that he had committed. Instead he employed faulty logic along the following lines: it was the NCOs who delivered the *coups de grace,* Lenz was an NCO, and therefore Lenz delivered *coups de grace*. In fact, his client claimed that he had stayed with the trucks on the outskirts of town, and Daab had confirmed it. Later, he had come into the village and had been standing next to Captain Kahn when the latter gave the signal to machine gun the men, but both Lenz himself and two other Germans had confirmed that he was not in any of the firing squads. After the executions, he had left the village and had seen the flames from a distance. He had not been at the church, counsel claimed, and it was incorrect to say that all the defendants had gone there. He was up a tree at the time, partly as a lookout, and partly as a punishment. Witnesses had stated that there were bodies nearby, but Lenz was not a sniper, as was obvious from his squint and the fact that his personal weapon was a submachine gun and not a sniper's rifle.

In summary, Lafeuillée-Viellard said that he had read in a newspaper that President Nussy Saint-Saëns had received a delegation of the families of Oradour and promised them that, "French justice will judge each according to his culpability." As regards Lenz, counsel concluded, "If you judge by his degree of culpability, you can only acquit."

The argument for the three German defendants who had admitted being in firing squads—Pfeuffer, Frenzel, and Daab—was more straightforward. Captain Kahn had told them that the targets were partisans and were to be executed on his signal. Kahn and an NCO had gone into the barns after the executions and administered the *coups de grace* to the victims who were still moving. These defendants, therefore, were simply obeying an order of Captain Kahn which they had no reason to doubt was a lawful one. Thus, Article 327 of the French Criminal Code (which indicated that a homicide was neither a crime nor even a misdemeanor if ordered by a legitimate authority) covered the case clearly. Did these soldiers have a free choice between executing the order or not? Did they even have time to reflect on that order? No. They were in the Waffen SS. They could not question Captain Kahn's statement that the targets were partisans and as such, given the prevailing condition of "total war," had to be executed. Counsel reminded the Tribunal of testimony describing how some Alsatian SS-men had been executed just for showing their distaste for Hitler. The defendants had no reason to doubt that Kahn would have had them shot if they had disobeyed his order. They also were at that point unaware of what had happened in the church.

M. La Chapelle then presented the case of a defendant named Frenzel, explaining how this young man, who had wished only for the life of a farmer, had been compelled to join the Hitler Youth at the age of fourteen, and had been inducted into the SS three years later. In no sense had he been a "volunteer." At Oradour, still only seventeen years old, he had believed that he was following a legal order in participating in the execution of partisans. As counsel put it:

"... [Frenzel] had been in the company for 120 days. This boy was armed only with a rifle. He fired, he said, only a single bullet. I am comforted to think that probably no Frenchman at Oradour was killed by that bullet. That sole act he committed was in obedience to an order" and that qualifies as an absolute excuse. For over eight years, Frenzel had been in prison. He had thus lost the most useful, productive years of his life.

M. Renaud, counsel for another German defendant named Daab, who had participated in the shootings at the Desourteaux garage, observed that by dividing the men into several groups who had all fired simultaneously upon Kahn's signal, each soldier had been led to think that there was only one execution taking place and a not a mass execution. "The operation was orchestrated and timed perfectly by Kahn," counsel said. "My client [Daab] said that "when we opened fire, I was under the impression that we had been chosen to execute twenty terrorists who had been identified in the village." [I note that this was a somewhat specious defense given that the various execution squads all led their victims away from the village green at the same time and in full sight of each other.]

The next day, Saturday, M. Moliérac undertook the task of summarizing the case for all the German defendants. He challenged the Tribunal.

"If a régime is on trial here, are these really the guilty men? Should we not look higher on the ladder of responsibility?" He then proceeded to an examination of the Nazi code into which the German defendants had been indoctrinated: "The watchword of these young men, as inscribed on their daggers, was 'Blood and Honor'. There was no more religion and no justice." He quoted the pre-war words of Martin Bormann, Hitler's deputy, "We must demoralize our adversaries by acts of terrorism, bombings and assassinations. We do not pretend to act as heroes. We must be hard. War is terribly bloody and cruel. Any means are good means. War is what I choose. The time for beautiful sentiments has passed. Our task is to sack the world. War is myself."

Moliérac also quoted the words of Field Marshall Keitel at Nuremberg, "I have lived my whole life in a traditional military milieu, and have never concerned myself with what was good or evil." He also cited the message of Jean Cocteau to the Americans, "The world will not be saved by arms nor by fortune; it will be saved by the minority who think." After a lengthy exposition concerning the moral and actual powerlessness of the individual soldier in the Nazi war-machine, Moliérac ended with the words of the witness from Alsace, Lévignac, who had lost two sons at Oradour, "I do not hate [the defendants] or wish for vengeance. I only ask that their remorse be as great as my sorrow."

The president then instructed the head of the guards to escort the Germans to the prison and to bring in the French defendants.

Chapter 22

The Case Against the Alsatians

In accordance with the decision to divide the trial, Nussy Saint-Saëns reopened the session without the German defendants present but with the Alsatians defendants including Boos in their stead. He explained that given the change in the law, it was now incumbent on the prosecution to demonstrate that the Alsatian defendants were co-authors of the crime. Counsel for ten of these defendants moved that their cases be dismissed on technicalities relating to abrogation of the Law of Collective Responsibility, but the Tribunal ruled against them.

Gardon then began to outline the case against the French/Alsatian defendants. Having issued a broad condemnation, he moved on to discuss them individually, starting with Boos. Boos was the only French volunteer among the defendants and possibly the only one in the Third Company. "…His subordinates have been unanimous in telling us that Sgt. Boos was a particularly brutal and vindictive Nazi. The behavior of Boos at Oradour on June 10, 1944 does not contradict these opinions. At the Desourteaux garage, he turned over the bodies with his boot, said Jean-Pierre E., before administering the coups de grace and setting fire to the corpses. Nor did it end there; Sgt. Boos killed two women near the church with a burst from his submachine gun. The bodies of these two unfortunates were later discovered under the debris in a nearby house."

Jean-Pierre E. confirmed that Boos went into the church, fired his machine gun, threw grenades, and ordered Jean-Pierre E. to bring firewood and straw. Boos had returned with some men on Monday, June 12 and had gone into the church, Gardon continued, after which the tabernacle had been found to have been broken into, and its contents looted.

When the trial opened again on Monday afternoon, February 9, Gardon examined the roles played by the other defendants. Three of them (Joseph B., Albert L., René Camille G.) had participated in firing squads, and three others (Paul G., Jean-Pierre E., Albert D.) had admitted, or had been identified by other defendants, as having shot people. Some of the rest had set fires, but others claimed to have done nothing but act as sentries outside the village. Gardon mentioned in mitigation that Paul G. had forewarned a *résistant* [Vigneau] that he was being watched. Another had stopped several people from entering the village. A couple of the men had served in the French army between 1939 and 1940, and others had joined up after having deserted in Normandy. Two had won the *Croix de Guerre*.

The prosecutor then returned to broader themes. He reminded the Tribunal that the French defendants were not on trial for war crimes but as criminals under the ordinary Penal Code. Gardon acknowledged that while they could reasonably claim to have been forcibly inducted into the Waffen SS, they were being judged for their behavior at a specific place and time. Forcible induction, he said, was an extenuating circumstance, but it was not an absolute defense. Gardon quoted the defense's claim that the men were only there because they had been forcibly inducted, and that any of the 130,000 others thus inducted would have done as they had. He said that he did not believe this, and that the fact of the post-Oradour desertions had only made things worse.

"Why did they wait three weeks to desert?" he wondered. "The truth, Gentlemen, and I say it to them openly, is that for as long as the war consisted only of the oppression of the civilian population they did not think [of deserting], but when they found themselves on the receiving end of Allied bombs and shells, four or five years of intensive Nazi propaganda proved insufficient to hold them."

In consequence, Gardon said, they could not be absolved of guilt. They had blood on their hands. They had acted as subordinates but their actions had been worse than the Germans' because the Germans were the enemy. The French/Alsatians had been killing their own brothers. They had seen the sacrifice that the mayor had been prepared to make for his compatriots but they had not been moved by it. They had cared nothing for the village that they had exterminated.

Gardon recognized that under the Penal Code, the *malgré nous* could plead duress, but he said the facts did not support it. He cited various examples including Mme Yvonne Gaudy's testimony that she had heard an Alsatian justify the massacre by citing the disappearance of Major Kämpfe, "What is the problem, they killed one of ours." For these men, Gardon requested sentences of hard labor or prison according to their ages and personal situations. "Against the French SS volunteer Boos, a fanatic Nazi, and a holder of the Iron Cross, who by the orders that he issued and the example that he gave, proved himself one of the principal actors in the slaughter at Oradour and concerning whom I search in vain for the smallest hint of an attenuating circumstance, I call for the application of the law in all its rigor. I demand the death penalty."

"To illustrate my thinking and my conviction, a scene from a Shakespearean tragedy will serve. In Richard III the Duke of Gloucester, covered with blood implores the Queen as follows:

Gloucester: 'Say that I slew them not?'

Lady Anne [the Queen]: 'Why, then they are not dead: But dead they are, and, devilish slave, by thee.'"

Chapter 23

The Alsatian Response

The defense counsel with the least enviable task in the courtroom was M. Laborde, the Bordeaux lawyer charged with defending Boos. Laborde tried to show that Boos had been accused by other defendants of more crimes than he had really committed, and that much of the testimony against him was inconsistent, contradictory, and vague and therefore not a proper basis for condemning a man to death. He reminded the Tribunal that Boos had been seventeen years old when he enlisted, and had been in prison since the war. He then went to considerable lengths to attempt to establish that Boos had not been involved in the crimes at the church.

Next, M. Burguburu pleaded on behalf of Paul G. The Parisian lawyer presented the human side of his defendant. His client, he said, had been born in a village of 500 inhabitants, had been raised by his grandparents, and had received letters of support from people of his village to the effect that he had always been a pleasant boy. Burguburu acknowledged the facts of his client's acts: that he had been on patrol in Oradour with a German and a Russian who had opened fire on three people who had been hiding in a hedge, and that he had followed suit, killing a woman. This was a consequence of the rule insisting that Alsatians were not to be left by themselves, Burguburu argued. Had Paul G. been alone, he would not have shot the woman.

In the church, Paul G. had obeyed Diekmann's order to bring firewood, but in doing so, he had been under clear duress because Diekmann had had a reputation for shooting soldiers who disobeyed his orders. It had been argued that Paul G. should have deserted earlier, before the Division started moving north after the Allied landing. But neither he nor his Alsatian comrades had been able to do so for the reasons established at the trial: that the French citizenry had thought at the time that all SS-men were volunteers, and so would not have helped them.

Fifteen days after Oradour, Paul G. had lost an eye in Normandy. Unlike the other Alsatians, he had been in prison since the war. Indeed, Burguburu pointed out, he had been condemned to death by a Limoges criminal court in March 1946 for the shooting of Mme Octavie Dalstein. Burguburu had been his defense counsel on that occasion, too, and said that the audience had been ready to lynch his client. They had applauded when the guilty verdict was announced. At the time, Paul G. had been eighteen years old.

M. Andre Moser started the pleading on Tuesday, February 10. He was referred to by *Le Monde*—a leading French daily—as the defense's "heavy artillery." He argued that for a criminal act to be proven, the prosecution had to show criminal intent as well as material facts. Moser argued that not only had the government failed to prove such intent but that it was demonstrable that the opposite was true, because the Alsatians had been forcibly inducted, and even the prosecutor had admitted that their behavior prior to induction had showed they were anti-German. He added that it was elementary that they were acting under duress, and with the possible exception of Boos or perhaps Paul G., none of them had done more than he was ordered to do.

Given that the prosecution had been silent on the question of intent, Moser said he considered that the prosecution was a scandal and an intellectual fraud. As for one of his clients, who apart from anything else was mentally retarded, Moser recognized that he had participated in two firing squads, but requested that this should be set against the fact that before Oradour he had twice attempted to desert. While he had admitted being in the firing squads, he had also claimed that he had shot over the heads of the victims. His client had not been a hero, Moser said, but he had not been a criminal, either.

In conclusion, Moser said that he accepted that the families of the victims would not be satisfied with legal niceties. Therefore, he said, he had a question for the Tribunal. "Put yourself beside him in that barn at Oradour—an eighteen-year-old youngster taken away from his homeland, without support. You are there beside him, rifle in hand, surrounded by Boos and the other vindictive officers. 'Fire!' comes the order. What would you have done? These are not heroes, certainly, but you cannot [rightly] claim that they are criminals. Remember, that even as the screams of the 642 killed at Oradour resound across history, the screams of the thousands of Alsatians tortured and killed by the same enemy are also to be heard."

Albert Schmidt, counsel to Jean-Pierre E., and former counsel to Wagner, the Governor of Alsace, reminded the Tribunal that Jean-Pierre E. had defaced photos of Hitler before he was forcibly inducted, but had then participated in the massacre at Oradour. "How, gentlemen, can you reconcile such gestures with those with which he is charged relative to Oradour except by duress?" Schmidt asked. To plead duress, he acknowledged, was neither noble nor fine, but society did not have the right to impose heroism on each of its members. M. Schmidt then quoted the American prosecutor at Nuremberg in a communication to President Truman, "If a person is put in a firing squad, he is not responsible for the validity of the sentence [of execution]. But the question can be modified by reason of his rank or the nature of the order he receives to the point that he has complete freedom of action."

M. Schmidt then posed an important question to the Tribunal. "What influence do you think your judgment will have on the conduct of future wars and on the conduct of European soldiers yet to be born?"

M. Richard Lux, whose forceful advocacy on behalf of Joseph B. and Albert O. had caused him to be expelled from the Communist party, took the floor at that point. "Before beginning, I would like to make a preliminary observation. From the beginning, this trial has provoked an outpouring of passion, and when the president said on January 12 that the martyrs of Oradour were present in the courtroom, I agreed with him. [But] I believe that the souls and the memories of the dead have been chased from this courtroom by the hate of certain individuals, who have tried to supplant justice. We have been constantly aware of these people, moving around the corridors, trying to plant their message in the minds of the Tribunal…" The president interrupted him by saying, "What goes on outside in the corridors or elsewhere whether in Limousin or Alsace does not interest us," he said. "Our concern is for the trial, and that takes place in this room."

Reluctantly, Lux abandoned the subject. Instead, after some general remarks, he focused on his client Albert O. The prosecutor claims that to determine intent, you only have to look at the behavior of the soldiers after the crime. Does not their desertion at the first chance they had show that they did not have the requisite criminal intent? "My client's case is the most straightforward of all. He was ordered to muster people. He did not want to go into one particular house, and so remained in the entrance. A woman, dependent on walking sticks was forced out. My client protested and for his pains was threatened, shot and wounded by Sergeant Staeger, leaving him unable to walk."

Lux argued that you only had to look at Albert O. to see that he did not want to help the SS to commit these crimes. After he deserted he fought with the French Army. His family kept the postcards on which he had written 'Vive la France'. He had added, "The war will be over soon. Hang on because we're going to finish off the Boches." The prosecutor had conceded that Albert O. deserted but had asked why he did not do so sooner. Lux continued, but how could more than 100,000 forcibly inducted men—five whole divisions—possibly desert?

In this connection, Lux said he had a copy of a German military document confirming the death sentence for an Alsatian who had been forcibly inducted in the Division Das Reich, and had deserted in the southwest of France. The man had been arrested by the French police and returned to the Division where he had been condemned to death. The judgment added that: "In recent times many men from Alsace-Lorraine have been inducted into the Division as recruits and among them there were ten cases of desertions. To discourage the others and to preserve discipline in the ranks, the death penalty has been chosen."

The next defense counsel to be heard was M. Mérius, who represented Albert L. He told the court that his client was a modest and simple man, and had always been honest, patriotic and loyal to France. "I have known Albert L. a long time, and for nearly fifteen years lived next door to him. The Germans recognized that men like Albert L.

had pro-French sentiments and it was for this reason that he was forced into joining the Waffen SS. Once in the Waffen SS, an Alsatian was surrounded so that it was possible to keep a close watch on him and prevent him from attempting to desert."

Mérius described the regime. At first, the Alsatians had not been permitted to leave the camp. Then, when they had finally been permitted to leave, they had always been accompanied by a German, and required to carry a weapon with which to intimidate the local populace. His client, Mérius said, had not lacked courage. In 1940 he had manned a tank that had achieved a rare combat success against the Germans, and won a *Croix de Guerre*.

Paul Minges then spoke on behalf of another Alsatian, Fernand G., who had been forcibly inducted in February 1944. Eighteen at the time of Oradour, he had deserted two months later in Normandy. Taken prisoner by the U.S., he had volunteered for the French Army, and at the end of the war re-enlisted to go to Indo-China. It was clear that Fernand G. had deserted not from fear or cowardice, Minges said, "but simply because the opportunity had presented itself. He had demonstrated his loyalty by fighting for the French after the Allied landing.

On Wednesday, February 11, the twenty-seventh day of the trial, Pierre Schreckenberg took the floor as counsel for Louis P., Henri W., Jean N., and Albert D. His first act was to lay the responsibility for Oradour firmly at the feet of the commandant of the Regiment Der Führer, Colonel Sylvester Stadler. The French authorities, he said, had had an opportunity to arrest Stadler in Vienna, but had failed to act. Nussy Saint-Saëns promised that the government would make further attempts to have the former SS officer extradited and tried. Schreckenberg then provided information on the number of Alsatian *malgré nous* in the Third Company and what had happened to them. There were "twenty-eight [out of a company of approximately 150 to 200 men] of whom fifteen fell in the uniform they hated, and thirteen are before you today."

Schreckenberg then pointed out to the prosecutor that desertion in time of war was universally punishable by death. He argued that the prosecutor demanded a lot of these forcibly inducted young men, themselves victims of a war crime. He demanded that they become heroes, and risk being shot themselves for disobeying an order to open fire.

Schreckenberg spoke of Henri W. who had been seventeen years old at the time of the massacre. His parents had been sent to a concentration camp and their restaurant business closed by the Germans. His brother had been sent to the Russian front and had died there. Henri W., therefore, could hardly have been said to have had pro-Nazi, anti-French feelings. If he had deserted, his parents would have been "liquidated".

Schreckenberg argued on behalf of Henri W. and his other clients that the defense of the Alsatians was actually more complex than the defense of the Germans. The Alsatians could offer as a defense the fact that they had been obeying the orders of a legitimate authority. Gardon had disputed that fact, choosing not to regard German officers as legitimate authorities in the case of French soldiers. But Schreckenberg said that he preferred to proceed on the basis of the absence of criminal intent which he argued his clients lacked. He concluded by demanding that if justice was to be done, those responsible for the massacre—General Lammerding, Colonel Stadler and Captain Kahn—should stand trial.

M. Jacques Kalb returned to the question of why the Alsatians had not deserted. Some who had attempted this when they were first forcibly inducted, he explained, had been executed in a Strasbourg jail. And there had been grave consequences for relatives, too, he said, describing a family where the mother had been sent to Auschwitz, the father to Dachau and the daughter to a soldiers' brothel. Of the class of 1942 from the town of Markalsen, two hundred and seventy-five young men, who had refused military service in the German Army, had been arrested, sent to Schirmeck, tortured, and inducted into the Waffen SS. In the SS, Kalb argued, the Alsatians had been prisoners in the truest sense of the word. Kalb ended his submission with a request that, in the interests of national unity and mutual patriotic respect, the ashes of the Oradour victims and those of the German oppression of Alsace be considered jointly symbolic.

The President Nussy Saint-Saëns then asked the Alsatian defendants if they had anything they wished to add in their defense. Only Boos spoke, saying, "I regret having been involved in this affair."

At that point, the French defendants were sent out and the Germans were brought in. The president first dealt with certain outstanding details, reporting that the investigation in Frayssinet had yielded no results, and confirming that the "ten commandments" identified by the prosecutor had not been issued to the Waffen SS or the Luftwaffe but to the Wehrmacht. Nussy Saint-Saëns then asked if any of the German defendants had any words to address to the Court.

Lenz rose to his feet clicking his heels and said his piece, "As a German, I sincerely regret the events at Oradour. I took no part in them, and with full confidence leave my fate in the hands of the Tribunal." Blaeschke stated that he had only discharged his function as a medical orderly, and that he had nothing to add to the arguments of his lawyer. Degenhardt denied that he had played any part in the massacre.

Others were content to associate themselves with the words of their comrades.

At 5:45 p.m. that evening, after twenty-seven days of sessions, the President Nussy Saint-Saëns declared the trial over, and the court filed out to commence its deliberations. As was traditional, the president requested that a guard be posted outside their chambers. Six camp cots had been prepared in one room and another for the President in a small antechamber. The judges had arrived at the beginning of the afternoon with their suitcases packed, prepared to stay as long as was necessary (Illustration 56). While the court deliberated, the ANFM (including Hébras, Godfrin and Machefer) and its supporters mounted a demonstration in Bordeaux which attracted several thousand participants, despite the bad weather. After the demonstration, and without waiting for the verdict, the ANFM families returned to Oradour.

56. Presiding Judge Marcel Nussy Saint-Säens arriving on February 11, 1953, with his suitcase prepared to stay for the duration of the Tribunal's deliberations on the verdicts.

Chapter 24

The Verdicts

The deliberations lasted just over thirty-two hours (Illustration 57), and it was 2:30 a.m. on Friday, February 13 when the officials finally filed into the courtroom. The six military judges were in their dress uniforms, with white gloves and military decorations, and were preceded by the President Nussy Saint-Saëns, in his red robe (Illustration 58). The president greeted the sleepy, thin ranks of guards, lawyers, and journalists in the courtroom. None of the defendants were present. The judges appear to have announced their verdicts in the middle of the night in part because they wished to minimize the risk of demonstrations inside or outside the courtroom.

Commencing with the ritual words, "In the name of the people of France…" the president detailed the responses to the 502 counts against the Germans, stating in each case whether the vote was unanimous or by a majority, in which case he indicated the number of votes for and against. This process lasted almost an hour. The president's voice became more and more strained as the hour went on. After a brief pause, he announced that the sentences were as follows. My speculations as to what may have influenced individual sentences are in brackets.

Those tried *in absentia*—Death, forty-two individuals in all, apparently a record, including the officers Kahn and Barth. For reasons not stated, two of the original names in the list of forty-four absent defendants were omitted.

Oradour-The Final Verdict

57. The nearly empty courtroom before the verdicts. The unused fireplace more visible in the center.

58. Judges standing for the rendering of the verdict at 2:30 a.m. on February 13, 1944. The prosecutor Gardon stands to the left. The defendants heard their fate from him afterwards in the prison.

Lenz—Death [While scant evidence was demonstrated as to his actual culpability, the presumption was that as the highest ranking NCO present he must have played an active role].

Blaeschke—Twelve years hard labor [In Britain he had admitted being involved in the Frayssinet hangings, but he denied Lenz's allegation that he had administered *coups de grace* in the Beaulieu shed].

Daab—Twelve years hard labor. [He was in Boos's firing squad in the Desourteaux garage.]

Bœhme—Ten years hard labor [He was involved in hangings at Frayssinet but tried to deny it].

Pfeuffer—Ten years hard labor [He was in firing squad at the Beaulieu shed].

Frenzel—Ten years imprisonment [He was also in the Beaulieu shed firing squad, but only seventeen at the time, and had only been in the SS four months].

Degenhardt—Acquitted [He only passed by Oradour late in the day on route to Nieul].

The Tribunal then repeated the process with the Alsatians. The penalties were determined as follows:

Boos—Death [He held the rank of sergeant, he was unrepentant, he admitted directing a firing squad and administering *coups de grace*, albeit he denied shooting women and participating in the murders at the church].

Joseph B., Fernand G., René Camille G., and Albert D.—Eight years hard labor [They were all in firing squads; Albert D. denied being in one but was contradicted by Boos].

Paul G.—Eight years imprisonment [He was seventeen years old at the time, his sentence was almost fully served already, and he saved the Resistance café owner; he killed a woman but was frank and remorseful].

Jean-Pierre E.—Eight years imprisonment [He was in a firing squad but was eighteen years old at the time, and testified against Boos].

Albert L.—Seven years hard labor [He was in the same firing squad as Joseph B., but testified more freely].

Louis P.—Six years hard labor [He was in the heavy machine gun group that did not participate in the executions in the barns].

Henri W.—Six years imprisonment [He was in the same group, but was only seventeen years old at the time].

Jean N.—Five years hard labor [He was thirty-one years old at the time and in the same group, but he showed contrition].

Albert O.—Five years hard labor [Also thirty-one years old at Oradour, he was wounded during the house-to-house searches, after which he played no further part; he was also contrite].

Alfred S.—Five years hard labor [He was in the same section as Louis P., Henri W. and Jean N., but eighteen years old at the time, and showed humanity especially in escorting the tram riders to the Masset house; and was awarded the *Croix de Guerre* in Indochina].

Louis H.—Five years imprisonment [He was seventeen years old at the time, and served in Indochina].

The expressions on the faces of the Alsatian lawyers as the sentences were read told the story of their disbelief and despair. Although it was no consolation, the Alsatian *malgré nous* generally were found guilty by a vote of only five to two whereas most of the rest of the verdicts were unanimous. If one more judge had voted for acquittal, they would have been freed under the so-called "acquittal by a minority in favor" rule. If three out of seven votes are against conviction, the court acquits. Presumably the two voting for acquittal had based their opinion on the fact of their forcible induction since that was the only relevant distinction between them and the Germans. Also of little consolation for the Alsatians and their counsel was the fact that for comparable participation, for example in firing squads, the French defendants got lesser sentences than the Germans; of course the latter had all been in prison since the war.

With the trial at an end, the president looked exhausted. When the photographers requested a last picture, he responded with one word, "Non." Afterwards the defendants were told the verdicts by the prosecutor in the prison. By and large, the Germans received the sentences with resignation. The time that they had already served meant that, with the exception of Lenz, they would be freed in two to four years. The Alsatians, however, who (except for Paul G.) had been at liberty since the war and had come to the trial as free men, were close to collapse.

Chapter 25

Fierce Reactions to the Verdicts

With the verdicts announced at 2:30 a.m., some newspapers like *Le Figaro* (which had held the presses) were able to run the story in that day's morning editions. The verdicts were also broadcast by radio. Reactions in Limousin and Alsace were swift. By 6:00 p.m., church bells were pealing throughout Alsace in protest at the severity of the verdicts. The ANFM, on the other hand, found the penalties inadequate, and insisted that death would have been the only appropriate sentence. In Germany, Chancellor Konrad Adenauer praised the relatively equal-handed treatment of the German and French defendants, but said that he hoped for clemency.

That weekend there were demonstrations in both Alsace and Limousin. In Alsace, Pierre Pflimlin (an Alsatian deputy and later president of the Council of Ministers) convened a meeting of all the Alsatian deputies except the Communist one, and moved into action. He sent a telegram to René Pleven, the Minister of Defense, requesting that he immediately suspend the judgments against the forcibly inducted Alsatian defendants. Pleven replied by telegram later that day, and advised Pflimlin that for technical reasons the suspension of the judgments was not possible. At the demonstration in Alsace, the monument to the war dead was draped in black (Illustration 59).

He went on to say, however, that he understood that Pflimlin meant to support a bill granting amnesty to those who had been forcibly induct-

59. Strasbourg Monument to WW I Dead draped in black to protest the verdicts.

ed—effectively, completely effacing from those so amnestied not only the penalties but the crime itself—and confirmed that such bill would be granted urgent consideration in the legislature. This was a momentous development, and Pleven's telegram, which became public, restored a measure of calm in Alsace. In Limousin, when the ANFM heard about the movement to seek an amnesty, they composed a letter to the government which listed the actions it would take if one were voted:

1. Return the *Légion d'honneur* awarded to the village of Oradour by President Auriol.
2. Refuse to transfer the ashes of the victims to the crypt built by government.
3. Refuse to accept government representatives at future ceremonies.
4. Display at the entrances to the ruins the names of those in parliament who voted for the amnesty.

The amnesty bill was fiercely debated in the legislature, the press, and the country in general. It was primarily supported by the center and right-wing parties and opposed by the Communists. The Socialists were divided. The essential argument of those who supported the amnesty was that national unity was the overriding consideration. Their opponents' response was that the verdicts against the French/Alsatian defendants had been fairly arrived at, and that the suffering of Alsace was a separate matter. Other arguments against the amnesty, both practical and emotional, can be summarized as follows:

1. Granting amnesty to the Alsatians would violate at least the principle of the constitutionally mandated separation of powers. More simply, it would state that the judges had judged wrongly, and turn the legislature into an appeal court.

2. When the abrogation of the Law of Collective Responsibility had been debated, the Alsatian representatives had said that the purpose of the proposed abrogation was to repeal the collective responsibility concept, and this had been unanimously approved without voting opposition from the Alsatian deputies. More simply, since the French/Alsatian defendants had been found guilty of crimes under the criminal law they should be punished.

3. Favoring one province over another would endanger national unity.

4. Granting amnesty would martyr the victims of Oradour a second time.

5. How could France hope to gain the extradition of General Lammerding and other officers if the Germans and the French were not treated equally?

6. The possibility of Alsace seeking autonomous status was an unspoken and unacceptable premise of the debate.

7. If granting amnesty to the forcibly inducted Alsatians implied that they had been acting against their will, then other collaborators, like those who had served Vichy, would seize on that as a defense. This

argument was popular among ex-*résistants,* a great many of whom were against the amnesty for collaborators or the *malgré nous.*

8. The amnesty bill was part of a surreptitious process of rapprochement with Germany. This could entail a common defense policy, which would allow Germany to rebuild its army. (The Communist argument)

The supporters of the amnesty argued that:

1. The Tribunal had not really listened to the Alsatian witnesses nor understood the real situation of those forcibly inducted. Nor had they really understood the travail Alsace had been through during the war, nor the long history of Alsace/Moselle as intermittently French and German. While being as subtle as possible, they also did not deny any autonomous sentiments—after all such sentiments had been a part of Alsace during different eras—as mentioned earlier in the summary history of Alsace/Moselle.

2. The legislature would not be overruling the Tribunal's decision, but merely considering the matter "on a different level," namely that of national interest.

3. The victims could take out civil actions (albeit against the French state and not the defendants).

4. The 13 Alsatians were part of a larger group, 130,000-strong, whose forcible conscription had been deemed a war crime in the trial of Governor Wagner.

5. The wrong people were tried at Bordeaux, as the officers were not there. One suggestion (not adopted) was to make amnesty conditional on the government achieving the extradition of General Lammerding and the other officers.

6. The word "amnesty" meant "forgetting." To simply "forget" the verdicts was not adequate compensation for the injury done to the honor

of Alsace at Bordeaux. The only acceptable compensation would be a reversal of the conviction. Schreckenberg (lead counsel for the Alsatians) claimed that according to the law faculties of Strasbourg and Bordeaux, the defense had reasonable grounds for pursuing this reversal.

In the end, on Friday, February 20, the Assembly adopted the legislation granting amnesty by a vote of 319 to 211 with 55 abstentions and 28 not voting. The Senate approved by a vote of 174 to 78. The law was printed in the Official Journal on Saturday and became effective on Sunday, February 22.

Having been sentenced to a total of eighty-two years imprisonment a week earlier, the thirteen *malgré nous* were now free to return to Alsace. Not only were they free, the effect of the amnesty was to expunge not only the penalty but any notion that they had committed a crime, although not standing as a reversal of the legal findings as Schreckenberg might have preferred. It is because the amnesty expunged the crime as to these defendants that I have been careful to use only the first name and the first initial of the last name of the *malgré nous* so as to not identify these defendants as the French law provides.

During the night of February 20-21, at 3:30 a.m. four vans left the prison in Bordeaux. While the law technically did not take effect until Sunday, there was no real possibility that it would be changed. The route was kept secret, but the fact that the amnestied Alsatian defendants were returning home was soon common knowledge. The three from the Haut-Rhin were delivered to Mulhouse, while the other ten went to Strasbourg in Bas-Rhin. The receptions, which occurred in the middle of the night, were discreet, with only a handful of officials, lawyers, and family members in attendance.

In Oradour and elsewhere in Limousin, there were demonstrations against the amnesty, and black crepe was placed on the war-memorials. On Sunday, the ANFM refused to join with the Communists in a demonstration in Oradour as they viewed their actions as politically motivated. As the ANFM had warned, they returned the village's *Légion d'honneur* to Paris, took down the marble plaque placed by General de Gaulle at the time of his visit in 1945; covered up the cornerstone of the new town laid by President Auriol in 1947; and, refused to put the ashes in the government-built crypt. They also erected signs (1) Listing the deputies who voted to abrogate the Law of Collective Responsibility (2)

The members of parliament who voted for amnesty and (3) The names of the thirteen *malgré nous* and their sentences (technically a violation of French law in light of the amnesty).

It goes without saying that there was no "right" answer to the amnesty question. At bottom, the issue was whether the threat to national unity was great enough to warrant the overriding of the judicial decision. It was possible that if the appeals had been allowed to run their course, the French/Alsatians might have had their judgments reversed. As Schreckenberg said, there were valid bases for appeals. Given the gravity of the massacre and the comprehensive nature of the proceedings, however, the Supreme Court might have elected to let the Tribunal's verdicts stand. After the Liberation, de Gaulle had been faced with an even more complex problem: how to balance the return to normalcy with the country's need to punish collaborators. Government sources originally estimated the number of collaborators executed by the Resistance after the war at nearly 100,000, although that figure was later regarded as way too high, with 10,000 the more likely number. In the event, de Gaulle had sanctioned the trials of Pétain and Laval and other prominent collaborators, but retained most of the civil servants who had served under Vichy.

The political battle over the fate of *Les Douze* was played out in the shadow of the upcoming spring municipal and legislative elections, and it is arguable that the factors which finally tilted the balance in favor of the amnesty were that Alsace was prosperous, well-populated and politically conservative, while the Limousin was poor, sparsely populated and Communist. There were also concerns about the unspoken threat of Alsatian separatism. If one more judge had voted for acquittal, the *malgré nous* would have left the trial free men, and perhaps the amnesty was a means of adding that one vote. But no decision would have given universal satisfaction, delivered uncontestable justice, or healed the wounds of Oradour. The final decision came down on the side of expediency and, in the eyes of de Gaulle and the legislature, at least, the greater good of France.

EPILOGUE

Chapter 26

The Oradour Mysteries Examined

Three principal mysteries surround the annihilation of Oradour. Why did the massacre occur? Why did it occur at Oradour rather than elsewhere? And, by whose order was it carried out? Arguably the easiest of these questions to answer is: why did the SS annihilate the village? The answer is that they wished to terrorize the Resistance and the civilian population of the region, and to discourage any further attacks on the Division and the German occupation forces in general. In the days following the Normandy invasion, the Resistance had made its presence felt very effectively. *Maquisards* had attacked the garrisons in Tulle and Guéret, harried the Division on its way north (Bretenoux), stepped up attacks on railroads and bridges (St. Junien), captured Kämpfe and Gerlach, and inflicted considerable damage on the morale of the German troops. All of this had to be stopped. There is also evidence that a secondary purpose of the operation was to 'blood' the comparatively raw Alsatian recruits, and to test Kahn's ability to lead the battalion, as he had to do after Diekmann was killed only a few days later.

Leaving aside the fictitious reasons for the Oradour massacre invented by the Germans and other revisionists, the massacre was clearly designed to intimidate. It was not a unique incident, but one that was typical of actions on the Eastern Front and on a smaller scale in the Ardennes and in Italy, notably the massacre of 560 people by the SS in the village of Santanna di Stazzema on August 14, 1944.

On the question of why the massacre was committed, Ecto O. Munn stated in his report that:

"The more plausible theory is that the S.S. [the Division] and the Gestapo wished to strike terror into the entire countryside in order to prevent uprisings such as had occurred at Tulle two days before and also in order to discourage the felling of trees across the roads and the blowing up of bridges which were seriously delaying the movement of the Division to the Normandy front."

Further confirmation of the operation's objectives comes from two reports by the Division relative to Oradour. The first noted that, "One operation of the Division Das Reich in the region near Limoges provoked an emotional reaction from the population." The second, dated four days later, observed that, "The action had a favorable influence on the morale of the troops."

Why Oradour? The various claims made by the Germans after the event—that a German medical unit had been attacked outside the village; that the Third Company had been shot at as it passed by; that the village harbored the *maquis*, and that Kämpfe was a captive there—were obvious fictions. According to Georges Guingouin and others, the idea of carrying out a major operation against the civilian population had been discussed by the SS several days before the massacre, although it appears that no specific target had been identified. If such an operation was contemplated before the early evening of June 9, that would eliminate the idea that it was a reprisal for the capture of Kämpfe.

There has been much speculation about when Oradour was selected for destruction. A probable time seems to have been around 9:00 a.m. the morning of the 10th at Division headquarters in Limoges or possibly at the meeting convened by Diekmann later that morning in St. Junien. The earliest time would have been the day before, either when Gerlach was sent to Nieul to secure billeting for the Third Company for the nights of the 10th and 11th or, more likely at a meeting of the Milice later in the day.

Testimony at the trial also described an attack on the Resistance at the Chateau de Morcheval near Nieul on the 11th by the Third Company. So when Gerlach was sent to Nieul on the 9th, the move from St. Junien was a logical precursor to an operation against the local *maquis* at the Chateau de Morcheval or against the village of Oradour, or both. When the question arose as to which village would be annihilated, issues of size and location made the choice of Oradour perfectly logical. It was midway between St. Junien and Nieul and of modest size, about 1,500 inhabitants. The Division was critically short of fuel so the short distance involved was important; the Company had been commandeering every available fuel supply in St. Junien and had been obliged to requisition two trucks (of the slow coal-gas variety) to bring bread and the baggage to Nieul that night. Probably Diekmann had hoped to save space for looted goods in the Division's own trucks.

As Diekmann would have discovered from the Milice and Gestapo, Oradour had no active Resistance, was of a manageable size, and was relatively well supplied with food and valuables. Moreover, as the historian Jean-Jacques Fouché has demonstrated, the Germans and the Milice were obsessive in their pursuit of Communists and Jews, classifying all such people as terrorists, whether active or not. There were several Communists and Jews in Oradour under German and Milice surveillance and it is possible that their presence figured in the choice. That said, Diekmann's briefing outside Oradour stated that the aim of the operation was to annihilate the whole village. There was no mention then, or subsequently of any attempt to single out Communists or Jews, or to search for Major Kämpfe, the *maquis,* or munitions.

Munn rejected the theory that Oradour-sur-Glane was mistaken for Oradour-sur-Vayres. In part that was on the basis of the testimony he took from a Resistance leader named Colonel Rousselier who said that Oradour-sur-Vayres was a larger village and close to the Division line of march as they came up from the south. Accordingly, Rousselier concluded that the idea the Division did not know it was there was improbable. In addition, he noted that the Gestapo which was well established in Limoges was thoroughly familiar with the surrounding villages.

So if not a mistake, what? Munn opined that:

"Oradour-sur-Glane, though small, was rather well known; its restaurants and shops were better than average; a few visitors from Paris spent the summer there; it was prosperous and worth looting. Besides, it was situated off the main road and easily controlled. Therefore, if an impression was to be made on the countryside, it would serve as well as any other place."

Munn interrogated a German officer, Hauptmann H. Schmidt, in a prison camp near Limoges. Schmidt had been attached to Verbindungstab (a liaison group), which had offices in the Hotel Central in Limoges where the Division Das Reich was headquartered. From Schmidt, Munn learned the identity of the unit that carried out the massacre. From other sources he learned the identities of Lammerding, Stadler and Diekmann (whose name he had correctly spelled albeit at the trial and even at the museum of the Centre de la Mémoire at Oradour to this day it is misspelled "Dickmann"). Copies of photos of Lammerding and Stadler as well as capsule biographies were attached to Munn's report.

Who ordered the massacre, and where does ultimate responsibility rest for Oradour? First, it is clear that orders from the German High Command provided the predicate for the annihilation of Oradour. Sperrle's February 1944 and June 5 orders encouraged severe measures against partisans and the civilian population. General Lammerding elaborated on these, as can be seen from his memo to General Kruger outlining the "brutal" tactics he intended to employ.

According to the German historian, Professor Ahlrich Meyer, Kahn claimed that he had been ordered to destroy the village by Diekmann. In his book, *The German Occupation of France*, Meyer quotes from a statement made by Kahn to German authorities on December 13, 1962. According to this statement Kahn arrived at mid-day on June 9. While he and his section heads were resting in a hotel, a liaison officer arrived, and told Kahn that Diekmann wanted to see him. When the two were face-to-face, according to Kahn, Diekmann said, "There is an order you are to execute, the destruction of the village of Oradour." I have checked the original wording with several German speakers who all agree that where the order came from is not clear from the statement. Kahn claimed that he had questioned the order and had suggested that Diekmann clarify it with the regiment; but Diekmann, Kahn said, had become angry, and had simply ordered him to prepare the operation.

In the course of his deposition, and despite the fact that Alsatian defendants had identified him as having played a particularly bloody role at Oradour, Kahn made several efforts to portray himself as a "good German." He claimed that after the men had been shot at Oradour, he had asked Diekmann, "Why kill the women and children. Isn't there enough blood already?"

Diekmann's response had been that it was out of the question not to finish the job. In judging this claim of Kahn's, one should bear in mind the witness at Bordeaux who said that an Alsatian woman had asked an Alsatian SS soldier to ask Kahn to let her out of the church, in response to which Kahn had brutally replied that he did not want any surviving witnesses.

There is no evidence that either Diekmann or Kahn ever claimed that the order had come from the regiment or the Division. After the war, Lammerding, Stadler, and Weidinger all claimed that Diekmann alone decided upon the massacre. Professor Meyer concludes that only a divisional or regimental commander could have ordered the massacre. In my opinion, it is probable that Lammerding or Stadler either gave a direct order to Diekmann or employed the indirect method of telling him that something drastic had to be done, and leaving him to use his imagination. Given that all concerned had seen service on the Eastern Front, it would not have taken a great deal of imagination on Diekmann's part to conclude what kind of action they had in mind.

What is beyond question is that in any war crimes trial, the irrefutable evidence of the general orders and prior actions like Frayssinet, the Tulle hangings, and the other actions against civilians would have been sufficient to convict Lammerding and Stadler. Their story vis-à-vis Oradour was that they had ordered Diekmann only to take hostages to trade for Kämpfe. When they learned what had happened, they claimed they had initiated a court-martial investigation against Diekmann which was only terminated upon his death. I note that the evidence showed that through motorcycle messengers to Limoges and St. Junien from Oradour, both Division and Battalion headquarters were kept informed. Given that no action was taken at the time to punish Diekmann, to relieve him of his command, or to curtail his actions in any way, the claims that he acted on his own cannot be viewed as credible. Moreover, the Germans already had more than enough hostages under their control in Limoges as demonstrated by Lammerding's offer to trade a significant number for Kämpfe.

In 1968, when asked by the French authors, Georges Beau and Léopold Gaubusseau, whether he considered himself responsible for the murders at Tulle and Oradour, given that he had commanded the Division that carried them out, Lammerding replied that he could not be held responsible for orders issued by his subordinates. While it is probably correct that an officer heading a chain of command is not *ipso facto* liable to prosecution for a subordinate's crime, the issuing of general orders authorizing such crimes such as those which Lammerding had issued would certainly justify a conviction. Lammerding had been condemned to death *in absentia* for Tulle and twice more for the actions of the Division.

In summary, the Division determined that a drastic action would serve the double purpose of safeguarding its passage north and of carrying out its orders to employ brutal measures against the Resistance and those who supported them. The annihilation of a village, furthermore, was a familiar exercise to the officers from the Eastern Front. Given the geography and the fact that a company-size unit was selected to carry out the operation, Oradour provided the ideal target. It simply fell to Diekmann and Kahn to carry it out.

Chapter 27

A Concluding Note about the Oradour Trial

My two strongest criticisms of the trial are that it took too long to convene, and that no officers were convoked to answer for the massacre. On the first point, it is clear that for obvious reasons, the judicial machinery was in disarray in the years immediately after the war. Resources were inadequate and there was a backlog of cases to deal with. As the war itself had receded into the past, other considerations had come into play, such as the intensification of the Cold War, the concomitant desire for détente with Germany, and a more general wish to consign the occupation and the war to history. For those involved in the Oradour tragedy, however, there would be no forgetting. In Limousine the failure of the military justice system to punish the known perpetrators was insupportable. In Alsace, there was continuing frustration at the rest of country's failure to understand what the region had suffered after Vichy had abandoned it to a German Governor.

As to the second issue, the general post-war turmoil and lack of resources clearly aided the escape of the officers. While the U.S. alone extradited over 2,000 German prisoners from German prison camps to France for trial in the 1947-1949 period, most remaining prisoners of war were released at the end of that period. The UK and Germany, meanwhile, agreed in 1948 not to process any extradition requests unless incontrovertible proof existed that the subject of the request was responsible for murder. The French later used that agreement as an excuse for why they had not submitted a formal extradition request to the UK for Lammerding who lived in their zone. They also claimed that until he sent a letter to the Bordeaux Tribunal in late 1952, they had not known where he lived. Christopher Weber in his 2004 TV documentary showed Lammerding's listing in the Dusseldorf phonebook of the era. In any event, no extradition requests were ever served in relation to the officers responsible until after the trial. That fact undoubtedly changed the nature of the proceedings, and probably resulted in greater penalties being imposed on the defendants in the Oradour trial than would have otherwise been the case.

At the same time, as I noted earlier, the Bordeaux trial was a model of procedure compared to most of the earlier French war crimes trials, which had been virtually summary. In terms of placing responsibility on individual defendants, the trial had produced little evidence that was not in the investigatory files—indeed, some of that evidence was contradicted by the defendants. The trial had also failed to elicit any request for forgiveness, although some defendants expressed regrets at having participated in the massacre.

The principal legal construct to emerge from the trial was the government's contention that while obedience to orders was a fundamental requirement in any army, it did not apply when the required action was manifestly criminal or constituted a flagrant war crime. All seven judges apparently accepted that view vis-à-vis the Germans. While those defendants were unable to avail themselves of the obedience defense under the 1944 Law, as the trial turned out, it was the Penal Code that was applied and the obedience defense was applicable although it was not sustained.

As for the Alsatian *malgré nous*, the 5-2 votes for conviction suggest that two judges would have accepted that forcible induction was a valid defense—it being the only general distinction from the Germans. As far as the seven judges were concerned obedience to orders was a valid defense neither for the Germans nor the Alsatians in the case of a flagrant war crime. As M. Hébras replied when I asked whether he agreed with Gardon, "While such a construct was admirable in theory, it was hardly practical in the case of unsophisticated and in many cases teenaged soldiers."

My own view is that it was helpful for the Tribunal to articulate such a construct and to find the defendants guilty under it, because it provided a lesson for the future. While it is debatable whether the defendants knew that certain orders (like those relating to the firing squads) were in flagrant violation of criminal or international law, no defense would have been possible if they had obeyed orders to fire into the church and to burn women and children alive.

The trial helped to broadcast to the world the immorality of using the killing of civilians as a military strategy. While one can certainly argue where the line should be drawn (for example where civilians are inevitably going to be killed in a military operation), the Oradour massacre was an unambiguous case.

I'd like to talk about the Alsatian defense. It was based primarily on the assertion that "but for" their forcible induction into the Waffen SS, which was itself a crime, the Alsatians would not have been at Oradour, and thus should be acquitted. In American law, and from what I am told, in French law as well, this kind of "but for" notion of causation is generally not valid, even in civil law. That is, but for being forcibly inducted (a crime) the Alsatians would not be guilty of anything they did at Oradour (or elsewhere) because "but for" the original crime they would not even have been there.

The Alsatian defense also claimed duress to which forcible induction combined with the regime in the Waffen SS was relevant. Here the prosecutor clearly had some difficulty. To negate duress he cited the Alsatians' failure to desert until Normandy. The response was that desertion had not been possible until the Alsatians were in a war zone where their absence could be attributed to death or capture, and before that they could not have deserted because the French were afraid to aid someone in an SS uniform. The prosecutor also attempted to show by anecdotal evidence of the soldiers' high spirits that they were not under duress, but he was unable to link such behavior to any specific defendant. Should the Alsatian defense have pressed harder on that weak point in the prosecution's case, and if they had done so, would they have prevailed? Given the gravity of the crime and the fact that the case concerned Frenchmen killing their fellow citizens, I do not think so, although it might have contributed to a reversal on appeal.

The Tribunal did not greatly concern itself with the issue of whether the Resistance should have been treated as the internal army of France and so protected by the Geneva and Hague Conventions (as de Gaulle had specifically demanded of the Germans). Ideally, fighting men or women in the Resistance (or comparable militias) should wear identifying uniforms or armbands, although obviously that was not feasible in the case of clandestine Resistance operators in towns and cities. Even for a *maquisard*-type fighter, I recognize that wearing uniforms or even armbands would deprive them of the advantages of not wearing such identification and might not avail them of the protections of the Conventions in any event. In a more perfect world, the resolution of the dilemma would be to make clear that even non-identified militia or spies are entitled to some kind of legal process and not summary execution, as even the Germans 10 point instructions to soldiers provided.

As to whether the Alsatians were murderers or victims or both, I leave it to the reader to decide. The fact that they were convicted points to the view that they were murderers, or aiders and abettors. The amnesty, however, although fundamentally a political act, had the effect of providing the extra vote that would have resulted in acquittals, perhaps based on the notion that their being forcibly inducted was an attenuating circumstance especially when paired with the argument of duress.

The Alsatians felt at the time, and some still feel today, that the trial was somewhat detached from reality, and that President Nussy Saint-Saëns was both biased against the defendants and ignorant of the suffering of Alsace under annexation. There were certainly criticisms of Nussy Saint-Saëns' conduct of the proceedings in the press, although they tended to reflect the emotions of the two opposing sides, especially the Communists and the Alsatians. Of perhaps greater concern, are the well-informed and thoughtful criticisms of him by Jean-Jacques Fouché and others. Fouché, in his book on the trial *Oradour La Politique et la Justice*, comments that the president seemed at times insensitive to witnesses, did not ask critical follow-up questions, seemed more interested in determining the composition of the different units within the Third Company than the crimes themselves, and failed to convoke several key witnesses such as Guingouin, the *milicien* Davoine and certain of the judicial police.

I acknowledge the validity of such criticisms. However, my overall view of President Nussy Saint-Saëns' conduct of the trial is that he did a credible job. Account must be taken of the historical context, the lack of resources available to the investigatory arm of the judiciary of which Nussy Saint-Saëns was himself very critical. Most importantly, there was a highly charged political atmosphere due to the presence of the *malgré nous* defendants. Finally, when one compares the Oradour trial to the virtually summary tribunals that had preceded this one, such as Tulle it stands out. No doubt the length and seriousness of the trial was largely attributable to the presence of the Alsatian *malgré nous* defendants and the top-flight nature of both the Alsatian and German counsel.

From the point of view of the Oradour survivors, justice was not served by the trial, let alone the amnesty. The two NCOs were sentenced to death. However, they received a reduction of their sentences to life imprisonment via a presidential pardon a few years later. Objectively speaking, the real injustice was that none of the officers responsible for Oradour faced trial at Bordeaux. It is ironic that it was the Communists in East Germany—almost forty years after the crime—who meted out the only punishment to an officer who participated in the massacre (Heinz Barth). Ironic, because it seemed to have been done at least in part as a propaganda ploy in the Cold War while (West) Germany and France were by then staunch allies (see the description of the Barth trial in East Berlin below).

President Marcel Nussy Saint-Saëns started the trial by saying that, "The real issue on trial here is Hitlerism," which was certainly true. At the same time, it is possible with the advantage of more than sixty years of distance (and history) to recognize that the Oradour massacre was an example of the way in which war almost inevitably brings out the worst in mankind. An even more disheartening view is held by some that it is human nature to act violently, and especially where acting under authority or out of fear. One does not have to accept that view to see that trials of those committing crimes against humanity serve to remind us that such behavior is abhorrent and at least risks punishment.

Returning to Oradour, my verdict on the massacre is that it was a military operation calculated to intimidate the civilian population and the Resistance. The preservation of the Oradour ruins has provided a unique memorial which annually impresses and educates hundreds of thousands of visitors. The 1953 trial represents another kind of memorial, access to which is obtained through books such as this, which I can only hope will serve in some way to discourage such crimes against humanity, and act as a reminder that obedience to orders is not a legitimate defense to such flagrant crimes.

Chapter 28

Aftermath

The Prisoners

Karl Lenz and **Georges René Boos** had their death sentences commuted by presidential pardon a few years after the verdicts. By 1959, they and all the other defendants were out of prison. This treatment was as much a matter of turning the page on the war as it was détente with the (West) Germans since most of the collaborators had also been freed by that time. Boos gave testimony to German judicial authorities in 1962, 1977 and 1979. In 1962, he said that Oradour had been intended as an initiation for the Alsatians, to prepare them for fighting in Normandy. In later depositions, the only fresh observation that he made about Oradour was that in his opinion, it had been a mistake to use raw recruits like the Alsatians because they got in the way of professionals like him. Although he took German citizenship when he left prison, and lived in Germany for sometime afterwards, he kept his French citizenship and is rumored to have returned to Alsace before he died.

The Oradour Survivors

Marguerite Rouffranche, who was forty-seven years old at the time of the massacre, lived to the age of ninety-one. Her significance as the sole survivor of the church can hardly be overstated. Her precise and indisputable testimony that the SS brought in and set off the explosives was essential. The German version, still purveyed by some revisionists, that the church blew up because of munitions stocked by the Resistance, would have been difficult to disprove otherwise.

Roger Godfrin, the only child who escaped from the school, died in 2001.

Robert Hébras and **Marcel Darthout** are very much alive and I see them from time to time. They are most interested in learning any new facts that come from my research and are patient in answering my questions. Each year, Hébras and Darthout speak at conferences and address many thousands of visitors to Oradour from France and neighboring countries. Many of these visitors are teenagers. Hébras and Darthout did not choose to make this their life work, but they do it willingly for their families and friends who did not survive. As they both say, they are no longer angry, but neither do they forget. They forgive the Germans, but can never forgive the Nazis.

The Germans

General Heinz Lammerding, the Division commander, was wounded in the kidney and the legs by a shell explosion on July 25 or 26, 1944 in Normandy. After hospitalization, he resumed his command in mid-October until January 1945, when he became the chief of staff of the Army of the Vistula (commanded by Heinrich Himmler). After Easter 1945, he was made commander of the SS Division Niebelung. According to an affidavit that he filed with German judicial authorities in 1962, Lammerding was captured by the Americans on May 2, 1945, put in a prison camp in Bavaria, but released relatively soon thereafter. He had used his real name but had concealed his rank and position. When he got to Düsseldorf, he obtained his identity card from the UK zone officials in his own name. In another statement, however, he said that he was taken by the Americans in civilian clothes in a hospital and released two hours later.

The recent declassification of some eight million U.S. intelligence services' records has brought to light a cold-blooded crime for which Lammerding was directly responsible. In a conversation among

German officers, secretly recorded by the British in February 1945 in a POW camp, Lieutenant Colonel Friedrich August Freiherr von der Heydte, commander of the Sixth Airborne Regiment, recounted how he captured two American doctors in Normandy. They were from the First American Paratroop Division. He handed them over to the Division Das Reich (to which his unit was attached), at which point they were summarily shot. Incredulous, von der Heydte asked the Division commander (Lammerding) why he had ordered the doctors' executions, and Lammerding replied: "One looked so Jewish and the other wasn't up to much either." Von der Heydte also described how an unnamed narrator had told him that in return for the murder of two SS men, an entire village (whose name he did not recall) had been annihilated. "Just imagine our bad luck when it turned out that it wasn't that village at all where the SS men had been shot," the narrator said with a smile.

After the war, Lammerding lived openly in Düsseldorf running his own construction business (the state of North Rhine Westphalia was his biggest client). Although he was not a defendant even *in absentia* at the Oradour trial, as noted above, he had three times been condemned to death *in absentia* by the Bordeaux Tribunal for other war crimes.

In addition to the aforementioned 1962 affidavit, Lammerding, Stückler, and Otto Weidinger gave an extraordinary interview in July 1968 to the French writers, Georges Beau and Léopold Gaubusseau. Except for minor details, the interview conforms to Lammerding's affidavit. He admitted that the Resistance had slowed the Division in its march northward to Normandy, but pointed out that even after they arrived on June 17, the Division was held in reserve for several days. As for Tulle, Lammerding continued to maintain that he did not arrive there until after the executions. Significantly, he admitted that events would not have changed had he arrived earlier, except that he would have ordered the hostages shot rather than hanged.

Why was Lammerding never extradited to France to be tried for the crimes at Tulle or Oradour? A reason often put forth by the French is that he was somehow protected from extradition by the United States. In his 1962 affidavit, Lammerding stated that at the time of the Bordeaux trial, when demands for his extradition had begun to intensify, his lawyer was negotiating with the Americans to gain permission for him to go to the U.S. zone (in Schleswig-Holstein), which he subsequently did.

It is a well-established fact that the U.S. employed ex-Nazis during the Cold War. Klaus Barbie, the former Gestapo chief charged with suppressing the Resistance and deporting Jews, (he was known as the "Butcher of Lyon") was quite clearly protected by the Americans. Although condemned to death *in absentia* by the French in 1947, he was recruited by an American Intelligence department the same year, and ran an extensive network reporting on former SS officers, French intelligence, and other matters. In 1951, the U.S. provided Barbie with a false identity and helped install him in Boliva, where the Nazi hunter, Beate Klarsfeld, eventually discovered him. Recently declassified U.S. intelligence files show that the U.S. obstructed attempts to identify Barbie for over ten years before his extradition in 1983. Barbie was finally tried in 1987. He was convicted, sentenced to life imprisonment and died in 1991.

With respect to Lammerding, in my view, the French were largely to blame. They made little or no attempt to seek his extradition during the active extradition period between 1947 and 1949. As Lux pointed out at the trial, the Alsatian members of parliament had questioned the government in early 1953 and found that no demand for extradition had been made which left them incredulous. At the time of the Bordeaux trial in 1953, a request for Lammerding's extradition was presented by M. René Pleven, to the British Ambassador in France and to the British High Commissioner in Bonn, but this extradition was requested relative to Tulle, not Oradour. The citizens of Tulle took the position that the notice of the hangings "By the Commanding General" (Lammerding), constituted proof of murder so it fell within the exception to which the UK and West Germany had agreed. However, the point was disputed, not least by Lammerding himself. He said that if he had issued the order personally, he would have used his own name. Had the story of the shooting of the two American doctors been known at that time, there would have been a strong case for extradition even under the German/UK accord of 1948, given that the doctors were military officers, not Resistance members.

On February 12, 1953, a meeting took place between Secretaries of State Georges Bidault of France and Anthony Eden of Great Britain, in the course of which Eden stated that he had never heard of Lammerding and saw little chance of extraditing him. He added the next day that he could not understand why the French could not lay this terrible chapter in their history to rest, given that the war had been over for eight years. On February 18, Pleven attempted to explain the Lammerding situation to the National Assembly; but his attempt to lay the blame at the door of the British was swiftly proved specious when the British demonstrated that no request for extradition of the former general had ever been received—a fact which the French were unable to deny. On February 27, after the trial was over, the British authorities in Germany, did, in fact, issue an order for Lammerding's arrest. At that point, the general and his wife left Düsseldorf to go into hiding in Schleswig-Holstein in the American zone. Later attempts to extradite him were fruitless because the West German constitution, which went into effect in 1954, prevented extradition.

A previously unpublished photo of Lammerding taken just a few years before he died is shown here (Illustration 60). He died on January 16, 1971 and his funeral drew several hundred former SS officers, including Otto Weidinger.

60. Previously unpublished photo of Lammerding a few short years before his death.

Former Captain **Otto Kahn** took command of the First Battalion of the Regiment Der Führer when Diekmann was killed in Normandy on June 29. He was wounded in August (he lost an arm), was hospitalized, and then served in a non-combatant role in Czechoslovakia until the end of the war. He was imprisoned by the Russians but released at the end of 1945. Thereafter, he lived for a time in Austria before moving to Münster in the British zone of West Germany. There is no evidence that he fled to Sweden, as was claimed at the trial. Kahn was twice condemned to death *in absentia* in France for his war crimes: once in February 1949 for his part in the Frayssinet affair, and once by the Bordeaux Tribunal for Oradour. These sentences notwithstanding, he died in Germany on April 14 1977 of natural causes. It appears that no request for extradition relating to Kahn was ever made.

Former Second Lieutenant **Heinz Barth** was arrested on June 14, 1981 in the town of Gransee in East Germany. He was sixty years old and living under his own name. Recent research by Andrea Erkenbrecher, a German academic, reveals that the Communist authorities there had learned of Barth's whereabouts and participation in the Oradour massacre at least ten years earlier when his son had filed papers and been required to list information about his family. The authorities even located a witness (not an officer) who had also been at Oradour and had been condemned to death *in absentia* at the Bordeaux trial. Notwithstanding this information, no action was taken against Barth or the witness until Barth's arrest in 1981.

In 1982, Robert Hébras received a visit from a gendarme who showed him a picture of a German officer and asked if he (Hébras) recognized him. Hébras said he did not. The gendarme explained that the officer was Heinz Barth, and shortly afterwards, Hébras, Darthout and other Oradour survivors traveled to East Berlin to testify at his trial. When an elderly man came limping into the courtroom with a cane (Illustration 61), Hébras found it hard to think of him as an assassin. After Hébras had given his testimony, he asked the judge to question Barth about what

61. Heinz Barth at his 1983 trial in East Berlin.

happened on the night of June 10 in the Dupic house, which was not burned down until the next day. It was thought that it had been used by the SS to rape some of the women of the village, and Hébras was anxious to discover whether his sister, Georgette, then twenty-two years old, had been one of the victims. Barth said that he did not know; that he had left Oradour around 9:00 p.m. for Nieul and had never come back. Darthout had the impression that the Communists were using the trial to demonstrate that they were more diligent than the West in punishing Nazi war criminals. Barth was convicted and sentenced to life imprisonment.

In 1989, while still a prisoner, Barth gave an interview to a German TV documentary team. The interviewer was aggressive in his questioning and Barth appeared to respond quite openly. When the Third Company stopped just outside Oradour, he said, Diekmann and Kahn had a short meeting with the officers and NCOs, telling them that they were going to encircle the village and "annihilate it." This was the first that any of them had heard of such a plan.

The TV interviewer also asked Barth about events in Czechoslovakia following the assassination in May 1942 of SS General Reinhard Heydrich. In reprisal for Heydrich's killing, the Germans conducted a massacre of civilians at Lidice, where the supposed authors of the assassination came from. While Barth said that he did not participate in the Lidice massacre, he admitted being assigned to a firing squad during reprisals nearby. He had asked to be excused this duty, he said, but had been told that he could not hope to be an officer if he declined, so had agreed to participate. He was twenty-one years old. Between that time and Oradour, he had spent time on the Eastern Front.

When pressed by the interviewer as to whether he had regretted what he had done at Oradour, Barth said that he mostly tried to forget about it. Oradour, he said, had been no worse than similar actions that he had seen on the Eastern Front. While he acknowledged his guilt, he considered a life sentence harsh (at that point he was already sixty-nine years old). Barth was released from prison in 1997 on the grounds of age and health (he was seventy-seven years old), having served fourteen years, more than any of the men of the Third Company. Having successfully appealed against a denial of his war pension, Barth saw the dawning of the twenty-first century before he died.

Otto Weidinger was attached to the Division on its march northward from Montauban as a commander in waiting. He took over the Regiment Der Führer from Stadler on June 14, 1944, when the latter was promoted and transferred. His only admitted involvement in Tulle or Oradour occurred when he was sent to Tulle from Brive in the middle of the night of June 8-9 to get a report, as other means of communication had broken down. Weidinger wrote a history of the Regiment Der Führer entitled (in English) *Comrades to the End*. The book repeats many of the German inventions about Oradour including the assertions that a German medical unit was found murdered just outside Oradour; that the Third Company was met with fire from *résistants* in Oradour when they arrived; that Resistance munitions were stored in the church; and that Diekmann had been approached by two collaborators who informed him that a German officer was being held in Oradour and was going to be executed. Kahn and Barth stated quite firmly in their post-war depositions to German authorities, that there were no German soldier's bodies or German vehicles found at Oradour, that no one had fired on them from the village, and that no search for Kämpfe had taken place there, and that the SS had set the explosives in the church.

In Weidinger's view, the use of Alsatians in France was a mistake because of their French loyalties. He also claimed that after Oradour, the Germans had intercepted a message from *maquis* headquarters calling for a cessation of attacks on Germans until the Division Das Reich had left central France. While there is no evidence that any such message was sent, it is also the case that there were no significant Resistance operations mounted against the Division as it moved north.

U.S. intelligence files show that Weidinger was extradited from the American zone on August 12, 1947, pursuant to a French request. This shows that where German officers were held in POW camps, the French asked for extradition which was routinely granted. In Lammerding and Kahn's cases where they were at liberty in Germany, the French either did not have the resources or the initiative to seek them out. Weidinger and a number of ex-Division Das Reich members were located by a French Commission in various Allied prison camps and, ironically, assembled at the Nazi concentration camp at Dachau 12 miles north of Munich, from where they were transported to a French prison. In June 1951, about four years after arriving in France, Weidinger along with seventy-six others was tried and acquitted (of association with a criminal organization) by the Bordeaux Military Tribunal, after which he was released and returned to Germany. Over 100 other SS members were discharged for lack of evidence, while fifteen were convicted. Weidinger died in Würzburg in 1990.

Sylvester Stadler, an Austrian, was the thirty-three-year-old commanding officer of the Regiment Der Führer at the time of Oradour. In his December 1962 deposition to German judicial authorities, he stated that he had ordered Diekmann to search for Major Kämpfe and to take significant hostages to use in exchange for him. Stadler was condemned to death *in absentia* by the Bordeaux Tribunal on July 10, 1951. U.S. intelligence files indicate that France had requested his extradition from the U.S. on February 10, 1947. A later notation showed that his file was closed "administratively" on January 31, 1948, with no further explanation. Note that Schreckenberg said that the French had the opportunity to arrest Stadler in Vienna and failed to do so. He was never tried in person in France, and in 1995 he died in Austria.

The Alsatian *Malgré Nous*

Only three of the *malgré nous* defendants, **Paul G.**, **Henri W.**, and **Albert D.**, are alive at the time of this writing, but they no longer grant interviews.

The President and the Lawyers

Marcel Nussy Saint-Saëns remained president of the Bordeaux Military Tribunal until 1955. Afterwards, he served on various courts of appeal, and ended his active judicial career as president of the Court of Appeals in Montpellier (1970-73). A cultured and literary figure, he wrote a wide variety of historical papers, including discourses on the Cathars and on the traditions and customs of the Basques, for which the Académie Française awarded him a prize in 1965. So far as I know, he never wrote about the Oradour trial.

Gratien Gardon, the prosecutor, was attached to the military justice headquarters of the army from 1954 to 1956. In 1957, he became the legal advisor of General Salan, commander of the French army in Algeria, for much of the eight-year war (1954-1962) against the *Front de libération nationale* (FLN). According to certain (not necessarily credible) sources, Gardon provided the legal support for the use of torture by the French during that war. In 1958, he became Inspector of Military Justice in Algeria. General Salan led the attempted putsch against the

De Gaulle government after the later granted Algeria independence, but Gardon was not implicated.

M. Richard Lux. In late February 2006, my wife and I were received by M. Lux and his wife at their apartment in Strasbourg. M. Lux is probably the only surviving lawyer who participated in the trial in Bordeaux. M. Louis Oster, whom we also met, was a law clerk for Mr. Schreckenberg at the time, but was not present at the trial. M. Lux supplied many interesting details, including the fact that, although the Tribunal voted anonymously, he learned that the two judges who voted for the acquittal of the Alsatian *malgré nous* were the highest ranking of the six officers. Because of their seniority, M. Lux thought they had the objectivity and the courage to differ from their colleagues (including the president).

On another point, he recalled that what he said to Boos, which the latter had misunderstood, was that he was making a mistake not to present any witnesses for himself—clearly not meant as a threat.

In general, M. Lux still feels that in terms of the *malgré nous*, the trial was a miscarriage of justice and argued in a radio broadcast on the occasion of the 50th anniversary of the trial that there should be a retrial. Surprisingly, given M. Lux's Communist background and disappointment at the conviction of his clients, he characterized Gardon and his conduct of the trial as objective, sagacious, and conscientious. When I asked M. Lux about the claim that Nussy Saint-Saëns had made a Freudian slip at the beginning of the trial and said, "Bring in the guilty," he did not have any recollection of it. Had it occurred, I would have thought it would have been a subject of conversation among the lawyers at the time, especially the Alsatian ones. In summary, M. Lux feels strongly that the French (and especially Nussy Saint-Saëns) had no appreciation then or now of what the Alsatians had been through under the German annexation.

The Resistance Leader Guingouin

On August 12, 1944, less than two months after Oradour, **Georges Guingouin** led a Resistance group against Limoges. They surrounded the town, and on August 22, General Gleiniger, commander of the 586th Wehrmacht headquarters garrison, capitulated. Many of the

Germans escaped, taking Gleiniger with them. He was later assassinated by the Gestapo for surrendering and dumped in the garbage pit of a cemetery.

Three months later, Guingouin was badly injured in an automobile accident but recovered in time to receive a medal as a *"Compagnon de la Libération"* from de Gaulle and was elected mayor of Limoges from 1945-1947. Later, however, he fell from favor with the French Communist Party leadership. A tract entitled "Document on the Actions of the Renegade Guingouin" was circulated and he was expelled from the party in 1952. Having served on a Resistance tribunal that ordered the execution of several dozen collaborators at the time of the Liberation, the former Resistance leader was disingenuously accused by the Communists of participating in their murder. The bitterness surrounding these events may explain why Guingouin was not called as a witness at the Oradour trial. As a result of the accusations against him by fellow Communists, Guingouin was arrested on Christmas Eve, 1953. He was imprisoned at Brive, and in February 1954, he survived an assassination attempt by two prison guards at least one of whom was a Communist. He had already survived two other assassination attempts. Although he was released from prison later that year, the legal process continued until 1959, when the case against him was dropped. Roland Dumas, who later became Foreign Minister under François Mitterrand, represented Guingouin. Guingouin thereafter resumed his profession as a teacher.

In 1995, Guingouin wrote a paper to the *Centre de la Mémoire* at Oradour. In it, he stated that on June 10, Lammerding had used a *résistant* who was a prisoner in Limoges (one Fernand Laudoueneix), to contact him. Lammerding had offered to release fifty prisoners in exchange for Kämpfe. Guingouin said that he had considered the offer acceptable, but that just as he was about to signal his agreement, the news of the Oradour massacre had reached him. From that moment onward, Guingouin said it had been impossible to accept Lammerding's offer, and Kämpfe (along with a German policeman) was executed by the Resistance shortly thereafter. In March 2005, Georges Guingouin was made a *Commandeur de la Légion d'honneur*. He died on November 4 of the same year at the age of ninety-two.

Comment on the Value of the Resistance

Today, French historians are increasingly prepared to debate the issue of whether the operations of the Resistance benefited France, given the reprisals that they engendered. A key element of that calculation is the question of whether the FFL led by de Gaulle would have been able to place France at the victors' table without the efforts of the Resistance. To some extent, the issue has been downplayed because of the brave exploits of the Resistance as captured in postwar books and films.

The view of the Resistance by the French population during the war is difficult to measure and it was certainly mixed. Those who supported the Vichy regime were necessarily opposed to the Resistance and were responsible for many denunciations. Those who opposed Vichy were generally sympathetic and often aided the Resistance. Reprisals ordered by the Germans in the wake of Resistance operations, certainly turned a part of the population against the Resistance, while of course making others even more resolute against the Germans and Vichy.

My own view is that the Resistance played a vital role in keeping the flame of liberty alive. It also obliged the Germans to devote significant resources to the occupation that might have been more useful elsewhere. Hitler expressly ordered the placement of the Division Das Reich in the southwest of France in part for the purpose of crushing the active Resistance there. That decision meant that the Division was not in Normandy when the Allies landed; it arrived days later and then only at half strength. Ultimately it was the invading Allies who defeated the forces of occupation in France, but the Resistance made a significant contribution to this defeat.

The Oradour 60th Anniversary

"Never has France forgotten. Never will France forget." These words spoken at Oradour-sur-Glane by the Prime Minister, Jean-Pierre Raffarin, on June 10, 2004, movingly captured the sense of occasion, and complemented those of the German Chancellor, Gerard Schroeder, delivered four days earlier in Normandy at the anniversary of the Allied landing. Concerning Oradour, Schroeder said, "I am ashamed of what was perpetrated by Germans." He also called the Waffen SS "inhuman and immoral."

62. Hébras and Darthout on the village green awaiting
Prime Minister Raffarin on the 60th anniversary.

Although Raffarin had been mayor of the town of Chasseneuil-eu-Poitou, only one and one-half hours away, this was his first visit to Oradour. The Prime Minister said that he had been moved beyond words by his walk through the ruins, and by the personal accounts of Marcel Darthout and Robert Hébras (Illustration 62). The stories were told in the two survivors' typically understated manner, but Raffarin had been in no doubt of the depth of their feelings. The two men spoke to the Prime Minister at the edge of the village green where, on just such a sunny afternoon sixty years earlier, the inhabitants had been assembled before being led to the slaughter by the SS. "We watched as the soldiers followed orders first to guard us and then to kill us," said Hébras. "They didn't want any survivors," Darthout added. Raffarin clasped both men and thanked them "for keeping the memory alive."

"We are overwhelmed," the Prime Minister told the crowd, several thousand strong, who were gathered in front of the memorial. "While we bear witness for the nation, this tragedy is first and foremost your own. Our collective pain represents your families' suffering." At the same time, he praised "the reconciliation with your [Alsatian] compatriots, with your country and with yesterday's enemy; this process has not been without its misunderstandings, but it must continue."

The morning had started at the church in the new town, just a few hundred yards from the ruined village. Most of the people attending the service were in the overflow area outside, watching the proceedings on two television screens. As a gesture of reconciliation, the Archbishop of Limoges (Monsignor Dufour), had invited the Archbishop of Alsace (Monsignor Dore) to be present, and the latter was accompanied by many of the highest officials of Alsace. "These ruins possess a symbolic force," said Adrien Zeller, president of the *Conseil Régional d'Alsace*. "Even if the forcible induction of 130,000 Alsatians was weighed against the massacre at Oradour," he continued, "one did not justify the other."

Ironically, the post-war reconciliation of France and Germany took but a few years (among the crowd, I knew, there was a specially invited group of German teenagers), while that of Limousin and Alsace has only recently begun to take effect.

A message from Pope Jean-Paul II, read by the Archbishop of Limoges, said that on Oradour's 60th anniversary, it was important to forget neither what had happened nor "the responsibilities of those persons implicated in the massacre." Then Cardinal Joseph Ratzinger (and now Pope Benedict XVI) after attending the ceremony at Normandy Beach as part of the German delegation led by Chancellor Schroeder went to the nearby cemetery at La Cambe to pay his respects to the 21,000 German soldiers buried there. He was almost certainly not aware that Adolf Diekmann was one of them.

After the church service in Oradour, a procession formed near the town hall. This was led by school children from Alsace and Limousin, who were followed by a forest of tricolor flags, carried by members of the ANFM and other organizations, mostly older men in civilian clothes with their chests festooned with medals. Next came the elected officials and other dignitaries, the survivors and their families, and a group of thirty girls in blue uniform dresses from a school near Paris for the female descendants of persons holding the *Légion d'Honneur*.

The procession went first to the Children's Memorial, and then returned through the town to the Memorial to the Dead of the First and Second World Wars, where ten minutes of silence was observed. There is a striking difference in the numbers of military dead listed for the two wars. For WW I there are 101 names, while for WW II only five. This is a consequence of France having surrendered only six weeks after the outbreak of WW II, many men of the village being held in POW camps and most of the rest of the men having been annihilated in the massacre prior to the Free French army's part in the liberation of France.

Accompanied by his Minister of Defense, Michèle Alliot-Marie, and Minister of Veteran Affairs, Hamlaoui Mekachera, Raffarin then walked from the north gate of the ruined village along Oradour's main street. The trolley tracks and electric wires were still in place, but the post office, Hébras's house and other buildings along the route were ruins. In the burned out carcasses of the 328 buildings, only a handful of rusted cars and twisted objects remained. As the Prime Minister's entourage reached the village green, a military band played a slow march and then, as police and military personnel snapped to attention, struck up *La Marseillaise*. When the Prime Minister had delivered his speech, he placed a wreath on the memorial. About eighty other officials placing tributes followed him.

It is noteworthy that after the contretemps over the amnesties in 1953, no government official was invited to the anniversary until 1974. President Mitterrand, who had first visited Oradour forty-seven years earlier as Minister of Veterans' Affairs with President Auriol, attended the fiftieth anniversary in 1994. On that occasion, Auriol had promised to establish the Law of Collective Responsibility, and to prosecute the members of the Third Company. Mitterrand (then a deputy in the National Assembly) voted for amnesty in 1953; thereafter for a long time he was *persona non-grata* in the village. In 1999, President Jacques Chirac said that Oradour was inscribed alongside history's genocides and the Shoah [Holocaust] on the roll of the worst horrors perpetrated by mankind. Chirac's statement was lent significance by the fact that four years earlier he had become the first president of the republic to formally acknowledge France's responsibility for the exportation to the death camps of over 70,000 Jews during the Vichy regime. At the time of the massacre at Oradour the existence of the Holocaust was unknown and thus Oradour was the most monstrous war crime then known.

It struck me and others present at the 60th anniversary that times are changing. Oradour has become a national and not merely a regional symbol. Given that the massacre was the worst committed on French soil in modern times, it has become an important memorial to France as a victim of Nazism. The massacre, as we have seen, had a specific military purpose: to dissuade the French from attacking the occupation forces and the Division Das Reich. While the annihilation of the village undoubtedly terrified the local population, and to that degree achieved its aim, it left a terrible and lasting stain on the German military. A clear moral emerges: such reprisals are not only morally reprehensible, but come at an incalculable long-term cost. The martyred village of Oradour-sur-Glane stands as a permanent reminder of this important historical lesson.

The End

63. Hébras and the author in the Library of the Centre de la Mémoire, summer 2006.

GLOSSARY OF TERMS AND ABBREVIATIONS

ADEIF. Association des Evadés et Incorporés de Force, the main organization of the veterans of the Resistance and the *malgré-nous* in Alsace

ANFM. Association Nationale des Familles des Martyrs d'Oradour-sur-Glane. The organization of the Oradour victims and their families.

AS. Armée Sécrète. The main non-Communist part of the Resistance in the southwest. The AS were often clandestine *résistants* maintaining regular jobs.

Chantiers de la Jeunesse. Work and indoctrination groups for youths sponsored by Vichy.

FFI. Forces françaises de l'Intérieur. Created on June 1, 1944 to unify the Resistance in France, it was dissolved after the Liberation and the personnel incorporated into the regular French army.

FFL. Forces Françaises Libres. French military forces under de Gaulle starting in 1940 after the Armistice.

FTP. Francs-Tireurs et Partisans (Français). Also referred to as the FTPF. The Communist Resistance. The term *«francs-tireurs»* means "free shooters." The origin is probably from the name given to the French guerillas in the 1870-71 Franco-Prussian War.

Gestapo. Geheime Staatspolizei. Literally "secret state police". The principal German instrument in France to coerce and control the population.

GMR. Guarde Mobile de Reserve. A French quasi military force organized and supported by Vichy.

Les Douze. Refers to twelve Alsatian defendants in the Oradour trial who were forcibly inducted in the Division Das Reich.

malgré-nous. Literally, "against our will". Refers to Alsatians/Mosellans forcibly inducted into the German military.

maquis. The term comes from "macchia" the kind of rough mountain brush found in the Corsican hills. By extension it refers to the members of the Resistance who hid in the countryside. An individual in the *maquis* was called a *maquisard*.

Milice. The word derives from the Latin "militia". Vichy created the Milice on January 3, 1943, under Pierre Laval as a French paramilitary force to repress the Resistance and other opposition.

MUR. Mouvements unis de Résistance. An association of Guallist Resistance groups with a generally political focus.

NARA. National Archives and Records Administration (US)

Nazi. National Socialist Workers' Party led by Hitler.

OSS. Office of Strategic Services. The American overseas intelligence agency (predecessor of the Central Intelligence Agency) organized by William "Wild Bill" Donovan.

Prefect. The representative of the national government in a department or other administrative area (in French *Préfet*); an extremely important position in France roughly equivalent in stature to an American Governor or British Governor General of a colony.

SA. Strumabteilung. Nazi militia "brown shirts". Largely replaced by the SS after the "Night of the Long Knives" on June 30, 1934.

SD. Sicherheitsdienst. Security and intelligence service under Heinrich Himmler—similar to but distinct from the Gestapo

SHAEF. Supreme Headquarters Allied Expeditionary Forces. The Allied Command in Europe

SNCF. Société nationale des chemins de fer. The French national railway.

SOE. Special Operations Executive. UK operation that sent a number of French speaking operatives to France to aid the Resistance including Violette Szabó (and in fiction, Charlotte Gray).

SRCGE. Service de recherche des crimes de guerre ennemis. An investigative service established by the government to conduct research on a regional basis into war crimes in France. It functioned from 1944 to 1946

SS. Schutzstaffel. Protection squad for the Nazi Party (see also "Waffen SS" below).

STO. Service de Travail Obligatoire. French forced to go to Germany to work in its factories and farms.

Vichy. The name of the collaborationist Government of France led by Marshall Petain and located in the spa town of the same name.

Waffen SS. Waffen means "armed." The SS was divided into two main parts—the Waffen SS, which was the military arm, and the Allgemeine-SS which was mainly concerned with police operations and running the prisoner of war and concentration camps. The Gestapo and the SD were the main part of the SS police operation.

Wehrmacht. Regular German Army.

RESOURCES

This book is the product of several years of research and writing. Since there have been many books written about Oradour-sur-Glane from many angles, the challenge was to write something aimed primarily at Americans—very few of whom have ever heard of Oradour or the massacre. For me, the principal interest was the drama of the massacre, the war crimes trial nearly nine years later, and the conflict between Alsace and Limousin which the trial engendered and which nearly split the country. Thus, my aim was to present the most up-to-date account of those events and the relevant subsequent developments. For such a book, I felt that footnotes would only be a distraction. In my legal career, I wrote one article that alone had 629 footnotes, but this book is different.

In terms of bibliography, much of my research took place in the extensive archives and library of the Centre de la Mémoire at Oradour. I visited many Resistance museums, mostly in the southwest of France, and talked to many survivors of the war. Rather than providing an extensive bibliography, I would offer the following suggestions for those interested in learning more.

> 1. A visit to Oradour, the martyred village and the museum of the Centre de la Mémoire at the site, is a moving experience. It is a twenty-minute drive from Limoges and four hours by car from Paris. The Centre has its own catalogue (in French). The Centre's own web site is at www.oradour.org (available in English soon).

2. Sarah Farmer's, *Martyred Village* (University of California Press, 1999 hardcover, and 2000 paperback), is an excellent and scholarly account of the massacre and surrounding events. Her book contains an especially insightful analysis of the meaning of memory and memorials in relation to these kinds of tragedies. Oradour is almost unique in its preservation of a place devastated by a massacre. Farmer's book also contains an excellent bibliography.

3. Jean-Jacques Fouché, a French historian, has written two of the most comprehensive books on Oradour, one of which has been translated into English as "Massacre at Oradour, France, 1944" (Northern Illinois U. Press 2005). The second book, concerning the trial and the politics surrounding it *"Oradour la Politique et la Justice"* (Lucien Souny 2004), only exists in French. The books contain exhaustive bibliographies which include some of the recent German sources.

4. Robert Hebras, one of the survivors, has written a short but powerful first-hand account of the massacre which is available in English at the Centre called, *Oradour-sur-Glane, The Tragedy, Hour by Hour* (*Les Chemins de la Mémoire*). He also co-authored, along with his friend André Desourteaux, a book in French called, *Oradour/Glane Notre Village Assassiné*. The book contains their personal accounts of the massacre, as well as many pictures of Oradour and its inhabitants.,

5. There is a documentary cassette about Oradour available with English subtitles at the Centre ("Oradour", Follin & Wilmart 1993) which contains interviews with many of the survivors as well as excellent commentary by Sarah Farmer.

6. Christopher Weber of Sunset Productions made a documentary about Oradour which has been shown enumerable times on French television. It contains much original research and footage. It is available in DVD (in French) *Oradour, retour sur un massacre* (May 2005).

7. The recent book (in French) by Ahlrich Meyer has added important information from German archives, *L'Occupation Allemande en France*, 1940-44 (Toulouse, Éditions Privat, 2002).

8. Two other Germans have made important contributions to the subject. Professor Claudia Moisel has written a book in German entitled *Frankreich und die deutschen Kriegsverbrecher* (English translation of the title, *France and the German War Criminals*, Goettingen, Wallstein, 2004), which was helpful in negating U.S. interference with French extradition requests for Lammerding. She also authored an article in French which provided much of the statistics in my book about war crimes and collaboration trials in France. It is entitled, *Les proces pour crimes de guerre allemands en France après la Seconde Guerre Mondial* (April 15, 2004, accessible at www. Ihtp.cnrs.fr). Andrea Erkenbecher wrote her thesis in 2006 based on her research in the German, including the East German (Stasi), archives that shed new light on the Barth episode.

9. The documents that I found at NARA with much help from Professor Norman Goda and NARA archivist Eric Slander have been given to the Centre de la Mémoire at Oradour.

10. After our meeting, M. Lux sent me a book entitled, *Guerre et Paix en Alsace-Moselle*, by Christophe Nagyos (La Nuee Bleue, 2005), which greatly informed my summary of the history of Alsace-Moselle.

This list is obviously very selective and emphasizes for the most part, material available in English and French. It is very important to know that the massacre in Oradour has been the subject of many books, pamphlets, articles, and web sites that contain revisionist versions of these events and some outright Nazi and neo-Nazi propaganda. Often, it is not easy to discern immediately what is true and what is not. I suggest caution in relation to such material.

ACKNOWLEDGEMENTS

Many people have provided help and encouragement for this project, and it is impossible to give thanks in proportion to individual contributions. Insofar as is possible, my gratitude will be conveyed in person. Here, however, is a partial list of those who have aided this endeavor.

In the area of research, the Resistance museums of the Limousin region (especially Brive, Cahors, Montauban, Tulle and Limoges) deserve special mention, as does the Bibliothéque Nationale in Paris. For help in locating key documents in US Intelligence files, thanks to Eric Slander at the National Archives and Records Administration and to Norman Coda. Reid Feldman and Eugene Fidell both aided me on French and US Military law respectively.

The foremost source for my research in France was the Centre de la Mémoire in Oradour. Its archivist Sandra Gibouin went to extraordinary lengths in support of this project. Jean-Jacques Fouché, whose books on Oradour I praise in the Resources section, was most generous with his knowledge and contacts as was Christophe Weber who made the TV documentary on Oradour.

Robert Hebras and Marcel Darthout have patiently submitted to interviews, the former repeatedly, and have not hesitated to relive their singular experiences for the benefit of this book. Hervé Machefer has helped guide me through some of the fine details of the French police investigation. Richard Lux, the lawyer who represented several of the Alsatians, and is probably the only surviving lawyer who participated in the trial itself, has provided me with invaluable information, not least concerning the history of Alsace's relationship with France. Others whose interviews enriched the story include my *belle mere* Odette Pontal, Lilly Lavaud, Simone Segalat and Jacquelin Patriarche.

A number of people agreed to read and comment on my draft. Their suggestions contributed mightily. They were: Norman A. Anderson, Peter Del Col, William F. Drake, Jr., Alain Hirsch, William S. Lamb, Christian Latand-Klein, Alan Lindgren, Fabrice Robert and Thomas S. Sherrard. Nadine Gudimard was my expert guide through the intricacies of photo acquisition and copyright. As can be seen from the list of illustrations, Cyril Guinet who graciously gave me permission to use them because his grandfather had told him never to forget Oradour found a large number in the old archives of Detective magazine. Luke Jennings, himself a published author and journalist who served as my editor, not only applied his magic touch to the text but also educated me along the way. The encouragement and critical help of Adam Sisman and his wife Robyn, both well-known authors, was vital. Robyn's mother Tamie Watters, who was one of my undergraduate English teachers at Principia College and later taught at Yale and Randolph-Macon, never stopped generously contributing to my education including in relation to this book. Any errors that have survived are mine alone.

My final thanks to my wife Claudie, who as well as unlocking certain intricacies of the French language and culture, provided the help and encouragement without which "Oradour – The Final Verdict" would have never been written.

Lightning Source UK Ltd.
Milton Keynes UK
UKOW05f0817010913

216317UK00002B/134/A